John Bowlby and Attachment Theory

John Bowlby (1907–1990) has been described as 'one of the three or four most important psychiatrists of the twentieth century'. In this book Jeremy Holmes provides a focused and coherent account of Bowlby's life and work, based on his writings and those of the 'post-Bowlbians', as well as interviews with members of his family and with psychoanalysts who knew him.

Bowlby's Attachment Theory is one of the major theoretical developments in psychoanalysis this half-century. Combining the rigorous scientific empiricism of ethology with the subjective insights of psychoanalysis, it has had an enormous impact in the fields of child development, social work, psychology, psychotherapy and psychiatry. Jeremy Holmes examines the origins of Bowlby's ideas, and presents the main features of Attachment Theory and their relevance to contemporary psychoanalytic psychotherapy. He looks at the processes of attachment and loss, and reviews recent experimental evidence linking secure attachment in infancy with the development of 'autobiographical competence'. He also provides fascinating insights into the history of the psychoanalytic movement, and considers the ways in which Attachment Theory can help in understanding society and its problems.

John Bowlby and Attachment Theory will be essential reading for all students of psychotherapy, counselling, social work, psychology and psychiatry, and for professionals working in those fields.

Jeremy Holmes is Consultant Psychiatrist/Psychotherapist at the North Devon District Hospital.

The Makers of Modern Psychotherapy
Series editor: Laurence Spurling

This series of introductory, critical texts looks at the work and thought of key contributors to the development of psychodynamic psychotherapy. Each book shows how the theories examined affect clinical practice, and includes biographical material as well as a comprehensive bibliography of the contributor's work.

The field of psychodynamic psychotherapy is today more fertile but also more diverse than ever before. Competing schools have been set up, rival theories and clinical ideas circulate. These different and sometimes competing strains are held together by a canon of fundamental concepts, guiding assumptions and principles of practice.

This canon has a history, and the way we now understand and use the ideas that frame our thinking and practice is palpably marked by how they came down to us, by the temperament and experiences of their authors, the particular puzzles they wanted to solve and the contexts in which they worked. These are the makers of modern psychotherapy. Yet despite their influence, the work and life of some of these eminent figures is not well known. Others are more familiar, but their particular contribution is open to reassessment. In studying these figures and their work, this series will articulate those ideas and ways of thinking that practitioners and thinkers within the psychodynamic tradition continue to find persuasive.

Laurence Spurling

John Bowlby and Attachment Theory

Jeremy Holmes

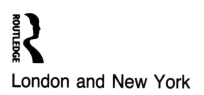

London and New York

First published 1993
by Routledge
11 New Fetter Lane, London EC4P 4EE

Simultaneously published in the USA and Canada
by Routledge
29 West 35th Street, New York, NY 10001

Reprinted 1994 and 1995

© 1993 Jeremy Holmes

Phototypeset in Times by Intype, London
Printed and bound in Great Britain by
Mackays of Chatham PLC, Chatham, Kent

British Library Cataloguing in Publication Data
A catalogue record for this book is available from the
British Library

Library of Congress Cataloguing in Publication Data
A catalogue record for this book is available from the
Library of Congress

ISBN 0-415-07729-X (hbk)
ISBN 0-415-07730-3 (pbk)

To Jacob, Matthew, Lydia and Joshua; also to Ben, Polly, Matilda and Flora; and in memory of Tabitha.

By the same author

The Values of Psychotherapy (with R. Lindley), (1991 [1989]), Oxford University Press.
A Textbook of Psychotherapy in Psychiatric Practice (Editor), (1991), Churchill Livingstone.
Between Art and Science: Essays in Psychotherapy and Psychiatry (1992), Routledge.
The Good Mood Guide (with R. Holmes), (1993), Orion.

Contents

Illustrations

Acknowledgements

The origins of this book can be traced to a phone call from Laurie Spurling asking me whom I would like to write about. John Bowlby sprang instantly to mind – so I must start by acknowledging my gratitude to him for that invitation, and for his subsequent editorial help and suggestions.

The next 'without whom . . .' is to the Wellcome Trust, who granted me a six-month Research Fellowship which enabled me to concentrate exclusively on the book, free from my clinical and administrative responsibilities. Sabbaticals are becoming rare enough in universities, and in the National Health Service are almost unheard of. Mine was a blissful period which not only enabled me to devote myself to the book, but also provided a perspective from which I realised how stressful and exhausting most NHS consultant posts are. So the Wellcome has saved me from burn-out (or postponed it for a while) as well as enabling the book to get written. Never was a psychotherapist so professionally indebted to a pharmaceutical firm!

Next I must express my gratitude to my colleagues in the Department of Psychiatry at North Devon District Hospital, and especially to Drs Roberts, Sewell and Van Buren, who gave their blessing to my absence, even though it meant more work for them, also to Dr Simon Nicholson, who cheerfully and efficiently took my place while I was away.

I am grateful to the Institute of Psycho-Analysis for granting me access to their archives.

Much gratitude is due to the many friends and colleagues who have taken time and effort to discuss Attachment Theory and to read all or part of the manuscript and have made many helpful suggestions which have improved its quality: Anthony Bateman,

Mary Boston, Peter Fonagy, Dorothy Heard, Matthew Holmes, Sebastian Kraemer, Brian Lake, Richard Lindley, Pat Millner, Oliver Reynolds, Glenn Roberts, Charles Rycroft, Anthony Storr, and Robert and Lorraine Tollemache. Needless to say, the defects of the book are entirely my responsibility.

I am very grateful for the help and encouragement I have had from members of the Bowlby family. By agreeing to be interviewed, and with their written comments, Ursula Bowlby, Mary Gatling, Sir Henry and Lady Phelps Brown, Juliet Hopkins and Marjorie Durbin gave me a fascinating window of reminiscence into their family and social life in the early part of the century.

My secretary, Patricia Bartlett, helped as always in countless ways to lighten the burden of my work and made my absence from the hospital possible by her combination of good humour, vigilance and efficiency.

Alison Housley and her staff in the library at North Devon District Hospital have been tireless in the promptness and enthusiasm with which they responded to my endless requests for references. Their contribution to making our hospital a true 'periphery of excellence' is incalculable.

Finally, I am grateful to Ros and Joshua Holmes, who, by providing me with a loving and secure base, enabled me to explore the world of Attachment Theory, and by expecting – without demanding – me to provide one for them, offered the necessary distraction without which one's work becomes stale and unbalanced.

Chapter 1

Introduction

When people start writing they think they've got to write something definitive . . . I think that is fatal. The mood to write in is 'This is quite an interesting story I've got to tell. I hope someone will be interested. Anyway it's the best I can do for the present.' If one adopts that line one gets over it and does it.

(Bowlby in Hunter 1991)

This book has four main aims. The first, and simplest, is to present John Bowlby's story of attachment – and we shall hear much about stories in the course of the book – in a condensed and coherent way. Bowlby was a lucid and prolific exponent of his own views, but the very comprehensiveness of his work, described by one critic as having a 'Victorian monumentality about it' (Rycroft 1985), can be daunting. Despite the clarity of his thought and the charm and epigrammatic flair of his literary style, the 1,500 pages of the *Attachment and Loss* trilogy (Bowlby, 1969b, 1973a, 1980), covering as they do every aspect of the subject in immense detail, are hard going for the faint-hearted reader. His later works, *The Making and Breaking of Affectional Bonds* (Bowlby 1979) and *A Secure Base* (Bowlby 1988), are more accessible, but as collections of essays they do not necessarily pull all his theories together into a whole. So there is a need for a survey of Bowlby's work, and also – here is a second objective – given that it is well over half a century since he published his first papers, a need to take an historical perspective on the evolution of his ideas.

The past thirty years have seen a second, and more recently a third, generation of researchers stimulated by Bowlby's seminal ideas first published in the 1960s. The 'post-Bowlbians' – Ainsworth, Main, Bretherton, Marris and Sroufe in the United States; the Grossmanns in Germany; Parkes, Hinde, Byng-Hall and Heard in Britain – have developed Attachment Theory into a major framework of developmental psychology in ways that are highly relevant to psychotherapy. Many of their findings have been collected into two important research symposia (Parkes and Stevenson-Hinde 1982; Parkes *et al.* 1991), but there is no single volume explicitly devoted to the exposition of contemporary Attachment Theory and little concerted effort has been made to consider its implications for psychotherapeutic theory and practice. The need for such a work is a third objective and justification for the present work.

A fourth and more compelling reason than these worthy but perhaps mundane considerations informs much of the purpose of this book. This is the attempt to come to grips with a curious enigma which surrounds Bowlby and his work. Apart from Freud and Jung, Bowlby is one of the few psychoanalysts who have become household names and whose ideas have entered the vernacular. The ill effects (or otherwise) of maternal deprivation; the importance of bonding between parents and children; the need for a secure base and to feel attached; the realisation that grief has a course to run and can be divided into stages – these are concepts with which people far removed from the worlds of psychology and psychotherapy are familiar. All may be traced, in whole or in part, to the work of John Bowlby.

Yet Bowlby's familiarity and acceptance by the general public and his influence in a number of specialist fields such as pediatrics, developmental psychology, social work and psychiatry have never been matched within the domain of psychotherapy. In his chosen profession of psychoanalysis his influence is honoured more often in the breach than the observance. Between his papers delivered in the late 1950s and early 1960s to psychoanalytic societies in Britain and the States, and polite obsequies of the early 1990s, there has for the most part been a resounding silence from the psychoanalytical movement in response to the challenges and opportunities which his work represents. A major aim of this book is to try to understand this discrepancy between public recognition and professional avoidance, and the attempt to remedy it by showing how Attachment Theory can inform the practice of adult psychotherapy.

The details of the relationship between Bowlby and psycho-analysis will emerge gradually in the course of the book but, as an overture, a brief summarising overview will now follow. The answers to the riddle of Bowlby's rift with the psychoanalytic movement can be found at three distinct but interrelated levels: Bowlby's own personality, background and outlook; the atmos-phere within the psychoanalytic society just before and in the aftermath of Freud's death; and the social and intellectual climate in the years surrounding and including the 1939–45 world war.

John Bowlby, described in an obituary as 'one of the three or four most important psychiatrists of the twentieth century' (Storr 1991), came from a conventional upper-middle class background. Cambridge educated, very 'English' in his reserve and empiri-cism, a 'nineteenth century Darwinian liberal' (Rycroft, 1985), he entered a psychoanalytical society in the 1930s that was riven between two warring factions led by Melanie Klein on the one hand and Anna Freud on the other (Grosskurth 1986). Melanie, a Berliner, divorced and separated from her children, the great innovator, faced the unmarried Viennese Anna, devoted to the orphans in her Hampstead nursery, defender of the true Freudian faith. Klein was powerful and domineering, but with a helpless side that meant that she depended on utter loyalty from her supporters. Anna Freud was shy and diffident, but with a steely determination not to be done down, and the confidence of her father's blessing.

The battle between the two women was ostensibly about theory. For Freud the Oedipus complex was the 'kernel of the neuroses' and he had had little to say about the early mother–infant relationship. Klein put the mother on the psychoanalytic map, arguing for the importance of phantasy in the early weeks and months of life; the primacy of the death instinct as an expla-nation for infantile aggression; and the need in therapy to lay bare and put into words these primitive impulses of infancy. Anna Freud – Antigone to her father's Oedipus – questioned Klein's speculations about the mind of the infant, continued to see the Oedipus complex arising at the age of two to three years as the starting point for the neuroses, and saw the role of therapy as strengthening the ego in its efforts to reconcile id and superego. Bowlby struggled to find his bearings in the charged atmosphere of the psychoanalytic society created by the rivalrous antagonism of these two daughters of the psychoanalytical movement, each vying for supremacy. With characteristic independence he steered a course between them, trying to work things out for himself. He took his stand on two main battlefields: the scientific status of psychoanalysis, and the role of the environment in the causation of neurosis.

Although both sides invoked the name of science in support of their ideas, this was, in Bowlby's view, little more than a genuflection to Freud's insistence that psychoanalysis should take its place as a new science of the mind. Bowlby saw both women and most of their followers as hopelessly unscientific. Neither Klein nor Anna Freud had any kind of scientific background. Both argued from intuition and authority rather than subjecting their claims to empirical testing. Neither had made any attempt to keep abreast of contemporary developments in science, or to revise Freudian metapsychology in the light of the emerging ideas about information processing and feedback which were to have such an impact on academic psychology and ethology. In rejecting Bowlby, his psychoanalytic critics on the other hand felt that by restricting himself to a narrow definition of science – to what could be observed and measured – Bowlby was missing the whole point of psychoanalysis. Any so-called 'science' of the mind which did not take account of the inner world of phantasy was worthless and certainly had no place within psychoanalytic discourse.

A similar polarisation took place around the role of the environment in the causation of neurosis. Bowlby was struck by the extent to which his patients had suffered from privation and loss, and horrified by the apparent disregard of real trauma as compared with an emphasis on the importance of autonomous phantasy in the Kleinian approach. Matters came to a head when Bowlby presented to the psychoanalytic society his famous film made with James Robertson (Robertson 1952; Bowlby and Robertson 1952b) documenting the distress shown by a small girl when separated from her parents on going into hospital. While Anna Freud endorsed Bowlby's views, the Kleinians in the audience were unimpressed, and felt that the girl's distress was due more to her unconscious destructive phantasies towards her pregnant mother's unborn baby than to the separation itself.

Bowlby was in an unusual position within the psychoanalytic society in that he was someone with non-Kleinian views who had been analysed and supervised by members of the Kleinian group (Joan Riviere and Miss Klein herself). Finding himself stuck in his analysis he decided to change to a non-Kleinian analyst, but extreme pressure was placed on him not to do so, to which, uncharacteristically, he submitted (Grosskurth 1986). He was cited by the Kleinians as evidence that they were not out to brainwash or convert all psychoanalytical candidates to their persuasion. As someone with evident ability and reputation he would have been quite a catch for whichever group he chose to join.

But both sides had reckoned without Bowlby's originality and ambition and preparedness to go out on a limb on his own. His discovery of ethology in the early 1950s provided the opportunity he was looking for to put psychoanalysis on a sound scientific footing. His World Health Organisation monograph (Bowlby 1951) and later observations of children separated from their parents enabled him to establish once and for all the importance of environmental trauma as a cause of neurosis and character disturbance. Attachment Theory was born, but rather than illuminating and strengthening Object Relations Theory as Bowlby had hoped, it was perceived by many analysts as a threat or even a betrayal. Bowlby had hoped to reconcile the warring factions within the society with his new theory, but instead they were for the most part united in either outright opposition or polite indifference to his ideas. Bowlby gradually drifted away from the society, and Attachment Theory came to stand as a discipline in its own right, owing much to psychoanalysis, but with links also to systems theory and cognitive psychology, and making a contribution as much to family and cognitive therapies as to psychoanalysis.

In retrospect the splits within the British Psycho-Analytical Society seem comparatively trivial. As Pedder (1987) puts it:

an innocent might . . . ask what all the fuss was about. Because really it could be argued that there was not a lot of disagreement. They argued about phantasy: how wide the concept should be. . . . They argued about . . . how early the Oedipus complex starts, whether at two or three or sooner. . . . They argued about the emphasis that should be placed on aggression and the death instinct, and whether neurosis is precipitated by the frustration of libido, as the Viennese thought, or [as the Kleinians saw it] by the awakening of aggression. . . . All these could be seen as matters of degree which you might think reasonable people could well discuss.

(Pedder 1987)

But as every psychotherapist should know, things are rarely that simple. The psychoanalytical movement was still struggling with the death of its founder, searching for a direction in which to go. The polarisation between those who idealised the dead leader (the Anna Freudians) and those who dealt with their depression by a kind of manic triumphalism, a celebration of the new (the Kleinians), can be understood in terms of the very concepts that those two groups espoused. A female principle was needed to balance the phallocentrism of the earlier Freudian movement. 'The King is dead, long live the Queen' might have been their slogan. But which queen should it be? The battle for psychoanalysis was going on against a backdrop of world war, of death, dislocation and genocide. The Kleinian emphasis on autonomous phantasy, on the death instinct, on the power of psychoanalysis to heal, irrespective of environmental factors, can be seen as a desperate attempt to bring some sense of order and the possibility of control – at times omnipotently – into a world in which one could not but feel powerless and helpless. Anna Freud's emphasis on the need to strengthen the ego was an effort to hold on to reason and sanity in the face of the irrational destructiveness unleashed by war.

Bowlby was perhaps the perfect scapegoat, with his cool Englishness, his social and intellectual powers, his espousal of a narrow version of science that could not encompass the cultural breadth of the Jewish-European intelligentsia, his comparative insulation from the full horrors of war, and his Whiggish belief in the possibilities of progress based on social and scientific reason. His attempt to open out psychoanalysis to ethology and contemporary science was premature. He threatened the closed world of psychoanalysis and, offered a cold shoulder, like others before him (Jung, Adler, Ferenczi, Reich), he gave up the fight after a while and moved away to follow his own interests.

The loss was both his and that of psychoanalysis. There is something in the kernel of psychoanalysis which Bowlby seems not to have fully assimilated. In comparison with Freud's and Klein's passionate world of infantile sexuality, Attachment Theory appears almost bland, banal even. An appreciation of the power of phantasy, and the complexity of its relationship with external reality, is somehow lacking in his work. It is not loss alone that causes disturbance, but the phantasies stirred up by loss – the lack of this appreciation makes Bowlby appear at times simplistic in his formulations. But in eschewing the scientific rigour which Bowlby saw it so badly needed, psychoanalysis was held back in its development as a discipline and a therapy, a setback from which it is only just beginning to recover (see Peterfreund 1983; Stern 1985). Perhaps there was something in the climate of the 1950s which made such a split inevitable. The divide between the 'two cultures' epitomised by the belief in the possibility of progress based on science advocated by C. P. Snow, and Leavis's moral condemnation of an illiterate and degenerate society was just too great to bridge (Holmes 1992). Psychoanalysis became increasingly identified with 'culture' – with the imagination, linguistics and the moral and aesthetic dimension (Rycroft 1985; Rustin 1991), while Attachment Theory gathered momentum as a part of scientific psychology, taking root in the United States in a way that seemed less possible in a Britain that was so split in its educational and bureaucratic structures between art and science.

But times have changed. The old certainties no longer hold. Psychoanalysis has lost its dogmatism and is much more open to empirical evidence and to cross-disciplinary influence. The Berlin wall which separated psychoanalysis from the superficiality but also the stimulus of other disciplines has come down. The debate about the scientific status of psychoanalysis, and the role of the environment in neurosis, continues, but it is no longer a matter of life and death. Each side can claim partial victories. Klein was right in her emphasis on the early weeks and months of life – there is abundant evidence of psychic life from the moment of birth (Stern 1985). She was probably wrong in her insistence on the universality of the paranoid-schizoid position – it seems likely that splitting and projection predominate only in anxiously attached infants. She was right to emphasise loss and separation as central themes in character formation from the earliest years, but wrong in the concreteness of her thinking – she believed that bottle feeding could never substitute for the breast and that the events surrounding weaning were critical determinants of character. It seems likely that it is the style and general handling of the infant that matters, not the specific events, unless these are overwhelmingly traumatic. In therapy she was right to emphasise the central importance of the relationship between therapist and patient, but wrong in her belief that only 'deep', 'Kleinian' interpretations would be effective: the strength of the therapist–

patient attachment is a crucial determining factor in the outcome of therapy, but the nature of the interpretations, as long as they are reasonably sensible, coherent and brief, is not (Holmes 1991). As increasing evidence of early trauma appears in the histories of patients with major character disorder (Grant 1991), Bowlby's emphasis on the importance of the environment as a determinant of pathology appears to be vindicated, but he also tended to be too concrete and specific in his hypotheses – it is not the loss of a parent in itself that is traumatic but the family discord or disruption surrounding it that causes the damage (Rutter 1981).

Klein showed how an individual's inner world shapes their perception of the object, and how, through projective identification, the object is coerced into feeling and behaving according to the projections it receives. In contrast with this near solipsistic account, Bowlby is concerned primarily with the impact of the object on the self. The self, which in his theories tends to be almost passive, is moulded by the inadequacies and absences of the object. We shall explore how the *interactive* view of self and object postulated by Winnicott (1965) and Bion (1978) and observed by developmental psychologists like Stern (1985) and Brazelton and Cramer (1991) offers the possibility of a long overdue climate of reconciliation and new understanding.

Bowlby was always careful to distinguish between the scientific and therapeutic aspects of psychoanalysis. As a scientist he was struggling for simplicity and clarity and for general principles, while therapy inevitably concerns itself with complexity and concreteness of the individual case. Much of the disagreement between Bowlby and psychoanalysis appears to rest on a confusion of these two aspects. Bowlby's main concern was to find a firm scientific underpinning to the Object Relations approach, and Attachment Theory, with its marrying of ethology to the developmental ideas of psychoanalysis, can be seen in that light. Although couched in the language of science, psychoanalytic therapy has come increasingly to be seen as a hermeneutic discipline, more concerned with meanings than mechanism, in which patient and therapist collaboratively develop a coherent narrative about the patient's experience. Such objectification and coherence are in themselves therapeutic, irrespective of the validity or otherwise of the meanings that are found. An extreme illustration of this comes from the finding that schizophrenic patients with complex and coherent delusional systems are better able to function socially than those who lack such meanings, however idiosyncratic (Roberts 1992). Bowlby's work has ensured that clinical hypotheses based on Object Relations Theory with a scientific underpinning of Attachment Theory are unlikely to be far removed from the truth, or to be tainted by totally unjustified speculation.

As we shall see in Chapter 6, recent developments in Attachment Theory suggest an exciting bridge between the narrative approach of contemporary psychoanalysis and the science of developmental psychology. There is a strong link between the kinds of attachment patterns found in infancy and the narratives that people tell about themselves several years later. Put briefly, securely attached children tell coherent stories about their lives, however difficult they have been, while insecurely attached children have much greater difficulty in narrative competence, either dismissing their past or remaining bogged down in it, and in neither case being able to talk objectively about it. The therapeutic implications of this are self-evident. Good therapy, like good parenting, provides the security and space within which a healing narrative can begin to emerge.

Psychoanalysis, perhaps more than it would care to admit, is influenced by the prevailing cultural climate. The Oedipus complex with its emphasis on castration anxiety reflected the patriarchy of its day. With the weakening of paternal power within the family came the rise of the female principle within psychoanalysis. The Society which Bowlby joined in the 1930s was dominated by strong women: Melanie Klein, Anna Freud, Joan Riviere, Sylvia Payne, Susan Isaacs, Paula Heimann and many others. Ernest Jones's power was waning, and Glover's grip on the Society was gradually being loosened. The main theorists of the post-war period – Klein, Bion, Winnicott and Bowlby – were all concerned with the role of the mother. A new phase of deconstruction has begun which emphasises the reciprocities of reader and writer, social, cultural and racial pluralism. We are entering an era of therapeutic co-constructionism – far removed from the *ex-cathedra* interpretations of classical therapy – where therapist and patient collaboratively build up a picture of their world and history. We have moved, perhaps, from the father principle, through the maternal, to the era of the sibling, in which, however different in their roles, there is a fundamental symmetry between patient and therapist.

This brings us to a concluding note about the nature of biography. A biographer is, in a sense, both patient and therapist in relation to the person he chooses to write about. As Gathorne-Hardy (1992) points out, there is an inevitable positive transference to one's subject; how else could one justify the long hours spent (far exceeding any psychoanalysis, however interminable) reading, studying, thinking about them? Biographers identify with their subjects, just as patients identify with their therapists, and see them in a way that is inevitably influenced and may be biased by their own themes and preoccupations. At the same time, biographers as 'therapists' have an opportunity to see their subjects as they really are: but with that privilege must also take into account their own counter-transferential tendencies towards voyeurism, prurience, envy, denigration and idealisation. Biographers should approach their subjects in the same spirit in which therapists see their patients: compassionately without becoming over-involved, with objectivity but without excessive detachment, with a sense of the uniqueness and specialness of the individual but without indulgence. The aim of this book is to form a working alliance with Attachment Theory and its originator – to see them in their strengths and limitations, their possibilities and blind spots. Although this book is not primarily a biography, some biographical preliminaries are therefore inevitably needed and it is to them that we must now turn.

Part I

Origins

Chapter 2

Biographical

> Parents, especially mothers, are much-maligned people.
>
> (Bowlby 1988a)

A family photograph, taken just before the First World War, shows Lady Bowlby surrounded by her six children. Her husband, Sir Anthony, the King's surgeon, is not there – he is, as usual, at work. She is flanked by her two favourite sons, John and Tony, aged about four and five, looking boldly and brightly into the camera. On her lap sits the baby Evelyn. The two older girls, aged eight and eleven, stand dutifully and demurely to one side. Finally there is two-year-old Jim, the weak member of the family, dubbed a 'late developer', lacking the physical and intellectual vigour of his brothers and sisters. A hand appears around his waist, partly propping him up. But whose hand can it be? Is it his mother's? No, hers are firmly around the baby – a rare moment of physical closeness, as it turned out. Can it be one of his older sisters? No, their hands are politely by their sides. It is in fact the hand of an invisible nurse, crouching behind the tableau vivant, the tiny and perfectionist 'Nanna Friend' who, with the nursemaids and governess, provided the child care in this fairly typical example of the English *haute bourgeoisie* on the threshold of the modern era.

Bowlby was notoriously reticent about his background and early family life. In the Adult Attachment Interview (see Chapter 6) he might have been rated as 'dismissive', giving the kind of response in which a person describes their childhood as 'perfectly all right' and refuses to be drawn further – a pattern that is strongly correlated with an insecure-avoidant pattern of attachment. But, as his book on Darwin testifies, Bowlby found the task of psychobiography worthwhile, making a strong case for considering Darwin's recurrent anxiety attacks as a manifestation of his inability to grieve loss, the pattern for which was set by his mother's death when he was eight. Whereas the main purpose of this book is an exposition of Attachment Theory, the aim of this chapter is to consider Bowlby's life and personality as a background to his ideas and to explore the relationship between them. The chapter is divided into three parts: the first is a chronological account of his life and career, touching on much that will be developed in subsequent chapters; the second consists of an assessment of his character, based on reminiscences of his family, friends and colleagues; and the third considers some of the major personal themes and preoccupations which inform Bowlby's work.

BOWLBY'S LIFE

Childhood and youth

Edward John Mostyn Bowlby was born on 26 February 1907. His father, whom he resembled in many ways, was Major-General Sir Anthony Bowlby (1855–1929), a successful London surgeon who had operated on one of Queen Victoria's sons, and was rewarded with a knighthood for his appointments as Royal Surgeon to King Edward VII and King George V, and a baronetcy on becoming President of the Royal College of Surgeons in 1920. John's grandfather, 'Thomas Bowlby of *The Times*', was a foreign correspondent for *The Times* who was murdered in Peking in 1861 during the Opium Wars when Sir Anthony was a small child. Anthony felt responsible for his mother, who did not remarry, and he only began to look for a wife after her death when he was forty. He was introduced by a mutual friend at a house party to the well-connected May Mostyn, then thirty, and pursued her (mainly on bicycles – they shared a love of the countryside and outdoor life) until they were married less than a year later. The train of May's wedding dress was embroidered with violets in deference to her dead mother-in-law as the statutory period of mourning had not yet passed. May was the eldest daughter of the Hon. Hugh Mostyn, who, despite grand origins (he was the youngest child, of ten, of Lord Mostyn of Mostyn in North Wales), was content to be a country parson in a remote Huntingdonshire village for all his working life. Bowlby's mother revered her father ('Grampy' in the Bowlby household) and invoked him as a model for all acceptable behaviour. She had little time for her mother, whom, when she was not having babies (May resented her numerous younger brothers and sisters and considered that first-borns were the only ones who really mattered) she described as 'always in the kitchen'.

John's parents were well into middle age by the time he was born: his mother forty, his father fifty-two. Each had had a special relationship with one parent and may have found the very different atmosphere of a large and vigorous family overwhelming. May had resented the demands of her younger brothers and sisters, and Sir Anthony was used to his bachelor ways. In any case, like many parents of their class and generation, they mainly entrusted the upbringing of their children to their numerous servants.

The children fell into three groups by age: the two older girls, Winnie and Marion, who were talented musicians from an early age; Tony and John, only 13 months apart; then Jim and Evelyn. Tony was their mother's clear favourite and could get away with almost anything. He later became a successful industrialist, and as eldest son inherited his father's title. John and Tony were close in age and temperament, good friends, but extremely rivalrous. They were treated as twins – put in the same clothes and in the same class at school. This meant that John was always making superhuman efforts to overtake his brother, who was equally as keen to retain his advantage. (Years later as a parent John would be renowned in the family for resisting his children's clamouring demands with the phrase, 'Now, don't bully me, don't *bully* me'.) They both teased and were concerned about their slightly backward brother Jim. John read delightedly in a newspaper about the miraculous effects of 'monkey gland extract' (presumably thyroxine), hoping that it would be the answer to their brother's difficulties, but of course they were disappointed. Jim struggled throughout his life, farmed not very successfully for a while and never married. It seemed contrary to the Bowlby spirit to have a family member who was not a 'success'. John's combination of competitiveness and his concern for disadvantaged and sick children may be not unrelated to his position between these two very different brothers. At fifteen he fought and defeated Tony when he discovered that he had destroyed a

picture that Jim had made out of dried flowers. The two older
sisters did not marry. According to John, 'the men they might
have married were killed in the First World War' (Bowlby *et al.*
1986) – a curiously unpsychological explanation. Evelyn shared
her brother's interest in psychoanalysis. She married the distinguished economist Professor Sir Henry Phelps Brown. Their
daughter Juliet Hopkins is a child psychotherapist at the Tavistock Clinic.

Bowlby describes his family as a 'straightforward, fairly close
– not all that close – but fairly close, professional class family
living a pretty traditional lifestyle, with nurses of course' (Bowlby
in Hunter 1991). Nanny Friend, whose hand appears in the photograph, joined the family when John's older sister Winnie was one
month old and after the children were grown up stayed with Lady
Bowlby until she died at the age of ninety-seven. She was highly
intelligent and well read, a disciplinarian, whose firm regime
would occasionally be lightened by her capacity for entrancing
and elaborate story-telling and by reading Dickens to the children
in the nursery.

Evelyn remembers life in their London house in Manchester
Square as rather joyless – regulated by order, innumerable clocks,
a sense of propriety, humourless governesses, and interminable
slow processional walks in nearby Hyde Park. Tony, in contrast,
describes a happy childhood. The reality perhaps was that they
had two childhoods – one in the country and one in the town.
Lady Bowlby boasted that she *never* worried about her children
and, especially in London, left them mostly to their own devices.
She would visit the nursery to receive a report from Nanny after
breakfast every day, and the children, clean and brushed, would
come down to the drawing room from 5 to 6 p. m. after tea,
where she would read to them, especially from her beloved
Children of the New Forest. May Mostyn had vowed that she
would never marry a 'city man', and Sir Anthony loved fishing
and shooting. Every spring and summer there was a ritual of
family holidays. At Easter the children were dispatched to Mar-
gate with the nurses while Sir Anthony and Lady Bowlby went
to Scotland for fishing. In July May would take the children to
the New Forest, in those days a wild and idyllic place. For the
whole of August and half of September the entire family
decamped to Ayrshire in Scotland, travelling by train in a
specially hired railway carriage. (Sir Anthony and Lady Bowlby

never owned a car: he used a brougham for his rounds in London and after his death she would travel around Gloucestershire in pony and trap well into the 1950s.)

On holiday John's mother seemed to come alive and, as 'Grampy' had done with her, ensured that her children were well versed in nature and country sports. From her and 'Grampy' they learned to identify flowers, birds and butterflies, to fish, ride and shoot, and John and Tony became and remained passionate naturalists. Sir Anthony seemed to be a fairly remote and intimidating figure, especially in London, but he gave the children special animal nicknames: John was known as 'Jack' the jackal (other nursery nicknames for John were 'Bogey' and the prophetic 'Admiral Sir Nosey Know-all'); Tony was 'Gorilla'; Evelyn 'Cat'. They saw little of him during the week but would walk with him in family procession across Hyde Park most Sundays to church, when he would instruct and occasionally amuse them with his deep factual knowledge about the world and its ways.

The war came in 1914 when John was seven. John and his elder brother were immediately dispatched to boarding school, because of the supposed danger of air raids on London. John later maintained that this was just an excuse, being merely the traditional first step in the time-honoured barbarism required to produce English gentlemen. The English preparatory school system took its toll: John was beaten for defining a 'cape' in a geography lesson as a cloak rather than a promontory, but, a resilient and self-assured little boy, he flourished. Sir Anthony was away in France as a surgeon-general for most of the war. When the war came to an end, John went as naval cadet to Dartmouth where he learned to sail, and gained a discipline and organisation which lasted a lifetime. Tony was destined to follow in his father's footsteps and become a surgeon, but he decided against this in his teens, feeling that it would mean 'failure' since he could never equal his father's eminence. This left the way clear for John to go into medicine, who, despite having passed out top in his Dartmouth exams, was already dissatisfied with the narrow intellectual horizons and rigidity of the Navy (as he was to become two decades later with the British Psycho-Analytical Society), as well as suffering badly from seasickness! Somewhat to John's surprise, Sir Anthony agreed to buy him out. Although not driven by a strong vocational pull, John felt that a medical career would be least unacceptable to his father and, together with a close Dartmouth friend, applied to Cambridge and duly entered Trinity college as a medical student in 1925. His intellectual distinction was already in evidence at university where he won several prizes and gained a first class degree in pre-clinical sciences and psychology.

Already mature and independent-minded, with an 'inner calm' (Phelps Brown 1992) that was to stand him good stead throughout his life, John's next move proved decisive. Rather than going straight on to London to study clinical medicine, which would have been the conventional thing to do, he got a job instead in a progressive school for maladjusted children, an offshoot of A. S. Neill's Summerhill. His father, who would undoubtedly have opposed such a move, had, in John's words 'fortunately' already died when John was twenty-one, so he was free to chart his own course. At the school he had two sets of experiences which were to influence the whole course of his professional life. The first was the encounter with disturbed children, with whom he found he could communicate, and whose difficulties seemed to be related to their unhappy and disrupted childhood. Like one of Lorenz's (1952) greylag geese, who were to play such an important part in the development of Attachment Theory, one boy followed Bowlby round wherever he went:

> There I had known an adolescent boy who had been thrown out of a public school for repeated stealing. Although socially conforming he made no friends and seemed emotionally isolated – from adults and peers alike. Those in charge attributed his condition to his never having been cared for during his early years by any one motherly person, a result of his illegitimate birth. Thus I was alerted to a possible connection between prolonged deprivation and the development of a personality apparently incapable of making affectional bonds and, because immune to praise and blame, prone to repeated delinquencies.
>
> (Bowlby 1981a)

The second seminal encounter at the school was with another man working there, John Alford, who had had some personal therapy, and who advised John to go to London to train as a psychoanalyst.

Psychoanalytical training

In the autumn of 1929, aged twenty-two, John came to London, to start his medical studies. He found these so tedious and wearisome that he started and managed 'Bogey's Bar', a sandwich bar patronised by his friends. While at University College Hospital (which was, and has remained, a home for would-be psychoanalysts wanting to acquire a medical degree) he entered the Institute of Psycho-Analysis, going into analysis with Mrs Riviere, a close friend and associate of Melanie Klein. His intention was to become a child psychiatrist, a profession which was then just emerging. After medical qualification in 1933, he went to the Maudsley to train in adult psychiatry, and then was appointed in 1936 to the London Child Guidance Clinic, where he worked until he became an Army psychiatrist in 1940.

The 1930s were a time of intellectual ferment. Progressive thought centred on Freud and Marx. Bettelheim vividly captures the atmosphere of debate:

> In order to create the good society, was it of first importance to change society radically enough for all persons to achieve full self-realisation? In this case psychoanalysis could be discarded, with the possible exception of a few deranged persons. Or was this the wrong approach, and could persons who had achieved full personal liberation and integration by being psychoanalysed create such a good society? In the latter case the correct thing was to forget for the time being any social or economic revolution and to concentrate instead on pushing psychoanalysis; the hope was that once the majority of men had profited from its inner liberation they would almost automatically create the good society for themselves and all others.
>
> (Bettelheim 1960)

Although by nature irreverent and at times iconoclastic, Bowlby tempered his rebelliousness with a belief in science and the need for evidence to back up ideas. He shared a house with his friend the Labour politician and academic Evan Durbin, who challenged his newly acquired psychoanalytic ideas – as did Aubrey Lewis at the Maudsley. While he believed in the practical efficacy of psychoanalysis, he was always sceptical about its theoretical basis. He came into conflict with his first psychoanalytical supervisor, 'a rather prim old maid . . . we never seemed to be on the same wavelength' (Bowlby 1991), but got on very well with his next, Ella Sharpe, who supported Anna Freud against Klein in the 'Controversial Discussions', 'a warm hearted middle-aged woman who had a good understanding of human nature and a sense of humour' (Bowlby 1991). He qualified as an analyst in 1937, and immediately started training in child analysis with Mrs Klein as his supervisor. Here too there was conflict, especially when Bowlby felt that she paid insufficient attention to the part played by the environment in causing his patient's disturbance – in this case a hyperactive little boy of three whose mother was having a breakdown and had been admitted to mental hospital.

Meanwhile, Bowlby was beginning to develop his own ideas, based mainly on his experience at the Child Guidance Clinic. There he worked with two analytically orientated social workers who introduced him to the idea of the transgenerational transmission of neurosis in which unresolved problems from a parent's own childhood can play a large part in causing and perpetuating the problems of their children.

> I was particularly struck by two cases, one of sibling rivalry in which the mother had herself been intensely jealous of her sister, and the other in which a father was deeply troubled by his seven-year-old son's masturbation and had dipped him under a cold tap whenever he found him touching his genitals, and who, it transpired, had himself fought an unsuccessful battle against masturbation all his life.
>
> (Bowlby 1977)

With his stress on the role of the environment in causing psychological difficulty, Bowlby was aligned with a group of British psychiatrists who, while influenced by Freud and sympathetic to the analytic cause, also maintained some distance from it. These included David Eder, a left-wing intellectual associated with the Bloomsbury Group; Bernard Hart, psychiatrist at University College Hospital, whose influential *Psychology of Insanity* Bowlby would certainly have read; W. H. Rivers, famous as an anthropologist as well as psychiatrist, who had applied Freud's ideas to victims of shell-shock in the First World War and who felt that the self-preservative instinct was as important as Freud's sexuality; and, above all, Ian Suttie, whose *Origins of Love and Hate* proposed a primary bond between mother and child, unrelated to infantile sexuality (Heard 1986; Pines 1991; Newcombe and

Lerner 1982), an idea which, as we shall see in Chapter 4, Bowlby was to develop and put at the heart of Attachment Theory.

In order to qualify as a full member with voting rights in the analytic society Bowlby had to read a paper. Many of his later ideas are to be found in embryonic form in 'The influence of the environment in the development of neuroses and neurotic character', which was published in the *International Journal of Psycho-Analysis* in 1940. It consists of a description of cases treated in the Child Guidance Clinic. He emphasises the scientific value of such one-weekly 'clinic cases' to complement more intensive analytic work. He boldly puts forward a 'general theory of the genesis of neurosis', in which environmental factors in the early years of a child's life are causative, especially separation from the mother through death or 'broken home'. He explicitly challenges the Kleinian view – actually something of a caricature, a product of the polarisation within the Society at that time, since Kleinians have never entirely denied the importance of the environment – that childhood phantasy is unrelated to actual experience: 'Much has been written about the introjection of phantastically severe parents, an imaginary severity being itself the product of projection. Less perhaps has been written recently about the introjection of the parents' real characters' (Bowlby 1940a). He cautions against unnecessary separation of children from parents – 'if a child must be in hospital the mother should be encouraged to visit daily' – and insists that

> If it became a tradition that small children were never sub-
> jected to complete or prolonged separation from their parents
> in the same way that regular sleep and orange juice have
> become nursery traditions, I believe that many cases of neur-
> otic character development would be avoided.
>
> (Bowlby 1940a)

He advocates working with the mothers of disturbed children so as to elucidate their own childhood difficulties which are interfering with their role as parents, and thereby helping them to feel less guilty. A second paper, 'Forty-four juvenile thieves, their characters and home life' (which led to Bowlby's wartime nickname of Ali Bowlby and his Forty Thieves), was also based on his work in the Child Guidance Clinic and continues the same ideas in a more systematic way. His capacity for coining a telling phrase emerges in his notion of the 'affectionless psychopath' –

a juvenile thief for whom the lack of good and continuous childhood care has created in him (it almost always is a him) an
absence of concern for others.

In this early work Bowlby shows a strong reforming drive: he
saw psychotherapy as preventative medicine which would help to
change not just individuals but also society. But he would not
have accepted Bettelheim's view that one had to choose between
Marx or Freud, nor was he prepared to swallow either whole.
His attitude towards extremism, whether Kleinian or communist,
might be compared with A. S. Neill's account of a wedding he
had attended:

> Filled with followers of Melanie Klein . . . they can't laugh;
> Melanie has evidently shown them humour is a complex which
> no normal man should have. To my asking what Klein was
> doing to prevent complexes there was a silence. I said: you
> can't analyse humanity but you can attempt to get a humanity
> that won't need analysis. No answer. Gott, they were a dull
> crowd. . . . Rather like talking to communists with a blank
> curtain that you could not penetrate.
>
> (Grosskurth 1986)

Several of John's friends of both sexes were acquired through his
more sociable older brother. Tony shared a 'staircase' at Oxford
with Evan Durbin, later to become a minister in the post-war
Attlee labour administration. Similar in physique, intelligence
and temperament, he and John soon struck up a close friendship,
based on shared intellectual interests and a love of walking (it
was hard to keep up with them as they strode rapidly through
the Cotswolds, deep in conversation). They collaborated in their
book *Personal Aggressiveness and War* (Durbin and Bowlby
1938). In Bowlby's contribution we see again later talents and
themes prefigured. He introduces psychoanalytic ideas in a common-sense (if slightly old-fashioned) way: in exemplifying the
concept of unconscious aggression he ways, 'It is impossible to
criticise some maids without paying for it in breakages. Plates
"come apart in my hands" far more frequently after the maid
has been reprimanded than when she has been praised' (Durbin
and Bowlby 1938). He surveys the literature on aggression in
apes and other higher mammals drawing parallels with human
behaviour, just as he was to do in the 1950s when he applied
ethological ideas to mother–infant behaviour. He also subjects

Marxist ideas about war to the same critical scrutiny with which he had approached psychoanalysis as an ideology, pointing out the dangers of any global theory of human behaviour.

Bowlby's friendship with Durbin continued until the latter's untimely death by drowning while on holiday in Cornwall in the late 1940s. Bowlby, who was on holiday nearby, was called in to help and in his typically practical way immediately organised with Durbin's close parliamentary colleagues a trust fund which supported the Durbin children through their education. Durbin's death was the most overwhelming loss of John's life, and certainly influenced his interest in the themes of grief and loss which were to figure so centrally in his work.

The war years

Bowlby volunteered in 1940 at the age of thirty-three, but was not called up and joined instead a group of Army psychiatrists whose main job was, by using statistical and psychotherapeutic methods, to put officer selection on a scientific footing – to put, as it was said, the 'chi' into psychiatry. His organisational and intellectual qualities soon showed themselves and he worked closely with members of the 'invisible college' (Pines 1991) of psychoanalytic soldiers like Wilfred Bion, Eric Trist and Jock Sutherland on the selection boards.

By 1944 the War Office had established a Research and Training Unit in Hampstead, of which Bowlby was a member. This enabled him to continue active participation in the affairs of the Psychoanalytic Society, riven at that time by factional fighting between the Kleinian and Freudian groups. Emerging from the 'Controversial Discussions' these differences were contained by the 'gentlemen's agreement' between the two ladies, Anna Freud and Melanie Klein. This established two training streams: 'A', the Freudians, and 'B', which comprised the Kleinians and 'Independents' (who later split off as a separate 'middle group' of which Bowlby was a member). The President of the Society, Sylvia Payne, herself an Independent, proposed Bowlby as Training Secretary in 1944, and despite not being a Training Analyst, and against strong opposition from Melanie Klein, his balance and organisational ability were recognised, and he was duly elected. Bowlby's passionate and uncompromising feelings were much in evidence at meetings of the Psycho-Analytic Society

during that period. As well as the Klein–Freud split there was a
more general division about the aims and methods of the Society.
Under Jones's and later Glover's leadership the Society had
adopted something of the features of a secret cell: purist, esoteric,
autocratically led, unwilling to sully itself with anything but the
'pure gold' of psychoanalysis, and refusing to have anything to
do with the analytic fellow travellers represented by the Tavistock
Clinic, who included several Christian psychiatrists like J. R.
Rees and Suttie, and which was referred to contemptuously by
the psychoanalysts as the 'parson's clinic' (Pines 1991). All this
was anathema to Bowlby, who believed in democratic methods
and was appalled by what he saw as the Society's indifference
towards the emergence of a National Health Service which was
clearly going to be established after the war. He advocated full
participation in the discussions between the Government and the
medical profession:

> We find ourselves in a rapidly changing world and yet, as a
> Society, we have done nothing, I repeat nothing, to meet these
> changes, to influence them or to adapt to them. That is not
> the reaction of a living organism but a moribund one. If our
> Society died of inertia it would only have met the fate it had
> invited.
>
> (King and Steiner 1990)

Bowlby and the progressives carried the day, and Bowlby was
delegated as a member of the Government's Mental Health
Standing Committee, where he proceeded to have the same effect
on the civil servants as he did on the older members of the
Society, and he was described in a Whitehall report as a '"live"
member, with embarrassing enthusiasm for his own speciality. An
advanced theorist who does not always give weight to practical
considerations' (Webster 1991).

Family life

Tony Bowlby married young: a beautiful musician and actress
whom he met through his sisters who were at the Royal Academy
of Music. John had had several tempestuous liaisons, but as his
analysis progressed and he approached his thirties, began to wish
to settle down. On holiday in the New Forest he encountered
the Longstaffs, a family of seven attractive daughters living with

their pipe-smoking mother whose father, Dr Longstaff, the famous alpinist, had abandoned her for a younger woman. Ursula, the third daughter, intelligent and beautiful but more diffident than her older sisters, attracted his interest. On a shooting holiday in Ireland she and John fell for each other. They were married in 1938. John, like his father, was some ten years older than his bride. Ursula proved a devoted and loyal companion. Although highly intelligent and literate, she had no knowledge of psychology, and claims not to have read any of his books except the biography of Darwin on which she collaborated extensively. She also helped to supply the quotations for the chapter headings in the 'trilogy'.

The Bowlbys had four children, the day-to-day care of whom John left almost entirely to Ursula. The family was afflicted by dyslexia, a condition unrecognised at the time, and his children's academic difficulties were a source of some sorrow and frustration to their father, although they were fully compensated by their practical and technical abilities. John had had little experience of close parent–child relationships, and found fatherhood a difficult role. He was, by contrast, in his daughter Mary's words, a 'brilliant grandfather' ('Grampy's' good influence making itself felt again) – tolerant, funny and adoring. John and Ursula's grandson, Ben, in the Bowlby tradition of independence and originality, received first-class honours in engineering for designing and building his own racing car – an 'external working model' (see Chapter 4). John, a slightly remote father, followed his own father's tradition of hard work and long holidays, so much so that his eldest son asked, around the age of seven, 'Is Daddy a burglar? He always comes home after dark and never talks about his work!' Family holidays were in Scotland, and a house was first rented and then bought on Skye where John, Ursula and the children could enjoy the walking, boating, bird-watching, shooting and fishing in beautiful and remote surroundings that repeated the pattern of his own childhood.

The Bowlbys and the Durbins had shared a house in York Terrace (where Adrian and Karen Stephens and Ernest Jones had their consulting rooms). This pattern was continued after the war when John's democratic ideas and recognition of the benefits of an extended network of friends and family when bringing up small children were realised, when he and Ursula and their growing family shared a large house in Hampstead with the Sutherlands (Jock Sutherland was soon to become director of the Tavistock Clinic) and with a young psychologist, later to become Mrs Mattie Harris, who became organising tutor of the child psychotherapy training programme at the Tavistock (Sutherland 1991).

The post-war years: the Tavistock Clinic

Immediately after the war the 'invisible college' of Army psychoanalysts re-grouped themselves around the Tavistock Clinic, hitherto ruled out of bounds by the autocratic Jones. An election was held and, although neither had previously worked there, Jock Sutherland was elected Director, with Bowlby as Deputy, given the specific task of developing a Department for Children.

John went about this with his usual energy, efficiency and determination. He established a clinical service, treating patients, seeing mothers and children together, spending one day a week in a well-baby clinic, supervising, and chairing case conferences. Together with Esther Bick he set up the child psychotherapy training and continued to support it, even when its Kleinian orientation began to diverge sharply from his own views.

About a third of his week was devoted to clinical and administrative duties. The rest was for research. One of John's unsung qualities was his ability to raise research funds. On the basis of his pre-war experiences in the Child Guidance Clinic, he had decided to make a systematic study of the effects of separation on the personality development of young children. He recruited James Robertson, a conscientious objector in the war who had worked as a boilerman in Anna Freud's Hampstead residential children's nursery, and who later became an analyst and filmmaker. Mary Ainsworth, later to become the co-founder of Attachment Theory, also joined the team, as did Mary Boston. The outcome of Bowlby's collaboration with Robertson was the famous film *A Two-year-old Goes to Hospital*, which showed the intense distress of a small child separated from her mother, made with a hand-held cine-camera without artificial light, almost impossible to watch dry-eyed, and which did so much to liberalise hospital visiting rules. As mentioned in the previous chapter, the film met with a mixed reception when shown to the Psycho-Analytical Society, the Kleinians being particularly unimpressed, a foretaste of the response Bowlby was to meet when he presented his breakthrough papers on Attachment Theory a few years later.

Bowlby's research interests, together with his Forty-four Thieves paper, made him an obvious choice when the World Health Organisation was looking for an expert to prepare a report on the mental health of homeless children. Bowlby travelled widely in Europe and the United States, meeting the leading figures in child development, and combined their views with his own in a review of the world literature, *Maternal Care and Mental Health* (Bowlby 1951). This was published in a popular edition as *Child Care and the Growth of Love* (Bowlby 1953), which became an instant best-seller, selling 450,000 in the English edition alone, and was translated into ten different languages.

Bowlby's reputation was by now secure and he was able to follow his innovative instincts without anxiety. He was keen to break down the ivory towerism of the Tavistock and to foster links with local health visitors, GPs and social workers. His efforts to establish liaison were blocked until the Minister of Health issued a directive asking the London County Council to pay more attention to mental health. The Chief Medical Officer of the LCC invited Bowlby to give a lecture on the subject. He refused, saying that mental health could not be properly taught by didactic methods, but offering to join a study group if one were set up. A week later he received a message from the Chief Medical Officer: 'Your "study group" is ready. When would you like to start?' (Mackenzie 1991).

Ainsworth (1982) believes that the idea of attachment came to Bowlby 'in a flash' when in 1952 he heard about and then read Lorenz's and Tinbergen's work in ethology, having been lent an advance copy of *King Solomon's Ring* by Julian Huxley. The ethological approach provided the scientific grounding that Bowlby believed was needed to update psychoanalytic theory. Seen psychobiographically, Attachment Theory might be seen as a return by Bowlby to the values of his mother which he had rejected when he became a psychoanalyst. Disappointed with his mother's self-preoccupations and favouritism, he turned to the many mothers of psychoanalysis – Klein, Riviere, Payne. But these too, partly through their own limitations, partly because they contained his hostile projections, disappointed in their turn. By marrying the biology of ethology with Freudian theory, he managed to reconcile the discordant elements in his personality:

his country-loving mother with her respect for nature, and the intimidating urban medical father whose success and intelligence were inspirational but whose Gradgrindian devotion to fact and duty dominated his life. Bowlby soon organised regular attachment seminars which were attended by a talented and eclectic group including the ethologist Robert Hinde and, for a time, R. D. Laing. A year as a fellow at the Centre for Behavioural Sciences in Stanford, California, gave him an opportunity to reread Freud and to prepare the breakthrough papers of the late 1950s, starting with 'The nature of the child's tie to his mother' (Bowlby 1958).

Bowlby remained active in the Psycho-Analytical Society in the post-war years. He was Deputy President to Donald Winnicott between 1956 and 1961, responsible for 'everything administrative' (Bowlby 1991). He set up and chaired the Research Committee, and initiated several other committees, including the Public Relations Committee; a committee to look at indemnity insurance for non-medical members (typical of Bowlby to be alert to the possible hazards to members uncushioned by the secure base of medicine); and the Curriculum Committee (set up to prevent trainings becoming interminable – another typically practical move).

While the society was happy to benefit from his organisational skills, Bowlby's theoretical papers, presented between 1957 and 1959, excited considerable discussion but little enthusiasm, and were received by the Kleinians with outright hostility. Typical comments were: from Guntrip, 'I think it is very good for an eminent psychoanalyst to have gone thoroughly into the relation of ethology to psychoanalysis, but my impression is that he succeeds in using it to explain everything in human behaviour except what is of vital importance for psychoanalysis' – (1962, letter to Marjorie Brierley, in Archives, Institute of Psychoanalysis); from Winnicott, although generally friendly and sympathetic to Bowlby's contribution (Malan 1991), 'I can't quite make out why it is that Bowlby's papers are building up in me a kind of revulsion although in fact he has been scrupulously fair to me in my writings'; and, from an anonymous analyst, 'Bowlby? Give me Barabbas' (Grosskurth 1986). The analysts found his patrician manner and 'orotund' (Rycroft 1992) delivery offputting, although these may well have been exaggerated in the intimidating atmosphere of the Psycho-Analytical Society at the time. Bowlby had an impish quality and a capacity for amusing tomfoolery which was clearly not evident to the analysts. Whether Bowlby did indeed betray psychoanalysis, or breathed new life into it, will form much of the discussion in subsequent chapters.

The trilogy

Partly no doubt because of his hostile reception, and partly because of his growing reputation elsewhere, Bowlby spent little time in the Psycho-Analytical Society after the mid–1960s although, unlike other distinguished dissidents such as Rycroft and Meltzer, he did not discontinue his membership. While continuing his clinical role at the Tavistock, in 1963 he became a part-time member of the Medical Research Council, which enabled him to devote yet more time to writing. The years 1964 to 1979 were devoted to his monumental trilogy *Attachment* (1969b), *Separation* (1973a), and *Loss* (1980). These have also been best-sellers, with the first volume selling well over 100,000, the second 75,000, and the third 45,000 (Bowlby *et al.* 1986). Colin Murray Parkes and Dorothy Heard joined him at the Tavistock in the 1960s. Like Bowlby, Parkes had been struck by the relevance of Darwin's ideas about grief to abnormal mourning, and a fruitful partnership developed (Parkes 1964, 1971, 1975). Bowlby was much in demand as a lecturer, especially in the United States where, through the work of Ainsworth (1969), Attachment Theory was exciting increasing interest.

Bowlby held numerous important positions and consultancies, and received many honours, including the CBE, Honorary Doctorates at Cambridge and Leicester, Honorary Fellowships of the Royal Society of Medicine and College of Psychiatrists, Fellowship of the British Academy, and several Distinguished Scientist awards and medals in the United States, including that of the American Psychological Association. As befits an innovator and original thinker, he was probably slightly more honoured abroad than at home, and neither received a knighthood nor became an FRS, both of which many thought were his due (Kraemer 1991). He did, however, do 'better' than his lifelong friend and rival, his brother Tony.

He retired from the NHS and the MRC in 1972, but remained at the Tavistock Clinic, dividing his time between London and his beloved Skye. He continued to encourage students and to receive many foreign visitors. During 1980 he was Freud Memorial Professor of Psychoanalysis at University College London, a post which gave him great satisfaction. His lectures from there and his trips abroad were collected in *The Making and Breaking of Affectional Bonds* (1979c) and *A Secure Base* (1988a). Mentally and physically active as ever, he began an entirely new project in his seventies, a psychobiography of Darwin (Bowlby 1990), which was published a few months before his death, and was well reviewed.

His eightieth birthday was celebrated in London with a conference with many distinguished speakers from around the world. The affection he inspired was palpable, as, garlanded with flowers, he embraced his many friends and colleagues to loud claps and cheers. A few weeks later he collapsed unconscious with a cardiac arrhythmia, but made a complete recovery, and was able to finish the Darwin biography. Three years later he suffered a stroke, while in Skye with his family, who had gathered as they did every year for the Skye Ball, where John had been a skilled exponent of Scottish reels. He died a few days later on 2 September 1990, and was buried at Trumpan on the Waternish peninsula, a hillside graveyard overlooking the cliffs of Waternish and the Ardmore peninsula. It was a favourite spot, wild and remote, from which John, with his great feeling for nature, often used to walk, and he had asked to be buried there. He had a traditional Skye funeral with three 'lifts' from the hearse to the grave. His friend Hyla Holden, a former Tavistock colleague, one of the bearers, concludes: 'his funeral and burial were in keeping with the straight-forward and loving simplicity which lay behind his formidable intellect' (Trowell 1991). His constancy and steadfastness of purpose are celebrated in the inscription on the headstone of pale grey Aberdeen granite, which reads: 'To be a pilgrim'.

BOWLBY THE MAN

What was John Bowlby like? In his work his greatest achievement was his bringing together of psychoanalysis and, via ethology, evolutionary biology. A similar capacity to reconcile divergent elements is to be found in his personality which, although remarkably coherent and consistent, contained many contradictory aspects: reserved, yet capable of inspiring great affection; quintessentially 'English' and yet thoroughly cosmopolitan in outlook; conventional in manner yet revolutionary in spirit; equally at home with the sophistication of Hampstead and in the wilds of Skye; outstandingly intelligent and yet not in a conventional sense an intellectual; a man of action who devoted his life to the inner world; determined in his convictions and yet without overt aggression; an explorer of the psyche who mistrusted the purely subjective; someone who believed passionately in the importance of expressing emotion, whose own feelings were an enigma; an *enfant terrible* who was always slightly formal.

It is hard to get an impression of Bowlby as a therapist because personal clinical material is so sparse in his writings. He is fierce in his opposition to rigid and punitive methods of child-rearing, detests the way in which children are deprived of love and affection in the name of not 'spoiling' them, and insists on the enduring nature of dependency which he refuses to see as a childlike quality to be outgrown, but rather an essential aspect of human nature. One guesses that he had first-hand experience of the child-rearing philosophy he rejects so vigorously. He consistently advocates flexibility and acceptance:

> An immense amount of friction and anger in small children and loss of temper on the part of their parents can be avoided by such simple procedures as presenting a legitimate plaything before we intervene to remove his mother's best china, or coaxing him to bed by tactful humouring instead of demanding prompt obedience, or by permitting him to select his own diet and eat it in his own way, including, if he likes it, having a feeding bottle until he is two years of age or over. The amount of fuss and irritation which comes from expecting small children to conform to our own ideas of what, how, and when they eat is ridiculous and tragic.
>
> (Bowlby 1979c)

The dangers of suppressing feelings is repeatedly emphasised by Bowlby:

> a main reason why some find expressing grief extremely difficult is that the family in which they have been brought up, and with which they still mix, is one in which the attachment behaviour of the child is regarded unsympathetically as something to be grown out of as soon as possible . . . crying and

other protests over separation are apt to be dubbed as babyish, and anger and jealousy as reprehensible.

(Bowlby 1979c)

Bowlby describes one such patient:

> I well remember how a silent inhibited girl in her early twenties given to unpredictable moods and hysterical outbursts at home responded to my comment 'it seems to be as though your mother never really loved you' (she was the second daughter, to be followed in quick succession by two much wanted sons). In a flood of tears she confirmed my view by quoting, verbatim, remarks made by her mother from childhood to the present day, and [describing] the despair, jealousy, and rage her mother's treatment roused in her.

(Bowlby 1979)

Bowlby himself came from a family in which there were two daughters, to be followed in quick succession by two much wanted sons, with a mother whose love her children may well have doubted (with the possible exception of Tony), so he probably knew what he was talking about. Even if he did not have a particularly loving mother, Bowlby had learned enough from her, and perhaps from his much-loved nursemaid Minnie who left when he was no more than four, to know what it takes to be one. In adult life he relied greatly on his wife Ursula's intuition and sensitivity. In a posthumously published self-portrait Bowlby modestly asserts:

> I am not strong on intuition. Instead, I tend to apply such theories as I hold in an effort to understand the patient's problems. This works well when the theories are applicable but can be a big handicap when they are not. Perhaps my saving graces have been that I am a good listener and not too dogmatic about theory. As a result several of my patients have succeeded in teaching me a great deal I did not know. . . . I often shudder to think how inept I have been as a therapist and how I have ignored or misunderstood material a patient has presented. Clearly, the best therapy is done by a therapist who is naturally intuitive and also guided by the appropriate theory. Fortunately, nowadays I meet many such people in clinical seminars, and among supervisees.

(Bowlby 1991)

One such was Victoria Hamilton, who confirms Bowlby's listening skills, painting a vivid portrait:

> a very unassuming person who at the same time displayed an unusual acuity. . . . My most constant image of John Bowlby . . . is of him sitting back in a chair, his legs crossed indicating an expression of relaxed concentration, and a very alert face. He had penetrating but responsive eyes, beneath raised eyebrows which expressed both interest and a slight air of surprise and expectation . . . a remarkable ability to listen to the thoughts and beliefs of others, combined with a capacity for objectivity and a rare facility with the English language. He could step back from an idea and reformulate it in a succinct articulate way. . . . Despite his somewhat military manner, expressed in a certain abruptness and stiffness very far from 'small talk', he was perfectly able to 'take turns', the essential ingredient of conversation.

(Hamilton 1991)

A lifelong friend, Jock Sutherland (1991), describes his first encounter with John during the war, in which he appeared 'somewhat formal and even aloof'. Sutherland and Eric Trist, another of John's half-century friends, speculated that Bowlby's description of the 'affectionless character' was based on empathic understanding (rather as Freud's discovery of the Oedipus complex was based on his own rivalry with his father):

> We speculated that John's own early experience must have included a degree, if not of actual deprivation, of some inhibition of his readiness to express emotional affection . . . so that he developed in some measure a protective shell of not showing his feelings as readily as many people do. . . . John's slightly formal and even detached manner struck many people on first knowing him Eric Trist and I were always convinced he was the possessor of a deep and powerful fund of affection – the source of his intensely caring concern for those who worked with him.

(Sutherland 1991)

John Byng-Hall, another Tavistock colleague, sees Bowlby as a perfect embodiment of his idea of the secure base, capable of holding together family therapists and child psychotherapists despite their very different philosophies, alert to real dangers faced by patients and therapists, and above all 'very reliable. I have images of him, even last winter [i.e. in his eighty-second year], shaking the rain off his green mackintosh and hat as he arrived on time for some evening meeting; while others sent their apologies' (Byng-Hall 1991).

Those clocks that Bowlby had grown up with did have their uses.

SPRINGS OF ACTION AND THOUGHT

It seems to be a characteristic of many outstanding men and women that they retain the freshness and innocence of childhood, however clothed it is with responsibility and the burdens of maturity. This was certainly true of Bowlby's great hero, Darwin (Bowlby 1990), with whom he strongly identified, and had much in common, although he would have been embarrassed by the comparison. Like Darwin, Bowlby had a boyhood love of outdoor sports, of the countryside and of exploration, with a keenness of intellect that was not precociously evident. Like Darwin, Bowlby had a strong and successful medical father; both seem to have aroused in their sons a rebelliousness hedged about with caution. Both were younger sons, with clever and rather overshadowing older brothers and sisters. Darwin's mother died when he was eight; Bowlby's was (at least in her London life) remote and self-centered. Both lived in times of social turmoil and had a strongly held but restrained sense of social justice, and of the responsibilities of the fortunate towards the disadvantaged, in the best Whig tradition. They both believed passionately in the power of reason to illuminate both the natural and social world. Bowlby admired Darwin's openness to all available evidence, as shown by the long hours he spent in smoke-filled public houses discussing breeding methods with pigeon fanciers in search of support for his theory of natural selection. Bowlby, too, mixed with mothers in nurseries and baby clinics, ever observant of patterns of attachment. Both showed generosity towards their supporters, and lacked rancour towards their detractors. Finally, it might be said of their theories that they have the quality of immediacy and 'obviousness' – of which it might be said, 'Why on earth did no one think of that before?' In retrospect it seems obvious that species have evolved by natural selection, that people are attached to one another and suffer when they separate – but it took child-like simplicity of vision combined with mature determination and attention to detail to root out the obvious and to create for it a secure theoretical base.

Bowlby describes an early boyhood memory of Darwin's concerning showing off:

> He recalls 'thinking that people were admiring me, in one instance for perseverance, and another for boldness in climbing a low tree, and what is odder, a consciousness, as if instinctive, that I was vain, and a contempt for myself'. This reference to self-contempt for being vain thus early in his life is of much significance, since we find it persisting as a major feature of his character into his final years.
>
> (Bowlby 1990)

Here we see Bowlby's extreme sensitivity to the uncertainties, miseries and vulnerability of childhood, to the gulf between a child's fragile self-esteem and a potentially hostile or indifferent world. Bowlby cared intensely about the mental pain of children, and his life's work was directed towards trying to prevent, remove and alleviate it. Behind the disturbed child's tough, 'affectionless' carapace Bowlby had a sixth sense for the sadness and sense of betrayal. Apparently bolder than Darwin, Bowlby kept his vulnerability well hidden. But in his rebelliousness we see perhaps the protest of the child who has been hurt and neglected. In his application and indefatigability we find the attempt to make good the unthinking damage the adult world so often does to children.

Many of Bowlby's metaphors were medical. Famously, 'mother-love is as important for mental health as are vitamins and proteins for physical health' (Bowlby 1953); 'deprived children . . . are a source of social infection as real and serious as are carriers of diphtheria and typhoid' (Bowlby 1953); 'the basic fact that people really do want to live happily together . . . gives confidence [to the family therapist], much as a knowledge of the miraculous healing powers of the body gives confidence to the surgeon' (Bowlby 1948).

Bowlby's ideas were forged in the era of two world wars. Millions died in the first war. The enormity of the loss went unmourned by society in the triumphalism of Versailles and the manic activity of the twenties. The second war saw the horror of the Holocaust, countless more deaths, and the disruption of the lives of children throughout Europe. As early as the 1930s,

Bowlby saw loss and separation as the key issues for psychotherapy and psychiatry. It was the men – the fathers, sons,
brothers, husbands, lovers – who died; it was a men's world that
went to war. And yet in Bowlby's work men are conspicuous by
their absence. It is *maternal* deprivation that made Bowlby's
name. Bowlby's strong identification with his much-absent father
comes through in his medical imagery, but he does not emerge
as a live figure in the family drama as depicted by Bowlby, or
indeed by the other outstanding analysts of his generation, Klein
and Winnicott. Bowlby's contribution, and that of his contempor-
aries, has been to rehabilitate the female principle, the missing
mother who until then was absent from social and psychoanalytic
discourse (Freud's main preoccupation was with fathers and their
children). In his concept of maternal deprivation it is as though
Bowlby was simultaneously reproving and idealising his neglectful
mother. Unlike Winnicott he seems uncertain of his intuitive
feminine side, just as he may have mistrusted his mother with
her fickle and uneven affections. In his theories of motherhood
it is as though Bowlby is *enacting* the male role – the guardian
of evidence and objectivity – without really examining it. His
father is there in the metaphors but not at the meal table. Bowlby's maleness is in the counter-transferential blind spot through
which he sees mother and child, but not himself seeing them –
a typical example of the modern 'patriarchal but father-absent'
family (Leupnitz 1988). To consider these and other issues we
must now turn to the topic for which Bowlby is best known, that
misnamed miscreant, maternal deprivation.

Chapter 3

Maternal deprivation

[The] evidence is now such that it leaves no room for doubt . . . that the prolonged deprivation of a young child of maternal care may have grave and far reaching effects on his character and so on the whole of his future life. It is a proposition exactly similar in form to those regarding the evil after-effects of German measles before birth or deprivation of vitamin D in infancy.

(Bowlby 1953)

Statements implying that children who experience institutional-isation and similar forms of privation in early life *commonly* develop psychopathic or affectionless characters are incorrect.
(Bowlby, Ainsworth, Boston and Rosenbluth 1956)

Psychotherapy can be seen as a branch of social psychiatry, using psychological methods to reverse or mitigate the damaging effects of environmental failure. This immediately raises two questions. First, given that the damage is already done, how can mere talk undo past miseries? Second, given that many people survive unhappy childhoods without developing psychiatric disorder, are therapists justified in attributing present difficulty to previous trauma? The two quotations from Bowlby above illustrate the transition between his career as a clinician and psychoanalyst to that of a researcher and theorist. The therapist, faced with the patient in front of him, naturally attributes his difficulties to the history of environmental failures he recounts. The researcher, with a control group and a sense of a population at risk rather than just one individual, is forced to more cautious conclusions.

The answer to both questions, in brief, lies in the fact that environmental failure is not merely impressed on a passive organism, but is *experienced* and given meaning by the afflicted individual. Psychotherapy is concerned with the way that stress is mediated psychologically – with why this person succumbs while others survive – and, by altering psychological responsiveness and the attribution of meanings, to change not the facts of history, but their context and significance. In this chapter I shall approach these issues through a discussion of 'maternal deprivation', and its corollary, 'that maternal care in infancy and early childhood is essential for mental health' (Bowlby 1952). However self-evident it may seem to us now – and this is largely the result of Bowlby's work – the idea of maternal deprivation as a cause of mental illness was in its day a revolutionary concept which became a paradigm (Kuhn 1962), setting the terms of debate and research in social psychiatry for the ensuing forty years.

CHILD CARE AND THE GROWTH OF LOVE

As Rutter (1981) points out, the phrase 'maternal deprivation', the central concept of Bowlby's WHO report *Maternal Care and Mental Health*, is a misnomer. His report was concerned primarily with privation (the absence of something which is needed), rather than de-privation (the removal of something that was previously there). The distinction is important because, as we shall see, the results of the complete lack of maternal care are almost always damaging to the child and have severe long-term consequences, while deprivation is less easy to define and much less predictable in its impact.

In its popular edition, *Maternal Care and Mental Health* was retitled *Child Care and the Growth of Love* – a significant shift, since it suggests a universal message about mothers and children rather than confining itself to questions of mental health. The book is far more than a scientific work (and indeed has been criticised for its handling of the evidence – Andry 1962), and is perhaps best seen as a landmark social document, comparable to the great nineteenth-century reports such as Elizabeth Fry's account of sanitary conditions in prisons, or Mayhew's descriptions of the plight of the London poor.

What marks *Child Care and the Growth of Love* out in the history of social reform is its emphasis on *psychological* as opposed to economic, nutritional, medical or housing difficulties as a root cause of social unhappiness:

In a society where death rates are low, the rate of employment high, and social welfare schemes adequate, it is emotional instability and the inability of parents to make effective family relationships which are the outstanding cause of children becoming deprived of a normal family life.

(Bowlby 1952)

The evidence

The central thrust of Bowlby's work is the effort to substantiate this claim and to consider its clinical, professional, ethical and political consequences. The evidence upon which the book is based includes Bowlby's own studies of juvenile delinquents, Goldfarb's comparison of institution-raised children in the United States with those who had been placed in foster homes, and the accounts of Anna Freud and Dorothy Burlingham from their residential nursery in Hampstead. All these studies strongly support the view that children deprived of maternal care, especially if raised in institutions from under the age of seven, may be seriously affected in their physical, intellectual, emotional and social development. Institution-raised children grow less well, and are retarded in their acquisition of language, and as they become older show evidence of impaired ability to form stable relationships – often tending to be superficially friendly but promiscuous (either metaphorically or literally) in their relationships. Based on his own finding that only two out of fourteen 'affectionless psychopaths' had not had prolonged periods of separation from their mothers in early childhood Bowlby asserts that 'prolonged separation of a child from his mother (or mother substitute) during the first five years of life stands foremost among the causes of delinquent character development' (Bowlby 1944; Bowlby 1952). It is worth noting that Bowlby was making very sweeping conclusions based on studies which had often only looked at relatively small numbers of cases – in his case fourteen, in Goldfarb's only fifteen, juvenile delinquents. By present-day standards these studies would also not be acceptable in that they often included no control groups, or, if they did, they were not rated blind by the researchers, who had a vested interest in establishing a link between deprivation and depravity. Bowlby was aware of these difficulties and, anticipating the modern vogue for 'meta-analysis' (based roughly on the Maoist principle that '600 million

Chinese people cannot be wrong'), suggested that, by combining many small studies, an overall trend emerges which is likely to have some validity.

Family care versus institutional care

Having established to his satisfaction that children without maternal care are indeed gravely disadvantaged, Bowlby goes on to contrast the quality of life in a family with that in an institution:

> All the cuddling and playing, the intimacies of suckling by which a child learns the comfort of his mother's body, the rituals of washing and dressing by which through her pride and tenderness towards his little limbs he learns the values of his own, all these have been lacking.
>
> (Bowlby 1952)

The tinge of sentimentality in this lyrical account has, as we shall see, been much criticised by feminist writers, as has his hymn of praise to what Winnicott was later to call the 'ordinary devoted mother':

> The provision of constant attention night and day, seven days a week, 365 days in the year, is possible only for a woman who derives profound satisfaction from seeing her child grow from babyhood, through the many phases of childhood, to become an independent man or woman, and knows that it is her care which has made this possible.
>
> (Bowlby 1952)

These much-quoted and sometimes derided overstatements have to be seen in context. The world was horrified in the 1990s by the revelation of the squalor and emotional deprivation in the orphanages of Romania. This was not just the result of a dictatorship but of an ideological devaluation of family life, and a belief in the power of public provision to overcome individual poverty. Bowlby was reacting against a similar trend to be seen throughout Europe and the United States in the post-war era, and indeed to a long tradition among the British middle classes, of which he had first-hand experience, of turning their sons and many of their daughters over first to nannies and then to institutional care in boarding schools from the age of seven! To the extent that Bowlby idealises motherhood – as opposed to offering a realistic appraisal of its central importance in child-rearing – this must be seen at least in part as a reflection of the deprivations which he and other members of his class had experienced in the nursery and at school. The long hand of the otherwise invisible nanny reached far.

The impact of Bowlby's advocacy has been enormous, and continues to the present day. It is now taken for granted, and enshrined in the 1989 Children Act, that individual care in foster homes is preferable to group care in nurseries, that 'bad homes are better than good institutions' (Bowlby 1952). The battle to replace institutional care for the mentally ill and mentally handicapped with care within the family, or at least provision of a family-type home atmosphere, is still being waged.

The need for professionalisation of child care

Critics have accused Bowlby of wanting to 'pin women down in their own homes' (Mead 1962). While it is true that he criticises cavalier attitudes towards elective separations of mothers from children under the age of three, he could rather be seen as arguing for a much greater valuation by society of motherhood – indeed, as being recruited in support of the feminist demand for state provision of 'wages for housework'. Whatever his views on housewives, he puts a strong case for the professionalisation for all child-care workers, including workers in day nurseries and children's homes, foster mothers and (we would now add, since this argument has also not been fully won) child minders. These workers must be skilled in understanding a deprived child's overwhelming needs: the craving for parental love; the need to idolise parents however flawed they are in reality; the importance of maintaining contact with absent parents, however fragmentary; the right to express pain, protest about separation, and to grieve loss. They must also be able to help parents in turn to recognise their children's and their own ambivalent feelings. He is intensely critical of case workers who 'live in the sentimental glamour of saving neglected children from wicked parents' (Bowlby 1952) (a comment still relevant today to the dilemmas presented by working with sexually abused children), and of actions which 'convert a physically neglected but psychologically well-provided child into a physically well-provided but emotionally starved one' (Bowlby 1952). All these principles are now enshrined at least in the theory of child-care practice, and for this too Bowlby is largely responsible.

Government action

Much of the debate about the de-institutionalisation of the mentally ill has centred on the question of funding. It was thought that community care must be cheaper than institutional care, and partly for this reason it received governmental support. Bowlby puts forward similar economic arguments in favour of family support for troubled children:

> There are today governments prepared to spend up to £10 per week [this was 1952!] on the residential care of infants who would tremble to give half this sum to a widow, an unmarried mother, or a grandmother to help her care for her baby at home. . . . Nothing is more characteristic of both the public and voluntary attitude towards the problem than a willingness to spend large sums of money looking after children away from their homes, combined with a haggling stinginess in giving aid to the home itself.
>
> (Bowlby 1952)

Although, thanks to Bowlby and others, much has changed, much remains the same. For some things may be worse than in 1952: the haggling stinginess has returned, but is now accompanied by an *un*willingness to spend large sums on public provision. The 1989 Children Act creates a partnership between parents and the local authorities to provide for 'children in need', à la Bowlby, with cash payments if necessary, but no extra funding has been made available for this.

Vicious and benign circles

A major idea which emerges in *Child Care and the Growth of Love* is that of cycles of deprivation: 'the neglected psychopathic child growing up to become the neglectful psychopathic parent . . . a self-perpetuating social circle' (Bowlby 1952). Today's emotionally deprived child becomes tomorrow's neglectful parent: adverse experiences become internalised by the growing child in a way that leads on to further adverse experiences, thus perpetuating the vicious circle of neurosis. Writing in an era of social optimism, and with what, sadly, in hindsight must be seen as some naïvety, Bowlby argued that, with concentrated social, economic and psychological effort, society could put these vicious circles into reverse, so that 'it may, in two or three generations, be possible to enable all boys and girls to grow up to become men and women who, given health and security, are capable of providing a stable and happy life for their children' (Bowlby 1952).

Psychoanalytical principles

One of the impressive features of *Child Care and the Growth of Love* is the way it presents psychoanalytical principles in an accessible and simple form. It is infused with the belief that it is always better to speak the truth, however painful, than to suppress it, and that to try to wipe the slate of the past clean is misguided and in any case impossible. Bowlby believed that children should be involved in any decisions about their welfare, and their own views and wishes taken into account – a principle which has only reached the statute book half a century later in the Children Act of 1989. He thought that children should be encouraged to express their ambivalent feelings about their parents. Children often believe themselves responsible for the calamities which befall them and their families, and child-care workers need to be aware of this and help put these feelings into perspective. For a child away from home 'the lack of a sense of time means that separation feels like an eternity', and this too needs to be understood. In a remarkable quotation from his psychoanalytic colleague Winnicott, a case is made that every child has a right to a primary home experience:

> without which the foundations of mental health cannot be laid down. Without someone specifically oriented to his needs the infant cannot find a working relation to external reality. Without someone to give satisfactory instinctual gratifications the infant cannot find his body, nor can he develop an integrated personality. Without one person to love and to hate he cannot come to know that it is the same person that he loves and hates, and so cannot find his sense of guilt, and his desire to repair and restore. Without a limited human and physical environment he cannot find out the extent to which his aggres-

sive ideas actually fail to destroy, and so cannot sort out the difference between fantasy and fact. Without a father and a mother who are together, and who take joint responsibility for him, he cannot find and express his urge to separate them, nor experience relief at failing to do so.

(Winnicott and Britton in Bowlby 1952)

These principles are as relevant today as they were when they were written. The tragedy of contemporary 'community care' is that, while the need to avoid the negative aspect of institutions has been grasped, the primary home experience as described by Winnicott remains elusive.

Bowlby's outrage

Perhaps the greatest single thread in Bowlby's work, one which comes through strongly in *Child Care and the Growth of Love*, is his pain and outrage at the unnecessary separation of children from their parents. He could take heart at the changes in pediatric and obstetric practice it has led to. The book ends with this passionate outcry at a 'developed' society which has forgotten the fundamental importance of human attachment:

Finally let the reader reflect for a moment on the astonishing practice which has been followed in obstetric wards – of separating mothers and babies immediately after birth – and ask himself whether this is the way to promote a close mother–child relationship. It is hoped that this madness of western society will never be copied by so-called less developed societies.

(Bowlby 1952)

Sadly, there is increasing evidence that Bowlby's fears are being realised.

Bowlby's work has excited considerable reaction, ranging from uncritical acceptance to outraged dismissal. His critics can be divided into two groups. First, there are those who question the social and political implications of his work, mainly from a feminist perspective. A rather different group of researchers have examined the factual basis of the concept of maternal deprivation. These workers, who include Bowlby himself, have modified and refined our understanding of the short- and long-term implications of maternal separation and mishandling for the developing child.

THE FEMINIST CRITIQUE

Feminists have aimed three broad kinds of criticism at the idea of maternal deprivation. The first, and most simple, merely accuses Bowlby of overstating his case. The studies upon which he bases his conclusions were of children who had experienced almost complete lack of maternal care. To generalise from these to the view that *any* separation of mother from child in the first three years of life is likely to be damaging is unwarranted (Oakley 1981). There is abundant evidence, they claim (and, as we shall see later, the facts support this view), that when a mother entrusts her child for part of the day to the care of a trusted and known person – whether a grandmother, a *metapalet* in a kibbutz, or a responsible baby minder – no harm is done. They argue, on the contrary, that *exclusive* care by the mother alone can lead to less rather than greater security for the child, and that Bowlby was wrong in his concept of 'monotropism' (that is, exclusive attachment of the child to one preferred figure). The reality is that the child has a hierarchy of attachment figures, of whom the mother is usually the most important, but that fathers, grandparents, siblings and other relations and friends also play a part, and that in the absence of one, the child will turn to another in a way that does not equate with the emotional promiscuity of the institution-raised child. They also point to the emotional burden on the mother alone with her child, who, despite (or because of) 24-hour proximity to her child may be emotionally neglectful even if she is physically attentive (Chodorow 1978). The dangers which Bowlby repeatedly identifies in his later work – role reversal between mother and child, threats of suicide, or saying the child will be sent away – can all be seen in part as consequences of this burden and the exclusivity which he advocates for the mother–child bond.

The second plank upon which the feminist critique rests is more complex, and consists of an attempt to locate Bowlby's ideas in an historical, anthropological and sociological context. It starts from the historical context of post-war Europe where, as New and David (1985) put it, Bowlby got an audience: women who had been working in munitions factories, obliged to send their children for nine or ten hours daily into indifferent nurseries, men who for years had been equating peace with the haven of the family, governments which saw the social and financial potential of idealizing motherhood and family life.

The collective sense of loss, and guilt, and desire for reparation found an answer in the idea of maternal deprivation. Children had suffered terribly as a result of the war, and this needed to be faced, as had the 'internal children' of the adults who had witnessed the horrors of war. The valuation and at times sentimentalising of the mother–child relationship in post-war Europe could be compared with a similar process in the nineteenth century in the face of the brutality of the Industrial Revolution. Bowlby's tenderness towards little children carries echoes of Blake and Wordsworth, Dickens and Kingsley. There had to be a safe place which could be protected from the violence of the modern world, and the Christian imagery of mother and child reappears, in his work, as an icon for a secular society.

A slightly different slant was offered in the suggestion that governments welcomed the idea of maternal deprivation in that it appeared to let them off the hook of providing child care, pushing it back to individual and family responsibility. Winnicott wrote to Bowlby warning him that his views were being used to close down much-needed residential nurseries (Rodman 1987). Bowlby had not, of course, argued that money should be withdrawn, but rather transferred from institutional care to home care, but, as in the more recent case of the mentally ill and handicapped, governments were less keen on this part of the argument.

The heart of the feminist case against Bowlby is that, like Freud, he had wrongly assumed that anatomy is destiny. Implicit, they argue, in the concept of maternal deprivation is a view of the biological 'naturalness' of an exclusive mother–child relationship which, as Margaret Mead (1962) puts it, is a 'reification into a set of universals of a set of ethnocentric observations on our own society'. Anthropology shows that what is normal is for child care to be shared by a stable *group* of adults and older children, usually, but not always, related, and usually, but by no means always, female. Maternal care is an important but certainly not exclusive part of this. For infants to survive in non-industrial countries such shared care is essential. As an Object-Relations theorist Bowlby rejects Freudian drive theory, but, once attachment theory was developed, offered an evolutionary-ethological account of the mother–child bond. Feminists object that he is using biology to justify what is essentially a cultural product of our own 'patriarchal but father-absent' society (Leupnitz 1988), with its nuclear families, small numbers of children, weakened kinship networks, mobile population, and fathers who are away from home for long periods, or absent altogether.

A more tenuous sociological argument (Mitscherlich 1963; Parsons 1964) suggests that the family structure which Bowlby implicitly advocates, with strong, closely bonded mothers and children, and peripheral fathers, fits the needs of modern capitalist society. Paternal authority has been replaced by that of the headmaster or boss in school, office and factory, producing a docile workforce, while the mother controls her children by bribes and threats, thus preparing them for the social manipulations of advertising and manufactured need which an ever-expanding consumerist economy requires. This pattern is offered as the norm for 'adequate' family functioning, as it is in the functionalist account offered by such influential writers as Parsons (1964). Leupnitz, from a feminist family therapy perspective, sees this as enshrining a state of affairs that suits men, but leaves wives who are obese, sexually dissatisfied, psychosomatically ill, and prone to depression (Leupnitz 1988).

Child Care and the Growth of Love was written about children who had lost their mothers, usually for good, and described the psychological consequences of that privation. Until recently, Europe had enjoyed an unprecedented period of peace and stability (warfare, starvation, genocide and mass migration have continued apace, exported to the developing world). The problems facing the modern family are not so much maternal deprivation as of paternal deprivation due to weak, absent or abusive fathers, and 'implosion' of the children onto unsupported mothers. Chodorow (1978) and other feminist psychotherapists have written about the psychological consequences of these changes. In summary, they lead to identity difficulties for both men and women. Lacking a strong father with whom to identify, boys differentiate themselves from their mothers and sisters by a disparagement of women, which conceals a dread of their phantasised omnipotence. It is this, according to Horney (1924), not Freud's castration anxiety, which underlies male fear of women and their difficulties in intimacy. The elusive search for 'success' is an attempt to please and appease the all-powerful mother. Girls, on the other hand, remain tied into their mothers, often taking on their pain and depression, and feeling intense guilt if they try to assert their independence and autonomy. The absent or seductive father makes a move towards him difficult or dangerous. Motherhood provides a temporary relief, but the girl again may feel caught in a mother–child dyad from which she still cannot escape, while the boy, now a father, feels excluded and jealous. As we shall see in later chapters, the Bowlbian concepts of avoidant and ambivalent attachment capture roughly these male and female patterns of anxious attachment in the modern family.

In summary, the feminist critique has questioned the logic of the implicit Bowlbian argument (one which in its simplistic form Bowlby would have been the first to repudiate) that since absent mothers lead to disturbed children, ever-present mothers will produce happy children. The feminists – in so far as it is possible to group them together – in turn have tended to overstate their case and failed to appreciate the importance which Bowlby has established for the role of the mother in her child's emotional development, both as a scientific fact and as a social and ethical principle. Bowlby's advocacy of the vital importance of mothers in the care of children, and the implications of his studies that good day-care facilities should be available for mothers who want or are forced by economic necessity to work, funded so that children can have individual and continuous relationships with care workers, should be seen as a step towards the liberation of women, increasing their range of choices and valuation by society.

Although still in print, it is now nearly fifty years since *Child Care and the Growth of Love* was first published. The terms of the debate have changed, so that, with less physical absence, but with ever-increasing difficulties in managing their lives, mothers are subject to enormous social pressures and their children are often the first casualties of this. For a more detailed examination of maternal deprivation from a contemporary perspective, and to a discussion of how children may be helped to escape or may remain ever more deeply trapped in deprivation we must turn now to the work of Michael Rutter.

MATERNAL DEPRIVATION REASSESSED

Rutter's monograph (Rutter 1981) and numerous papers (for example, Rutter 1972; Rutter 1979) comprise the definitive empirical evaluation and update of Bowlby's work on maternal deprivation. His contribution has been to amass further evidence, and, based on this, to begin to tease out the many different social and psychological mechanisms which operate under the rubric of maternal deprivation.

Bowlby, it will be recalled, claimed that maternal deprivation produced physical, intellectual, behavioural and emotional damage. He further argued that even brief separations from the mother in the first five years of life had long-lasting effects, and in general that these problems perpetuated themselves in a cycle of disadvantage as such children themselves became parents. Rutter has examined each of these points in turn.

On the question of intellectual and physical disadvantage, and the effects of brief separation, it seems that Bowlby was only partially right, and often for the wrong reasons. While it is true that institution-raised children are intellectually disadvantaged, this is mainly in verbal as opposed to performance intelligence, and this is a consequence of the child's 'verbal environment', not the lack of parents *per se*. Children brought up in large families are similarly disadvantaged. It is lack of verbal stimulation that is the problem for the deprived children, not lack of mother. A similar picture emerges with 'deprivation dwarfism', which has been shown to be due, as might be expected, to lack of food intake rather than some mysterious emotional factor, and can be rapidly reversed by attentive feeding, whether by a nurse or mother.

Acute separation distress is also probably less damaging, and more complex than Bowlby first saw it. Preparation and care by known figures reduces distress, and even without these there is no evidence of long-term effects from a single brief separation however painful it may be at the time. An important point comes from Hinde's rhesus monkey studies (Hinde and McGinnis 1977), which show that the effects of separation depend on the mother–child relationship *before* the event: the more tense the relationship, the more damaging the separation. These kinds of findings indicate a move towards a more subtle appreciation of the nature of bonds, and away from simplistic event-pathology models. What matters is not so much the separation itself but its meaning and the context in which it happens.

A similar conclusion applies to the relationship between anti-social behaviour and maternal deprivation. First, as Rutter (1979) puts it, 'the links are much stronger looking back than they are looking forward'. In 'Forty-four juvenile thieves', Bowlby found that a quarter of the thieves had had major separations from their parents in infancy, and in the sub-group of 'affectionless psychopaths' only two out of fourteen had not experienced maternal deprivation. In his later follow-up study of children who had been in a tuberculosis sanatorium he found that, compared with controls, the differences in social adjustment, while in the *direction* of less good adjustment for the sanitorium children, were not all that marked, and that at least half of the deprived children had made good social relationships (Bowlby *et al.* 1956). Second, the implication of the phrase 'maternal deprivation' is that antisocial behaviour is specifically linked to the loss of mother. Rutter's work (1971) suggests that antisocial behaviour is linked not to maternal absence as such, but to family discord which in divorcing families is often associated with temporary separations from mother. Children who have lost their mothers through death have a near-normal delinquency rate, while the rate is much raised when parents divorce, especially where there is a combination of active discord and lack of affection. Here too, presumably, it is the way in which the loss is handled, its antecedents (how secure the child has been with the separating parents), and meaning for the child that matter.

The importance of these refinements of the maternal depri-vation hypothesis is that they mark a move away from Bowlby's medical analogy, exemplified by the Vitamin D-rickets compari-son, to a psychological model which takes account of an indi-vidual's history, and of the way untoward events are 'processed' psychologically. It seems more plausible that maternal depri-vation should act as a general 'vulnerability factor' (cf. Brown and Harris 1978) which raises a child's threshold to disturbance rather than as a causative agent in any simple sense. Delinquency is such a complex phenomenon, dependent on non-psychological issues such as policing policy, quality of schools and housing that it would be unlikely to be the result of any one single factor, however important childhood deprivation may be.

For children unfortunate enough to be entirely deprived of

maternal care, recent research has served to confirm Bowlby's original claims. Tizard's (1977) follow-up studies on institution-raised children have shown that, as the maternal deprivation hypothesis predicted, these eight-year-olds were more attention-seeking, restless, disobedient and unpopular compared with controls, while as infants they had shown excessive clinging and diffuse attachment behaviour. Her studies also indicate that, as Bowlby suggested, the period six months to four years may be critical for the capacity to form stable relationships, since children who had been adopted after four, despite forming close and loving bonds with their adoptive parents, remained antisocial in their behaviour at school.

DEVELOPMENTAL PATHWAYS THROUGH CHILDHOOD

Subsequent studies have also generally confirmed Bowlby's concept of cycles of disadvantage. People brought up in unhappy or disrupted homes are more likely to have illegitimate children, become teenage mothers, make unhappy marriages and to divorce. Parents who physically abuse their children tend to have had childhoods characterised by neglect, rejection and violence. Girls from disrupted homes when they become mothers tend to talk less to their babies, touch them less and look at them less (Wolkind *et al.* 1977). But not all children from unhappy homes suffer and fail in this way. A complex model is needed to explain individual differences that takes into account the child, the parent, events and their appraisal, and the social environment. This can be conceptualised as a series of pathways through childhood that lead in a more or less positive direction. A number of varied influences will determine which path a particular child takes (Rutter 1981). Figure 3.1 attempts to summarise these.

As will be discussed in more detail in Chapter 6, there is good evidence that parents' own childhood experiences are important in influencing the way they respond to their child. Events around the birth are also important: mothers separated from their babies soon after birth are less confident and competent as mothers in the subsequent months. The sex and birth position of the child matter: parents are more relaxed and less punitive with second children than with first-borns. Male children are generally more vulnerable to family discord than are females. The death of a parent is more damaging for a same-sex child than if they are

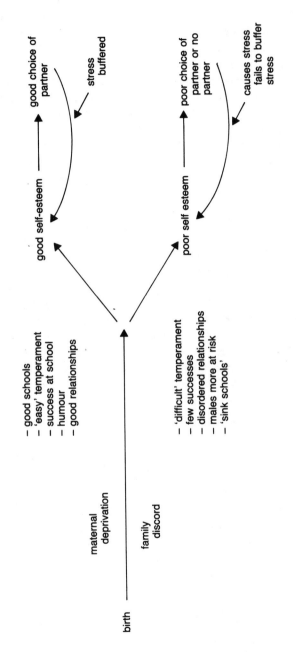

Figure 3.1 Developmental pathways from maternal deprivation

the opposite sex. Temperament plays an important part too: children who are less adaptable and more prone to negative moods are more likely to be targets of parental criticism than their more easy-going siblings, and are more likely to develop a childhood psychiatric disorder. Even in discordant homes, if the child has a good relationship with one parent or with a grand-parent, this acts as a protective factor against conduct disorder. Finally, the social environment is important. Inner-city areas have much higher rates of childhood psychiatric disorder than country or small-town areas, and even within inner cities some schools are much more successful in helping their pupils to avoid delin-quency than others.

IMPLICATIONS FOR PSYCHOTHERAPY

Key issues for adult psychotherapists are the need to clarify more precisely the links between early childhood difficulty and emotional disorder in later life (Rutter 1986); the question of how some people survive and are even strengthened ('steeled') by adversity, while others go under (Rutter 1985); and the need for a model that will suggest at what points in the process psycho-therapeutic intervention is likely to produce change (Holmes 1991).

Social psychiatry tends to emphasise present adversity in the causation of neurosis, while psychoanalytic explanations stress the past. The evidence suggests that both current and past dif-ficulties are important, and that *self-esteem* is a crucial factor linking the two. Looking at adverse experiences in childhood, those who, despite loss or difficulty, manage to maintain a sense of self-esteem do well. Self-esteem in turn rests on two main foundations: self-efficacy and good relationships. Success at school – in social relationships (especially the capacity to generate humour), athletic prowess, musical ability or scholastic achieve-ment – is correlated with better adjustment in institution-raised children in adult life (Rutter and Quinton 1984). There are likely to be a series of interlocking benign or vicious circles here. Good self-esteem means a child will be likely to cope with deprivation – chronic illness in a parent, for example – and the fact of coping will in itself enhance self-esteem, and give the individual a feeling that they will be able to cope in the future. This in turn will influence their choice of partner and the kind of relationship they have with them. Conversely, as Beck *et al.* (1979) and Ryle (1990) argue, depressed people will expect themselves to cope badly, will perceive themselves as doing so, may do so in fact, all of which will be experienced as depression-reinforcing 'failure'.

Apart from coping and competence, the second important childhood component of self-esteem derives from good relationships. Psychotherapists have long suggested that a history of at least one good relationship in the past predicts good outcome in therapy (Malan 1976), and this too is confirmed by empirical studies. An important point about both self-efficacy and good relationships is that they can generalise, so that one positive feature will lead to good self-esteem, despite an otherwise gloomy picture. The opposite is the case in depression (Brown and Harris 1978), where adverse experiences are generalised into a global feeling of hopelessness.

Bion mocked the early psychoanalytic fellow travellers like Suttie for their simplistic overemphasis on past trauma: 'doctor put it in the past' (Pines 1991). Equal in importance to past influences in the adult outcome of maternal deprivation is, as several studies have shown, the quality of a person's current intimate relationships. Vulnerable women who experience loss are protected from depression by the presence of a confiding relationship with a spouse or partner (Brown and Harris 1978). Parker and Hadzi-Pavlovic (1984) found that people whose parents die in childhood are less prone to depression in adult life if they have an affectionate spouse. Rutter and Quinton (1984) report similar findings for institution-raised women, who in general have more psychosocial difficulties than controls, and were much more likely to react badly to stress, unless they had a supportive husband in a harmonious marriage. This suggests another important vicious circle, since maternally deprived girls are more likely to marry unstable and similarly deprived men: childhood difficulty leads to low self-esteem, which makes for poor choice of sexual partner, which in turn leaves women unprotected from stress in adult life. As Bowlby (1952) puts it, there are 'strong unconscious drives which lead husbands and wives to create the very problems of which they complain', and so produce 'the distorted light in which they see the behaviour of their spouse'.

There are important implications of these findings for psychotherapy. There is an implicit contradiction in the psychoanalytic emphasis on the overwhelming importance of early experience – and even more so phantasies in early childhood – in determining adult difficulty and the claims for the efficacy of psychoanalytic therapy. If continuity between childhood and adult life is so strong, how is psychoanalysis likely to reverse it? The recent evidence suggests a much more subtle relationship between past and present, in which a person's partner plays a crucial role in determining outcome. Caspi and Elder (1988) found that 'difficult' children were more likely to demonstrate ill-tempered parenting and poor social control in adult life, but this only emerged if they were married to non-assertive men. Difficult behaviour in childhood made it more likely that these women *would* marry non-assertive men, but when they did not, then poor parenting was avoided. As we shall see in Chapter 8, therapy, through empathy and limit-setting, may play a similar role to marriage in helping to modify maladaptive behaviours. This may be particularly applicable to those whose early experiences have made it hard for them, despite a longing for intimacy, to sustain close relationships at all (Parker *et al.* 1992).

Apart from very severe cases, there is no simple one-to-one correlation between childhood mental states and adult difficulty. There are a number of environmental, and to some extent accidental, mediating factors which determine whether outcomes are favourable or not: the area a person grows up in, the school they go to, whether or not they happen to meet the right person at the right time. Nor is there a simple relationship between environmental stress and disturbance; the meaning and context of a particular event is critical. A teenager who storms out of the house after a row about what time he should come home, followed by the threat of 'You'll be the death of me', and who returns to find that his father *has* died suddenly is going to be more vulnerable to difficult relationships (perhaps characterised by avoidance and inhibition of anger and therefore poor conflict resolution), than one whose parent dies peacefully over several months with good opportunities for grieving. Also, it is important to see the 'victim' of deprivation not as a passive recipient of stress, but as an active agent, in a dynamic relationship with his environment, trying to make sense of experience, to master it and to cope as best he can, but also, via the benign and vicious circles of neurosis, as an active participant in his own downfall or deliverance.

CONCLUSIONS

Maternal deprivation emerges from this account not as the cause of neurosis, but as one, albeit vital, vulnerability factor among many in a complex web of developmental influences. Because nothing succeeds like success, and nothing fails like failure, these influences may summate in retrospect to give the impression of a simple choice between primrose or thorny paths, but there are in fact many roads less travelled (Frost 1954) and it is the psychotherapists' task to explore these. The circularity of neurotic patterns both in the present and over time is a central unifying concept, and suggests how and why many different kinds of intervention may be effective. Analytic therapy may be an example of how one good relationship can counteract many adverse influences: the nature of that good relationship will be considered further in Chapter 8. Cognitive-behavioural therapy concentrates on increasing a person's sense of self-efficacy, and reducing generalisation of bad feelings so that self-esteem remains intact despite loss. Family and marital therapy tackle relationships directly, thereby enhancing the buffering against stress. All types of time-limited therapy assume that if a person can be helped to re-engage with the benign cycles of normal life (although feminists argue that the definition of what constitutes a 'normal' family needs to be contested), then outcomes will be good, since, in Bowlby's (1952) words, 'there is in almost all families a strong urge to live together in greater accord, and this provides a powerful motive for favourable change'.

We have moved from simple privation to the complexities of relationships, from loss to the nature of the bond that is broken, from a simple model of environmental trauma to a consideration of its psychological impact. The stage is set for Bowlby's move from maternal deprivation to Attachment Theory, and after a short literary diversion, we shall, in the next and following two chapters, follow him there.

OLIVER TWIST: AN INTERLUDE

Dickens' *Oliver Twist*, with its mixture of realism, caricature, and fairy-tale, can be seen as a classic account of maternal deprivation. Oliver, orphaned at birth, brought up 'by hand' for the first few months of his life, spends his childhood in the 'parochial' orphanage, 'where twenty or thirty other juvenile offenders against the poor-laws rolled about the floor all day, without the inconvenience of too much food or too much clothing'. Protesting against the 'tortures of slow starvation', he 'asks for more', is sent out to work for his pains, and, after running away from further cruelty, falls among thieves and so begins his career as a delinquent, much as Bowlby would have predicted. But here, despite many reversals and cruel twists, his fortunes change. He is rescued first by the kindly Mr Brownlow, and a second time by the loving Rose Maylie. He is recognised as being in some way different from the run of juvenile thieves. In two crucial passages he is watched over by these parental figures in his sleep:

> The boy stirred, and smiled in his sleep, as though these marks of pity and compassion had awakened some pleasant dream of a love and affection he had never known . . . some brief memory of a happier existence, long gone by.

Later, anticipating Winnicott's (1965) concept of 'being alone in the presence of the mother', Oliver once again sleeps after a terrifying escapade of attempted robbery in which he is wounded, watched over by the tender Rose Maylie:

> It is an undoubted fact, that although our sense of touch and sight be dead, yet our sleeping thoughts, and visionary scenes that pass before us, will be influenced . . . by the *mere silent presence* of some external object. [Italics in the original]

The book ends, of course, happily, with Oliver's affluent parentage established, evil (in the shape of Monks, Sykes and the Bumbles) vanquished, and with the beginning of secure attachment:

> Mr Brownlow . . . from day to day filling the mind of his adopted child with stores of knowledge, and becoming *attached* to him, more and more, as his nature developed itself. . . . [My italics]

The universality of Dickens' message means that each generation can bring to the story its own themes and preoccupations. For the Victorians it was a social tract documenting the iniquities of the poor laws, and a contrast between the cruelties of the bad father and the benign love of Mr Brownlow. But this is no sentimental Victorian morality tale. The powers of good and evil are evenly balanced. Mr Brownlow's benign Bowlbian view of the perfectibility of human nature is contrasted with the cynical realism of his friend Mr Grimwig, who, at least in the short run, wins his wager that Oliver will take Mr Brownlow's money and run.

A Kleinian reading might see in its exaggerations and description of unbearable hunger an account of the 'bad breast' and the projection into it of the child's hatred and rage. As Oliver's bad feelings are balanced by good 'therapeutic' experience, so he becomes strengthened in his resolve to escape from the clutches of Fagin and Sikes, and sees them and the Bumbles no longer as phantasmagoric creatures of enormous power but as the seedy petty criminals which they are.

The Bowlbian perspective on *Oliver Twist* starts with the mystery of Oliver's parentage. The book opens with the description of a *place* – the orphanage where Oliver was raised. It ends with a *name* – Agnes, Oliver's mother, a name on a tomb:

> There is no coffin in that tomb. . . . But, if the spirits of the dead ever come back to earth, to visit spots hallowed by the love – the love beyond the grave – of those whom they knew in life, I believe that the shade of Agnes sometimes hovers round that solemn nook.

In finding his story, Oliver has found his lost mother even though he has never met her in reality, and can never do so, not even in her coffin. The movement from the concrete attachment to person and place of childhood to the possession as adults of a story, of a name which has been internalised, is a theme common to literature and to psychotherapy. The book is closed, the parents who nurtured (and failed to nurture) us are no longer there, but their characters remain with us – for good or ill. Therapy recreates past attachments so that they can live inside us again. The progress from attachment to narrative is part of the Bowlbian story too: we shall examine it more closely in the final section of the book.

Part II

Attachment Theory

Chapter 4

Attachment, anxiety, internal working models

All of us, from the cradle to the grave, are happiest when life is organised as a series of excursions, long or short, from the secure base provided by our attachment figures.

(Bowlby 1988)

In this and the following chapter we shall outline the main features of Attachment Theory, starting with the first of the two great themes described poetically by Bowlby as the 'making and breaking of affectional bonds'.

Bowlby was in some ways, like Freud, a late starter. Although he had a substantial body of related work behind him, it was not until around his fiftieth year, in a series of papers published between 1958 and 1963 (Bowlby 1958, 1960, 1961), that he began to formulate the main outlines of Attachment Theory. Perhaps psychological theorising, like novel writing, but unlike poetry or mathematics, requires a certain maturity; perhaps, like Freud too, Bowlby's revolutionary spirit was combined with a cautiousness of personality that meant that he needed to be absolutely certain of his ground before attempting to challenge the heavens. Bowlby had always felt some unease about the scientific status of psychoanalysis: his discovery of ethology in the 1950s provided him with the scientifically secure base from which to make his conceptual advance: 'The time is already ripe for a unification of psychoanalytic concepts with those of ethology, and to pursue the rich vein of research which this unification suggests' (Bowlby 1953c).

THE THEORETICAL AND EXPERIMENTAL
BACKGROUND TO ATTACHMENT THEORY

Bowlby's earlier work had shown that separated or bereaved children experienced, no less than adults, intense feelings of mental pain and anguish: yearning, misery, angry protests, despair, apathy and withdrawal. He had shown too that the long-term effects of these separations could sometimes be disastrous, leading to neurosis or delinquency in children and adolescents, and mental illness in adults. In separating parent from child a delicate mechanism had been disrupted, a fundamental bond broken linking one human being to another. What is the nature of that bond, and how does it develop? These were the questions Bowlby set out to answer.

He had at his disposal two sets of theories. The first was psychoanalysis which, as we have seen, he had embraced and struggled with for the preceding twenty years. The second was ethology, to which his attention had only recently been drawn, when he read the English translation of Konrad Lorenz's *King Solomon's Ring* (1952) in draft form; soon after, he encountered Tinbergen's (1951) work, and began to collaborate with Robert Hinde (1982b, 1987). Other important influences were the ideas of Kenneth Craik (1943) who, like Bowlby, was a product of the Cambridge Psychology Department, and Ian Suttie (1935), whose book *The Origins of Love and Hate* was influential in the thirties and had contributed to Bowlby's views on social psychology.

Psychoanalysis offered two different accounts of the infant–mother bond: drive theory and object-relations theory. Both of these were, in Bowlby's eyes, seriously flawed. The first, 'classical', drive-theory account came from Freud's early formulations. Here the bond which links mother to infant is libido, or psychical energy. The newborn infant lives in a solipsistic world of 'primary narcissism' and experiences a build-up of tension – the need to feed, to suck the breast as an expression of his infantile sexuality. The mother provides the vehicle for the discharge of this libido. If she, or her breast, is absent, tension arises due to undischarged libido which is felt by the infant as anxiety. The baby learns to love the mother because she feeds him, and so reduces the inner tension which is felt as anxiety. Bowlby calls this the 'cupboard love' theory of relationships.

In *Inhibitions, Symptoms, and Anxiety*, Freud (1926) changed his theory of anxiety from one of dammed-up libido to the theory of *signal anxiety*. Here anxiety is felt whenever there is actual or threatened separation 'from someone who is loved and longed for'. The basis of this love, however, remains satisfaction of physiological need:

> The reason why the infant in arms wants to perceive the presence of its mother is only because it already knows by experience that she satisfies all of its needs without delay. The situation, then, which it regards as a 'danger' and against which it wants to be safeguarded is that of non-satisfaction, of a *growing tension due to need*, against which it is helpless.
>
> (Freud 1926)

Despite this retention of a physiological substratum to relationships, Freud now emphasises that 'it is the absence of the mother that is now the danger'. This shift towards regarding anxiety as based on object-loss is a decisive move towards the *Object-Relations* viewpoint that has become the predominant psychoanalytic paradigm, especially in Britain (Greenberg and Mitchell 1983). For Melanie Klein, the infant is linked psychologically as well as physiologically to the mother and her breast from birth. She sees an intimate link between the physiological processes of feeding and elimination, and the beginnings of mental and ethical structures in the mind of the infant. The satisfying, nourishing, comforting breast is the prototype of the 'good object'; the absent, withholding, empty breast is the 'bad object', containing not only the actual failures and unresponsiveness of the mother, but also the infant's reactions to those failures, projected into and attributed to the 'bad breast'.

For Bowlby, both Freud and Klein failed to take the all-important step of seeing attachment between infant and mother as a psychological bond in its own right, not an instinct derived from feeding or infant sexuality, but *sui generis*:

> The young child's hunger for his mother's love and presence is as great as his hunger for food. . . . Attachment Theory provides a language in which the phenomenology of attachment experiences is given full legitimacy. Attachment is a 'primary motivational system' with its own workings and interface with other motivational systems.
>
> (Bowlby 1973a)

He based his new theory of attachment partly on the findings of ethology, partly on his theoretical critique of psychoanalysis.

As a keen naturalist Bowlby had been particularly struck by the phenomenon described by Lorenz (1952) of following responses in some avian species. Newly hatched goslings follow their mother (or a mother-surrogate), and exhibit analogues of 'anxiety' (cheeping, searching) when separated from her, despite the fact that she does not directly provide them with food. Here bonding seems to be dissociated from feeding. The converse example is provided by Harlow's (1958) monkey studies, which became available around the time Bowlby was publishing his first papers on Attachment Theory. Harlow, in an article with the tongue-in-cheek title 'The nature of love', described how he separated infant rhesus monkeys from their mothers at birth and reared them with the help of surrogate 'wire mothers'. In one series of experiments the infant monkeys were presented with a wire 'mother' to which a feeding bottle had been attached, and another 'mother' without a feeding bottle, but covered with soft terry nappy material. The infant monkeys showed a clear preference for the 'furry' mother, spending up to 18 hours per day clinging to her (as they would with their real mothers) even though they were fed exclusively from the 'lactating' wire mother – a finding which Harlow, arguing as forcibly against a behavioural 'derived drive' theory of bonding as did Bowlby against the psychoanalytic 'secondary drive' hypothesis, concluded, 'is completely contrary to any interpretation of derived drive in which the mother form becomes conditioned to hunger-thirst reduction'.

Geese demonstrate bonding without feeding; rhesus monkeys show feeding without bonding. Thus, argues Bowlby, we must postulate an attachment system unrelated to feeding, which, adopting a biological approach from which psychoanalysis had increasingly become divorced, makes sound evolutionary and developmental sense.

By thinking in terms of primary attachment and bringing the ideas of neo-Darwinism to bear on psychoanalysis, Bowlby identified what he saw as some fundamental flaws in psychoanalytic metapsychology. First, it overemphasises internal dangers at the expense of external threat. The biological purpose of the attachment system is protection from predators which would have been a vital necessity in the environmental conditions in which early man evolved. Infants and small children need to stay close to their mothers at all times, and to signal separation if they are to remain safe from predation. Suttie (1935) called this an 'innate need for companionship which is the infant's only way of self-preservation'. Bowlby criticises psychoanalysts for their over-civilised view of man in which they discount environmental threat, and emphasise instead the projection of 'internal' dangers (feelings of rage and hatred, for example) onto a neutral or benign environment. Even in an urban setting external dangers are far from negligible and children who are victims of injuries in the home or from traffic accidents and sexual attacks are likely to be unprotected and unaccompanied.

Second, Bowlby is critical of the psychoanalytical picture of personality development in which each 'phase' – oral, anal, phallic and genital – succeeds each other in a linear fashion. He questions the idea that normal development can be derived from considering pathological states, and is unhappy with the idea of regression to fixation points as an adequate model of psychological illness. He contrasts Freud's 'homuncular' model in which each stage is predetermined according to some pre-existing plan of development, with an 'epigenetic' model (Waddington 1977) in which several lines of development are possible, the outcome of which depends on an interaction between the organism and its environment. Thus, although the developing child has a propensity to form attachments, the nature of those attachments and their dynamics will depend on the parental environment to which he or she is exposed. Also, the development of the attachment dynamic can be considered as a process in its own right independent of other dynamics – for example, sex or feeding – just as the different organs of the body develop relatively independently of one another.

Bowlby also rejects the teleological 'Lamarckian' view in which the 'purpose' of psychological functions can be determined by some *a priori* goal: for example, the 'purpose' of attachment is not the reduction of physiological need, but, in evolutionary terms, to increase the fitness of those possessed of it, so protecting them from predators. Finally, he is critical of 'hydraulic' models of drive-discharge, seeing human behaviour rather in terms of control theory whose aim is the maintenance of homeostasis. Infant monkeys separated from their mothers respond with a rise in pulse rate and a fall in body temperature. In humans,

Brazelton and Cramer (1991) have shown that mothers who have to return to work within a year after giving birth show higher levels of physiological disturbance than those who are able to stay with their babies, and that there is a correspondingly higher incidence of infection in the infants. Secure attachment provides an external ring of psychological protection which maintains the child's metabolism in a stable state, similar to the internal physiological homeostatic mechanisms of blood-pressure and temperature control.

The group of analysts to whom Bowlby felt his ideas were closest were the 'Hungarian School', especially Ferenczi (1955) and Michael Balint (1964). Ferenczi, originator of the famous phrase 'it is the physician's love which cures the patient', had fallen out with Freud over his emphasis on Freud's insistence on the 'real' (as opposed to transferential) nature of the relationship between patient and therapist, and his rather dubious propensity to kiss and hug his patients when he felt it necessary. Balint, his pupil, had postulated a 'primary love' and a primitive clinging instinct between mother and child that are independent of feeding. Bowlby also saw an affinity between his ideas and those of Fairbairn (1952) who, like Bowlby, had jettisoned drive theory in favour of primary object-seeking, and who refused to see adult dependency as a relic of orality, but rather conceived of development as a movement from infantile to mature dependence.

As described in the Introduction, the reaction of the analytic world to Bowlby's challenge was, on the whole, unfavourable. The Kleinians saw him as having betrayed analytic principles, contaminating psychoanalysis with behaviourism, trying to expunge the heart of psychoanalysis – its account of the inner world of phantasy. Anna Freud and her supporters could hardly fail to notice that the Oedipus complex and infantile sexuality – for them, the cornerstones of the psychoanalytic edifice – played virtually no part in Bowlby's writings. What started out as an attempt by Bowlby to modernise psychoanalytic metapsychology and to find a sound biological underpinning for Object-Relations Theory became, in the face of the rejection of his ideas by his psychoanalytic colleagues, increasingly to look like a new psychological paradigm. As we shall see in Chapters 6 and 8, recent developments in 'post-Bowlbian' research have opened out the possibility of reconciliation. But first we must focus more clearly on the nature of attachment theory.

WHAT IS ATTACHMENT THEORY?

Attachment Theory is in essence a *spatial* theory: when I am close to my loved one I feel good, when I am far away I am anxious, sad or lonely. The child away from home for the night plays happily until she hurts herself or bedtime approaches and then feels pangs of homesickness. The mother who leaves her child with a new baby minder thinks endlessly about her baby and misses her dreadfully. Attachment is mediated by looking, hearing and holding: the sight of my loved one lifts my soul, the sound of her approach awakes pleasant anticipation. To be held and to feel her skin against mine makes me feel warm, safe and comforted, with perhaps a tingling anticipation of shared pleasure. But the consummation of attachment is not primarily orgasmic – rather, it is, via the achievement of proximity, a relaxed state in which one can begin to 'get on with things', pursue one's projects, to *explore*.

Definitions

It is useful to distinguish between the interrelated concepts of attachment, attachment behaviour, and the attachment behavioural system (Hinde 1982a), which represent roughly the psychodynamic, the behavioural and the cognitive components of Attachment Theory.

'*Attachment*' is an overall term which refers to the state and quality of an individual's attachments. These can be divided into secure and insecure attachment. Like many psychodynamic terms, 'attachment' carries both experiential and theoretical overtones. To feel attached is to feel safe and secure. By contrast, an insecurely attached person may have a mixture of feelings towards their attachment figure: intense love and dependency, fear of rejection, irritability and vigilance. One may theorise that their lack of security has aroused a simultaneous wish to be close and the angry determination to punish their attachment figure for the minutest sign of abandonment. It is though the insecurely attached person is saying to themselves: 'cling as hard as you can to people – they are likely to abandon you; hang on to them and hurt them if they show signs of going away, then they may be less likely to do so'. This particular pattern of insecure attachment is known as 'ambivalent insecurity' (see below and Chapter 6).

Attachment behaviour is defined simply as being 'Any form of behaviour that results in a person attaining or retaining proximity to some other differentiated and preferred individual'. Attachment behaviour is triggered by separation or threatened separation from the attachment figure. It is terminated or *assuaged* by proximity, which, depending on the nature of the threat, may vary from being in sight, to physical closeness and soothing words without touching, to being tightly held and cuddled.

Attachment and attachment behaviour are based on an *attachment behavioural system*, a blueprint or model of the world in which the self and significant others and their interrelationship are represented and which encodes the particular pattern of attachment shown by an individual. The ambivalently attached person we have described might have a working model of others as desirable but unreachable, and of themselves as unworthy of support and love, and/or of an unreliable and rejecting attachment figure with a protesting, attacking self.

An attachment relationship can be defined by the presence of three key features (Weiss 1982).

1 Proximity seeking to a preferred figure

As parents of toddlers well know, small children have a maddening propensity to follow their attachment figures wherever they go. The distance at which the child feels comfortable depends on such factors as age, temperament, developmental history, and whether the child feels fatigued, frightened or ill, all of which will enhance attachment behaviour. Recent separation will lead to greater proximity seeking, or 'mummyishness', as Robertson's (1952) film so beautifully demonstrates. The extent of the proximity required will also depend on circumstances. A three-year-old collected from playgroup after her first day may rush up to the parent and bury her head in his lap and want to be held and cuddled for a long time. A month later she may be content to slip her hand quietly into that of her collecting parent and continue chatting to her friends as she walks down the road.

Of central importance to attachment theory is the notion that attachment is to a *discriminated* figure (or small group of figures).

Bowlby originally explained this by analogy with the phenomenon of imprinting in which young birds will attach themselves to any mobile figure to which they are exposed at the 'sensitive period' in their development. Studies on primates suggest that imprinting does not occur in the same way as in birds, and that attachment, rather than being an all-or-none phenomenon, develops as a result of a gradual process of genetically programmed development and social learning (Rutter 1981; Bretherton 1991b).

The fact that attachment is, in Bowlby's word, 'monotropic' – that is, occurs with a single figure, most usually the mother – has profound implications for psychological development and psychopathology throughout the life cycle.

> It is because of this marked tendency to monotropy that we are capable of deep feelings, for to have a deep attachment to a person (or a place or a thing) is to have taken them as the terminating object of our instinctual responses.
>
> (Bowlby 1988a)

Monotropy is by no means absolute: a small child's attachments can best be thought of as a hierarchy usually, but not necessarily, with the mother at the top, closely followed by the father (or, rarely, the father followed by the mother), grandparents, siblings, godparents and so on. Inanimate objects such as transitional objects are also important.

Attachment Theory accepts the customary primacy of the mother as the main care-giver, but there is nothing in the theory to suggest that fathers are not equally likely to become principal attachment figures if they happen to provide most of the child care. The theory is a two-person psychology and has little to say directly about the different roles of mother and father, and of sexuality in psychological life. This has the advantage that its findings are perhaps more generally applicable across cultures than mainstream psychoanalysis, but means that it does not address the fact that individuals' identity is intimately bound up with their sexual roles.

Three-person psychology enters into Attachment Theory via separation and loss. The growing child has to learn that the figure to whom he is attached must also be shared with her sexual partner and other siblings, which forms the basis for the Oedipal situation, and makes separation and loss an inherent part of the attachment dynamic. For Melanie Klein (1986), the 'depressive position' represents the realisation that the loved and gratifying breast/mother and the hated and rejecting breast/mother are one and the same. For Bowlby, the human dilemma turns on the central importance of an attachment that cannot be entirely reliable, must perforce be shared, and will be lost, eventually (and often prematurely). The capacity to separate from attachment figure(s) and to form new attachments represents the developmental challenge of adolescence and young adulthood. The cycle repeats itself as parents attach themselves to their children only to let them go as *they* reach adolescence. Finally, as death of one's loved ones, and one's own death approaches, the 'monotropic' bond to life itself has gradually to be relinquished.

2 The 'secure base' effect

Mary Ainsworth (1982) first used the phrase 'secure base' to describe the ambience created by the attachment figure for the attached person. The essence of the secure base is that it provides a springboard for curiosity and exploration. When danger threatens we cling to our attachment figures. Once danger passes, their presence enables us to work, relax and play – but only if we are sure that the attachment figures will be there if we need them again. We can endure rough seas if we are sure of a safe haven. Anderson (1972) made a naturalistic study of mothers and their toddlers in a London park. The mothers sat on the park benches, reading or chatting while their children toddled and played on the surrounding grass. He found that each child had an invisible radius – a Maginot line – beyond which it would not venture to go. When it neared the limit it would begin to look anxiously towards the mother. Attachment exerted an invisible but powerful pull on the child, just as heavenly bodies are connected by gravitational forces. But unlike gravity, attachment makes its presence known by a *negative* inverse square law: the further the attached person is from their secure base, the greater the pull of attachment. The 'elastic band' which constitutes the attachment bond is slack and imperceptible in the presence of a secure base. If the secure base becomes unreliable or the limits of exploration are reached, the bond tugs at the heart-strings.

The example of the mother who leaves her child with the child minder and then worries about and misses her dreadfully suggests that attachment behaviour is not confined to infancy and applies to care-givers as well as care-seekers. Heard and Lake (1986) have extended the secure base concept in their model of an adult attachment dynamic in which they postulate a fundamental need for 'companionable interaction' based on 'preferred relationships in the attachment network'. These comprise, as in parent-child attachment, a mixture of support and exploration, with a sense of psychological proximity as the precondition for such companionship. Where no secure base exists, the individual is in a state of 'dissuagement', and resorts to defensive manoeuvres (such as splitting off anger; inhibition of sexuality; or conversely compulsive sexualisation of relationships) in order to minimise the pain of separation anxiety, and, if needs be, to manipulate support at the expense of truly reciprocal companionship.

Violence and a social facade

Jennifer, a successful painter, was forty when she entered psychotherapy. Her complaint was that she could never be her 'real self' in close relationships. In social situations she could be jolly and cheerful and was well liked; by herself she often felt depressed and anxious, but could cope, especially when she was painting. In her marriages (she had had two) she never felt at ease, unable to share feelings openly or to feel relaxed with her husbands. She had rather desperately sought some affirmation of herself through affairs, but in the end these left her feeling empty and valueless. Naturally enough these patterns were repeated transferentially in therapy and she bent her best efforts towards trying to please, seduce and sometimes (via projective identification) to exclude her therapist. She dated the death of her straightforward 'companionable self' and the shattering of her secure base to an incident where her much-feared father (who had been away at the war for the first three years of her life) was playing with her older brother and sister when Jennifer was about four. She tried to gain his attention but was ignored; she pinched his leg harder and harder until suddenly and terrifyingly he threw her across the room. From that day (and similar episodes were repeated in various ways throughout her childhood) she could only get attention, playfulness, support from others by means of pleasing them, controlling them, or vicariously caring for herself through her care for them (this characterised her relationship with her mother, herself chronically depressed). This illustrates in an extreme form a typical family pattern of absent-father/depressed-mother that so often underlies the lack of a secure base, and leads to defensive postures by the children who grow up in such an atmosphere. Progress in therapy only began when this woman had tested her therapist again and again for his reliability and had, inevitably, found him wanting, but still felt safe enough to reveal the extent of her disappointment and rage towards him.

3 Separation protest

Try to prise a limpet away from its rock and it will cling all the harder. The best test of the presence of an attachment bond is to observe the response to separation. Bowlby identified protest as the primary response produced in children by separation from their parents. Crying, screaming, shouting, biting, kicking – this 'bad' behaviour is the normal response to the threat to an attachment bond, and presumably has the function of trying to restore it, and, by 'punishing' the care-giver, of preventing further separation. The clinical implications of separation protest are very important and will be dealt with in subsequent chapters. For example, Ainsworth used it in devising her 'strange situation', the basic tool used for classifying the quality of attachment in children (see Chapter 6), and the analysis of patient responses to weekend and holiday 'breaks' are a basic theme in analytic psychotherapy (see Chapter 8).

A remarkable feature of attachment bonds is their durability. The persistence of attachment in the face of maltreatment and severe punishment has enormous implications for child and adult psychopathology. Harlow's monkeys clung ever more tightly to their cloth 'mothers' even when 'punished' by them with sudden blasts of compressed air (Rutter 1980)! It is hard to explain this phenomenon on the basis either of the psychoanalytic 'cupboard love' theory, or of reward-reinforcement learning theory. It is explicable along the ethological lines of Attachment Theory since stress will lead to an enhancement of attachment behaviour even when the source of that stress is the attachment figure itself. The 'frozen watchfulness' of the physically abused child is eloquent proof of the phenomenon of ambivalent attachment and its inhibition of normal exploration and playfulness.

THE DEVELOPMENT OF THE ATTACHMENT SYSTEM

The human infant is born in a state of great immaturity (a consequence, evolutionary biologists suggest, of the need to get the huge human brain through the pelvic floor before it is too late!). It is not surprising therefore that, unlike in ducks, monkeys and other animals, the human attachment system takes several months to develop. Only after six months does the baby begin to exhibit the full triad of proximity seeking, secure base effect and separation protest that we have described. The ontogeny of the attachment system can be conveniently divided into four phases.

1 0–6 months: orientation and pattern recognition

Although newborn babies cannot distinguish one person from another, they are highly responsive to human contact. Centrally important in this process is the sight of the human face, which evokes intense interest. The onset of the smiling response around four weeks marks the beginning of the cycles of benign interaction that characterise the relationship between the baby and his caregivers. The baby's smile evokes a mirroring smile in the mother; the more she smiles back the more the baby responds, and so on. As we shall see in Chapter 6, maternal *responsiveness* is a key determinant of the quality of attachment as development proceeds. Winnicott (1971) famously states: 'What does the baby see when he or she looks at the mother's face? I am suggesting that ordinarily what the baby sees is him or herself.' He goes on in the same paper to suggest that what happens in psychotherapy is 'a long term giving the patient back what the patient brings. It is a complex derivative of the face that reflects what is there to be seen' (Winnicott 1971).

Daniel Stern (1985), from a perspective of developmental psychology, and Kenneth Wright (1991), from a psychoanalytical viewpoint, both see the mutual looking between mother and baby as a key element in the development of an internal world in which attachment can be represented and regulated. The invariability of the mother's face, the recognition of it as a pattern, give the baby a primitive sense of *history*, of continuity through time that is integral to the sense of self. To evoke her smile provides a sense of *agency* and effectiveness. Her mirroring response is the first link between what is perceived *out there*, and what is felt *in here*.

For Wright the mother's face is the first symbol; her face is not part of the self and yet, because it is responsive, feels intimately connected to the self. In the Kleinian account of the origin of symbol formation – based on Freud's idea of hallucinatory wish-fulfilment – images are thought to arise as a consequence of *loss* or absence: 'no breast; so imagine a breast', thinks the Kleinian infant. Wright proposes a more harmonious theory in which the separation is simply spatial: the face is *over there, held off* and so is available for thinking about, contemplation, meditation. To watch a 3-month-old baby at the breast is to get *visible* proof of the rhythm of feeding and mutual gazing that constitutes the mother–child relationship at this stage. Freud, in his discussion of Leonardo (Freud 1910), seems to see looking as a sort of visual incorporation, a drinking in with the eyes, rather than a modality of relating with its own dynamic. The complexity and specificity of the visual world, as opposed to the gustatory world, is what makes looking the basis of attachment: 'Wine comes in at the mouth, love comes in at the eyes.' The world is mapped through the visual system: the mother's face is imaged on the retina and visual cortex before it is imagined in the inner world. We shall consider later some of the implications of the failure of this mirroring process.

As with looking, so with holding, a term used by Winnicott (1971) in his phrase 'the holding environment' to denote not just the physical holding of the baby by the mother but the entire psychophysiological system of protection, support, caring and containing that envelops the child, without which it would not survive physically or emotionally. The reliability and responsiveness of the holding environment form the nucleus of the emergent attachment patterns as the child begins the process of separation-individuation.

In the second half of the first six months the beginnings of an attachment relationship starts to be evident. The baby becomes much more discriminating in his looking. He listens out for and responds differently to his mother's voice; cries differently when she departs compared with other people; greets her differently; and begins to put his arms up towards her in a request to be picked up. She in turn responds to the physiological and social cues from her baby in a way that leads to the establishment of a mutual system of feedback and homeostasis. An interactive matrix is established, felt as a mutual 'knowing' of each other that is the hallmark of a secure mother–infant relationship.

2 6 months–3 years: 'set-goal' attachment

In the second half of the first year several developmental changes occur which mark the onset of attachment proper. Children removed from foster homes into permanent adoptive homes before 6 months show little distress, whereas after that watershed they show increased crying, clinging, apathy, and feeding and sleep disturbance (Bretherton 1985). Around 7 months the baby will begin to show 'stranger anxiety', becoming silent and clingy in the presence of an unknown person (Spitz 1950).

These changes coincide with the onset of locomotion in the child, which entails a much more complex system of communication if the baby is to remain in secure contact with the mother. The immobile baby is bound to remain where he is. The mother of the mobile baby needs to know that the child will move towards her at times of danger, and the child needs to be able to signal protest or distress when necessary to a mother who now feels she can put him down for a few minutes.

Bowlby conceives the attachment system at this stage as being based on 'set-goals', which he compares to the setting on a thermostat, maintained by a system of feedback control. The 'set-goal' for the infant is to keep 'close enough' to the mother: to use her as a secure base for exploration when environmental threat is at a minimum, and to exhibit separation protest or danger signalling when the need arises.

Figure 4.1 attempts to summarise the features of the attachment system at this stage. Several points should be made about this diagram. First, attachment behaviour, although usually discussed from the point of view of the attached person, is a *reciprocal relationship*. The parent is simultaneously offering complementary care-giving behaviour that matches, or should match, the attachment behaviour of the child. For example, when put in a new situation the child will, through *social referencing*, make eye contact with the mother, looking for cues which will sanction exploration or withdrawal. Second, and as a consequence, parent–child attachment systems can be seen in terms of continuously monitored *distance-regulation* (Byng-Hall 1980),

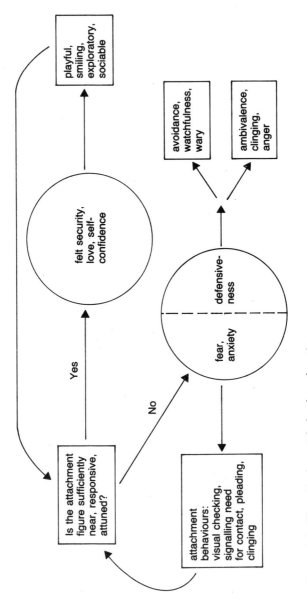

Figure 4.1 The attachment behavioural system

with many opportunities for problematic variants. The over-anxi-ous parent may inhibit the child's exploratory behaviour, making them feel stifled or smothered; conversely, the neglectful parent may inhibit exploration by failing to provide a secure base, lead-ing to feelings of anxiety or abandonment. Third, inherent in the model is the notion of an internal map or 'internal working model' which represents the relative whereabouts of the self and attachment figure. To the analytically minded psychotherapist this may seem like a rather uninteresting predominantly 'cogni-tive' map, but this would be mistaken. What is stored in the 'internal working model' is not so much an ordnance survey picture but an *affective* model which, if it could be translated into words, might be along the lines of 'I feel tense when my mummy goes out of the room so I must keep a good eye out for her and scream if necessary', or 'when my mummy comes so close to me while I am playing I feel uncomfortable, so I'll try to move away a bit, without discouraging her so much that she loses interest' (cf. Beebe and Lachmann 1988).

We have moved from a discussion of set-goals which keep toddler and parent in eyesight and earshot of each other to the idea of a *relationship*, and to a consideration of what internal processes might regulate it. This brings us to the attachment system in its fully fledged form which, Bowlby maintains, is estab-lished by the third birthday and persists from then on throughout life.

3 3 years onwards: the formation of a reciprocal relationship

As Bowlby first conceived it, the attachment system in the toddler was something like a 'homing device' in which the child was programmed to focus on the parent with the 'set-goal' of main-taining proximity. With the advent of language and the expanding psychological sophistication of the three- to four-year-old a much more complex pattern arises that cannot be described in simplistic behavioural terms. The child now can begin to think of his parents as separate people with their own goals and plans, and to devise ways of influencing them. If the mother is going to leave the child for the evening he may plead, bribe, charm or sulk in an attempt to maintain attachment, rather than crying or clinging as he would have done a year or two earlier. Attachment Theory at this point merges into a general theory about relationships (or 'affectional bonds', as Bowlby likes to call them) and how they are maintained, monitored and may go wrong.

INTERNAL WORKING MODELS

A key concept here is that of the 'internal working model'. This is Bowlby's way of describing the internal world of the psychoanalysts, but couched in characteristically practical terms. The idea of an internal 'model' of the world derives from Kenneth Craik's (1943) influential *The Nature of Explanation*, in which he argues that

> Thought models, or parallels reality . . . the organism carries a 'small-scale model' of external reality and its own possible actions within its head which enable it to react in a fuller, safer, and more competent way to the emergencies which face it'.

Wright (1991) has remarked how, until the advent of Winnicott's influence, the *work* ethic dominated the language of psychoanalysis: *working* through, getting the patient to *work* on their problems, forming a *working* alliance, and Bowlby's internal *working* models. Wright sees Winnicott as representing the female, maternal influence, a reaction against the paternal force of Freud. Bowlby in turn was in part reacting against the powerful women who had trained him, his analyst Joan Riviere, and supervisor, Melanie Klein. The idea of a 'working model' implies a practical mechanism, a down-to-earth title which he claimed 'allows for greater precision of description and provides a framework that lends itself more readily to the planning and execution of empirical research' (Bowlby 1981c).

Although derived from the psychoanalytic perspective, the idea of internal working models is perhaps closer to that of cognitive therapy (Beck *et al*. 1979) (itself also a development of and a reaction against the psychoanalytic paradigm). The developing child builds up a set of models of the self and others, based on repeated patterns of interactive experience. These 'basic assumptions' (Beck *et al*. 1979), 'representations of interactions that have been generalised' (Stern 1985), 'role relationship models' and 'self–other schemata' (Horowitz 1988), form relatively fixed representational models which the child uses to predict and relate to the world. A securely attached child will store an internal working model of a responsive, loving, reliable care-giver, and of a self that is worthy of love and attention and will bring these assumptions to bear on all other relationships. Conversely, an insecurely attached child may view the world as a dangerous place in which other people are to be treated with great caution, and see himself as ineffective and unworthy of love. These assumptions are relatively stable and enduring: those built up in the early years of life are particularly persistent and unlikely to be modified by subsequent experience.

Bowlby wished to recast psychoanalytic theory in terms of a systems approach in which feedback loops are a key element. They underlie the 'epigenetic' stability of psychological phenomena: the benign circles of healthy development, and the vicious circles of neurosis in which negative assumptions about the self and others become self-fulfilling prophecies.

THEORIES OF NEUROSIS: AVOIDANT AND AMBIVALENT ATTACHMENT

Bowlby uses the notion of faulty internal working models to describe different patterns of neurotic attachment. He sees the basic problem of 'anxious attachment' as that of maintaining attachment with a care-giver who is unpredictable or rejecting. Here the internal working model will be based not on accurate representation of the self and others, but on *coping*, in which the care-giver must be accommodated to. The two basic strategies here are those of *avoidance* or *adherence*, which lead to avoidant or ambivalent attachment (see Figure 4.2).

In avoidant attachment the child tries to minimise his needs for attachment in order to forestall rebuff, while at the same time remaining in distant contact with the care-giver whose rejection, like the person's own neediness, is removed from consciousness by what, based on Dixon's (1971) concept of perceptual defense, Bowlby calls 'defensive exclusion'. The ambivalent strategy involves clinging to the care-giver, often with excessive submissiveness, or adopting a role-reversal in which the care-giver is cared for rather than vice versa. Here feelings of anger at the rejection are most conspicuously subjected to defensive exclusion. A third pattern of insecure attachment, 'insecure disorganised', less common than the first two but probably associated with much more severe pathology, has also been delineated. All three patterns will be discussed in more depth in Chapter 6.

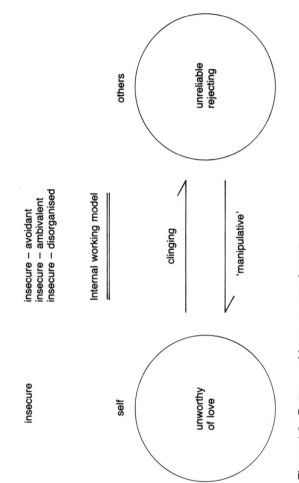

secure

insecure

insecure – avoidant
insecure – ambivalent
insecure – disorganised

Internal working model

others

unreliable
rejecting

clinging

'manipulative'

self

unworthy
of love

Figure 4.2 Patterns of insecure attachment

Although these strategies have the function of maintaining attachment in the face of difficulties, a price has to be paid. The attachment patterns so established are clearly restricted and, if repeated in all relationships, will be maladaptive. Also, defensive exclusion means that models cannot be updated in the light of new experience. Bowlby visualises the coexistence of incompatible models – for example, 'the good mother who lets me come near to her (if I look after her)', and the 'bad mother who rejects me and makes me angry (and who I'll try not to think about)' – which lead to sudden changes of mood and poor adaptation. A central problem created by defensive exclusion is the lack of opportunity for emotional processing of painful affect, particularly evident in pathological mourning, which leads to the persistence of primitive feelings of hate and abandonment and restricts emotional growth and development.

ATTACHMENT IN ADULT LIFE

This consideration of internal working models has been a necessary diversion in our discussion of attachment across the life cycle. It is through internal working models that childhood patterns of attachment are carried through into adult life and, as we shall discuss in Chapter 6, are transmitted to the next generation.

As children grow older and begin to reach adolescence they tolerate increasing periods of separation from their parents. Does this mean that the attachment 'phase' has been outgrown, to be superseded by, say, 'adult genitality'? According to Bowlby's 'epigenetic' model, emphatically not! As he sees it, attachment and dependency, although no longer evident in the same way as in young children, remain active throughout the life cycle. For adolescents the parental home still remains an important anchor point, and the attachment system will become re-activated at times of threat, illness or fatigue. The turbulence of adolescence can be seen in Bowlbian terms as springing from the complexity of detachment and re-attachment which the adolescent must accomplish. To disengage from parental attachments, to mourn that loss, to move on via the transitional phase of peer group attachment to the pair-bonding of adult life is no easy task.

Bowlby saw marriage, or its equivalent, as the adult manifestation of attachment whose companionship provides a secure base allowing for work and exploration, and a protective shell in times of need. Like Fairbairn (1952), but unlike Freud (1929) for whom affection was 'aim-inhibited sexuality', Bowlby saw bodily pleasure not as an aim in itself but as a 'signpost to the object', and so tends rather to downplay the role of sexuality in marriage. Just as the mother–infant relationship cannot, in Bowlby's eyes, be understood as primarily based on feeding, so adult pair-bonding cannot be adequately explained by sexuality. Sex without attachment and sexless marriages are both all too common, and suggest that the attachment system and sexual behaviour are separable psychological entities, however much society might wish that this were not so. 'In sickness and in health' is a reminder that the psychological purpose of marriage is to provide a secure base and an attachment system which can be awakened in times of need. The unconscious operation of the attachment system via internal working models probably plays an important part in the choice of marital partner and relationship patterns in marriage. Holmes (1993) has described a pattern of 'phobic-counterphobic' marriage in which an ambivalently attached person will be attracted to an avoidant 'counter-phobic' spouse in a system of mutual defence against separation anxiety.

The steeplejack's wife

A young woman developed multiple phobic symptoms soon after the birth of her first baby. At first her fears were of harming the baby; later she became severely agoraphobic, and took to phoning her mother several times a day for reassurance. She insisted on moving house so as to be within easy reach of her mother. Her mother 'helped' by looking after the baby for much of the day, and would herself telephone frequently to check if the baby was 'all right'. When the patient told her mother of a dream in which her son had fallen under a lorry, the mother (who was unlikely to have read Freud) told her that this meant that she wanted to kill her son! As a child the patient had lacked a secure base with this mother whom she felt neglected her in favour of two younger sisters, one of whom had been chronically ill with kidney disease, while the other was epileptic, and to whom she had devoted all her attention.

In an initial phase of individual therapy she was able to link her fears of harming the baby with aggressive feelings towards her younger sisters and her angry dependency on her mother, but her symptoms persisted. Marital therapy was then offered. At the first session she proudly announced that her husband – unlike herself – was afraid of nothing. He accepted the compliment rather diffidently, but confirmed that he had been more or less self-reliant since the age of ten, when his parents had divorced and he and his younger brother had been left to fend for themselves on the rough estate where they lived. He worked as a scaffolder on high buildings. When asked if it was true, as his wife believed, that he was frightened of nothing, he confessed that he had slipped on a plank that morning and had been very scared, and that since the birth of the baby he had been much less of a daredevil. His wife seemed surprised at this revelation, but visibly relaxed and perked up. He then admitted that he saw it as his task to conceal his fears and worries from his wife because of her 'illness'. For example, he resented his mother-in-law's intrusions into their family life, but was petrified by the idea of confronting her. Given the task of answering the phone when she rang, and explaining that his wife was too busy to speak, he became quite shaky and said that he would much rather be asked to go up a chimney-stack in a high wind! The patient was asked to rehearse him in this by role-playing her mother, and the session ended in laughter, with a much less anxious patient and subsequent good clinical improvement.

This example shows how attachment patterns are stored as internal working models. The patient saw herself as uncared for, unworthy of care and therefore unable to care for her baby, whom she perceived, in a sense correctly, as in danger of neglect or attack. Lacking a secure base inside herself she was unable to provide one for others, and her anger and frustration about this lack of care interfered with her capacity to look after her baby. The intrusiveness of her mother and the detachment of her husband (due in turn to their own faulty attachment patterns) served to reinforce her sense of an absent secure base. Her demandingness and dependency represented a desperate effort to create an ideally safe attachment, and her protest about the lack of it. Giving her an opportunity to nurture her husband made her feel better about herself, and the affective release of anger and laughter in the sessions enabled her to revise her internal working models towards a more realistic assessment of her capacities. We shall discuss in Chapter 6 important evidence showing how, as Winnicott (1965) suggested, the advent of parenthood calls into being the new parent's own attachment history. As the life cycle unfolds, each parent is presented with new challenges to their capacity to hold, respond to, attune with and release their children. With increasing age the depth and strength of attachment bonds increases. At the same time losses begin to accumulate. Divorce, and separation and death begin to take their toll. We shall see in the next chapter how Attachment Theory provides a schematic map of the painful terrain of depression, disappointment and bereavement.

CONCLUSION: THE MEDIATION AND PSYCHOPATHOLOGY OF ATTACHMENT

Bowlby's original mission was to find links between major life events such as parental loss or neglect and the development of psychiatric symptoms in children and adults. In 'Forty-four juvenile thieves' he linked such disruptions with the two major psychiatric disorders of childhood: conduct disorders and phobias. He anticipated that there would be connections between problems of attachment in childhood and adult conditions such as depression, agoraphobia and psychopathic disorders. He made a fundamental distinction between *secure* and *anxious* attachment, seeing the latter as the precursor of developmental difficulty and adult psychiatric disease.

In his early formulations he saw anxious attachment as resulting from gross disruptions of parenting such as parental death or divorce. He also incriminated major qualitative difficulties in parenting which included depression and unresponsiveness on the part of a parent; threats of suicide directed at the child; threats to send or give the child away; and situations of role reversal in which the child is expected to 'mother' the parent and be a caregiver for her, either overtly, or as in the case of the steeplejack's wife, by becoming an 'ill' child to whom the anxious parent can cling.

Bowlby the systematiser and theoretician relied greatly on collaborators to provide the experimental evidence upon which his ideas rested. James Robertson's (1952) research and films confirmed his ideas about maternal deprivation, and Mary Ainsworth (1982, 1989) is generally seen as the co-author of Attachment Theory. Since his original formulations the research of Ainsworth and her students has extended and to some extent modified Bowlby's original ideas. In particular, the focus has shifted away from gross disruptions of care such as bereavement, which, as discussed in Chapter 3, do not in themselves necessarily result in psychopathology if conditions are otherwise favourable. The contemporary emphasis is much more on the subtleties of parent–child interaction which contribute to the qualitative features of the attachment bond. Maternal *responsiveness* and the ability to *attune* to her child are seen as key features in determining the security or otherwise of attachment bonds.

We have assumed in this chapter that the mother is likely to be the primary care-giver in the first year of life. Changing patterns of family life mean that this is not necessarily the case. The evidence, such as it is (Brazelton and Cramer 1991), suggests that fathers are as capable of providing responsive attunement as mothers, and for the purposes of the arguments presented in this and subsequent chapters mothers and fathers should for the most part be considered as interchangeable. But here too there are subtle differences. Mothers are more likely to offer a containing 'envelope' for infant activity, while fathers tend to interact more intensely but for much shorter periods, in which can be found the beginnings of organised play as development proceeds.

Other important new themes to emerge from the work of the post-Bowlbians have been the emphasis on narrative and 'autobiographical competence' (Holmes 1992) as manifestations of secure attachment. These and other research findings relevant to Attachment Theory will be reviewed in Chapter 6. But we must turn now to the second of Bowlby's great themes, the breaking of affectional bonds, and the need for affective processing so as to mitigate the psychological impact of separation and loss.

Chapter 5

Loss, anger and grief

A liability to experience separation anxiety and grief are the
ineluctable results of a love relationship, of caring for
someone.

(Bowlby 1973a)

Towards the end of his long life Bowlby advised one of his former
research students: 'Always choose a central topic when doing
research. That way you know you can get sufficient data. That's
why I studied separation. You can't miss it. Whatever people
say, it is there in the data' (Hamilton 1991). As we have seen
in Chapter 3, Bowlby's insistence that people *had* missed the
significance of separation and loss as a cause of unhappiness,
delinquency and psychiatric illness met a receptive audience in
the post-war era of recuperation and reparation. The early work
of Bowlby and his associates on loss comprised a systematic
description of the psychological reactions to separation and
bereavement in children and adults (Bowlby 1953b: Bowlby *et
al.* 1952; Parkes 1964); once Attachment Theory was in place,
he could then go on to develop a theoretical account of mourning,
based on psychoanalysis but supplemented by the insights of
ethology (Bowlby 1980).

EARLY STUDIES

Bowlby's first attempts to understand the effects of separation
on psychological development were retrospective studies based
on the histories of children and adolescents referred to the child
guidance clinics where he worked. In his study of 'Forty-four
juvenile thieves' (Bowlby 1944), 40 per cent of the offenders had

had prolonged separations of 6 months or more from their mothers or foster-mothers during the first five years of their life, compared with only 5 per cent of controls. Of the 'affectionless' thieves, twelve out of fourteen had had prolonged separations, compared with only five of the remaining thirty. Bowlby saw two main factors as being of etiological significance. First, the separation itself:

> Thus the essential factor which all these separations have in common is that, during the early development of his object-relationships, the child is suddenly removed and placed with strangers. He is snatched away from the people and places which are familiar and whom he loves and placed with people and in surroundings which are unknown and alarming.
>
> (Bowlby 1944)

This must have struck many a sympathetic chord in readers who had survived six years of wartime evacuation, enforced separation and bereavement.

The second factor connecting delinquency and the 'affectionless character' with separation was the 'inhibition of love by rage and the phantasies resulting from rage'. The separated child responds to the absence of his parent with feelings of fury and destructiveness. Normally, as Klein and later Bion described, the soothing presence of the parent would enable these phantasies to be modified by reality, and therefore to give up their dominance in the child's mind. But if the mother is absent, or is herself aggressive and liable to retaliate rather than accept her child's anger, the growing child may be left harbouring phantasies of revenge and hatred which then become manifest in delinquent behaviour. This may be accompanied by an indifference born of

> [the] determination at all costs not to risk again the disappointment and resulting rages and longings which wanting someone very much and not getting them involves . . . a policy of self-protection against the slings and arrows of their own turbulent feelings.
>
> (Bowlby 1944)

We see in this early work the prefigurings of three of Bowlby's most insistent themes: the centrality of loss as a determinant of disturbance, the importance of the mother in neutralising and defusing the destructive effects of rage in response to loss, and the use of affective withdrawal as a defense against the pain of unmet longing or anger faced alone. Bowlby had already identified the importance of *expression* of anger, rather than its repression, and the role of the parents in fostering or holding this back, in his pre-war study of aggression:

> Take the child away from the fire, deny it a second piece of cake, but avoid being angry or hurt or disapproving if a scream of rage or a kick on the shins is the immediate consequence of thwarting a child's will to happiness. To permit children to express their *feelings* of aggression, whilst preventing *acts* of irremediable destruction is, we suggest, one of the greatest gifts that parents can give to their children.
>
> (Durbin and Bowlby 1938)

As we saw in Chapter 3, Bowlby's own retrospective findings were buttressed by his review of the world literature on the effects of separation, and here too he emphasises the importance of *active protest* as a mark of a positive response to separation: 'a violent reaction is normal and an apathetic resignation a sign of unhealthy development' (Bowlby 1965).

PROSPECTIVE STUDIES: CHILDREN IN HOSPITAL

Together with James Robertson (Robertson and Bowlby 1952b), Bowlby was next able to establish by direct observation the effects on children of temporary separation from their parents. They studied the reactions of children who were taken into hospital, which in those days required almost complete absence of contact with parents during the admission (for fear of cross-infection), and a series of constantly changing carers in the hospital ward. Profound effects were noted, especially in the younger age groups. The children initially became tearful, crying and calling bitterly for their parents, and rejecting the staff's attempts to mollify or distract them. Later, bored indifference and apathy seemed to take over, with the children isolating themselves from their peers, sitting listlessly staring into space, playing and eating little. Finally, children appeared to 'recover' and to become active once more, but if hospitalisation was prolonged their relationships with adults and other children appeared superficial and self-centered compared with before.

These three phases were described by Bowlby as the stages of *protest, withdrawal* and *detachment*. Feelings of protest re-emerged when these separated children were reunited with their parents, who were subjected to a mixture of rejection (even to the point of failing to recognise them), angry attacks and clinging in the days following return from hospital. Some of these changes were long-lived and could be detected up to two years later. They also found that the effects of separation could be mitigated by a number of common-sense measures including regular hospital visiting by parents, preliminary reconnaissance visits to the hospital ward, allowing children to take familiar comforting objects like teddy-bears with them when they went into hospital, and in the case of separations not involving hospital, placing them with adults who were previously known and trusted. All of these moves have by now become part of routine parental and pediatric practice.

AN ANATOMY OF MOURNING

The 1960s saw two important developments in the understanding of the psychological impact of loss. First, Bowlby was joined at the Tavistock by Colin Murray Parkes who undertook a systematic study of bereavement in adults which complemented and confirmed Robertson's (1952) earlier work with children (Parkes 1975). Second, the crystallisation of Attachment Theory provided a theoretical basis on which to understand these empirical findings.

Bowlby's theory of bereavement is essentially an extension of his theory of separation anxiety which we have considered in the previous chapter. He sees anxiety as realistic response to separation or threatened separation of a vulnerable individual from his care-giver. Since care-seeker and care-giver form a reciprocal partnership, and since the attachment dynamic continues throughout adult life, separation anxiety will arise whenever the parent–child, adult–spouse or adult–companion relationship is threatened. The components of separation anxiety include a subjective feeling of worry, pain and tension; angry protest, whose function is to register displeasure and to punish the errant partner so as to prevent repetition; and a restless searching for the missing person.

Bowlby sees the grief reaction as a special case of separation anxiety, bereavement being an irreversible form of separation. He believes that the psychological response to the trauma of separation is biologically programmed in the same way that the inflammatory response is an orderly sequence of physiological responses to physical trauma – redness, swelling, heat and pain. The early phases of grief consist of an intense form of separation anxiety. The later phases result from the confusion and misery that arise from the realisation that the secure base to whom the bereaved individual would turn for comfort in distress is the very person who is no longer available. With this in mind, let us look now at the four phases of mourning (Bowlby 1980, 1982a, 1988a) in more detail.

Stage 1: numbing

A soldier wounded on the field of battle may feel no pain and continue to fight until help is at hand. In the same way, perhaps, the very earliest response to a sudden bereavement may be an apparent calmness based on emotional shutdown in which all feelings are suppressed, or reality denied, until the bereaved person is in a safe enough situation to let go a little.

A bereaved wife in the casualty department

A young scaffolder was brought into the casualty department dead, having fallen from a tall building. There were no external signs of injury. When his wife arrived she was completely and chillingly calm, expressing no emotion, simply saying: 'Oh, but he's not dead, he's asleep, doesn't he look beautiful and peaceful.' It was only when, several hours later, her mother arrived that she began to sob and wail uncontrollably.

Stage 2: yearning, searching, anger

Bowlby places the *search for the lost object* at the centre of the mourning response. There may be physical restlessness and wandering as the bereaved person goes from room to room, from place to place, scanning, looking, hoping that their lost loved one may reappear. A similar process goes on psychologically in which the bereaved person goes over in their mind every detail of the events leading up to the loss, in a kind of compulsive 'action replay', hoping that some mistake may have been made and that past events can be made to turn out differently.

Freud (1917) saw the purpose of this mental searching as that of detachment: 'Mourning has a quite precise psychical task to perform: its function is to detach the survivor's memories and hopes from the dead.' Bowlby, by contrast, sees purpose in evolutionary rather than teleological terms, and views the mental searching of the bereaved as an attempt to recover and be reunited with the lost object. Similarly, Bowlby's understanding of the prevalence of visual images of the dead person that so often haunt the bereaved is of an intense 'perceptual set' towards the sight and sound of the lost person that can lead to misinterpretation of auditory and visual clues. Just as the 3-month-old infant quickens at the sound of his mother's footsteps and scans his visual field anxiously until he can meet her greeting smile with his, so the bereaved person is desperately trying to track down his missing attachment figure. Following Darwin (1872), Bowlby sees the facial expressions and crying of the bereaved as a resultant of the tendency to scream in the hope of awakening the attention of a negligent care-giver, and the social inhibition of such screaming.

Anger too is part of the normal response to separation: 'almost every separation has a happy ending, and often a small or large dash of aggression will assist this outcome' (Bowlby 1961c). Bowlby emphasises again and again the importance of the expression of anger if the bereaved person is to recover:

> Only if he can tolerate the pining, the more or less conscious searching, the seemingly endless examination of why and how the loss occurred, and anger at everyone who might be responsible, not even sparing the dead person, can he gradually come to realise and accept that loss is in truth permanent and that his life must be shaped anew.
>
> (Bowlby 1982a)

The anger so often seen towards potential comforters whose aim is to help the bereaved person 'come to terms' with the loss, or towards doctors responsible for the care of the dead person, can be understood in this light too. They represent the loss of hope that the loved one might somehow be alive. Their cold comfort can trigger an angry outburst in one who, already weakened by the stress of loss, wants nothing less than to be reminded that the loss is indeed irrecoverable. If only someone can be blamed then this allows the 'secret hope that perhaps in some miraculous way to seek out the villain will lead to recovery of loss' (Bowlby 1961c).

The lonely widow

Marion was fifty-five when her husband died suddenly of a heart attack. Childless, they had been married for thirty years and had returned to the United Kingdom after years of living overseas, having lost all their possessions in a fire. Marion had relied on her husband for everything, sheltering behind his competence and social confidence. She 'coped' well at first after his death, but then was admitted to hospital after taking a large overdose. She had only been found in time because the milkman had noticed uncollected bottles and raised the alarm. When she recovered she explained how furious she had felt when her doctor (who had failed in her eyes to save her husband's life) had summoned her for a cervical smear test, without apparently realising that she had had a hysterectomy some years previously.

Therapy with her meant withstanding a torrent of fury about the unfairness of life. She blamed the doctors, the laxity of modern society (the England she had returned to was such a different place from the one she had left), the insurance companies, the Government – everyone. She agreed reluctantly to try not to kill herself, although she continued to insist that life without her husband was futile and meaningless. Contrary to expectation, exploring her childlessness, of which the GP's summons had reminded her, did not lead to feelings of sadness about her lack of children. Instead she revealed how she, unlike her husband, had never wanted children since she feared that this would divert his care and attention from her, as she felt had happened with her mother in her family (she, like Bowlby's mother, was the oldest of six) when her younger siblings were born. A history of excessive dependency and exclusive monotropism is a significant predisposing factor towards prolonged grief reactions (Parkes 1975).

Stages 3 and 4: disorganisation and despair: reorganisation

The diagram of the attachment relationship (Figure 4.1) shown in the previous chapter depicted a dynamic equilibrium between care-seeker and care-giver, constantly monitored, quiescent at times of exploration, activated at times of stress. Bowlby (1980) likens the shock of loss to a see-saw in which one person is suddenly removed, and quotes C. S. Lewis on his widowerhood: 'So many roads once; now so many culs-de-sac.' The basic dilemma of the bereaved is, as we have said, that the loss removes not only the loved one, but also the secure base to which the bereaved person would expect to turn in their hour of need.

Loss throws the inner world of the sufferer into turmoil. All the assumptions and expectations which depended on the presence of the loved one are now thrown into question. Where can the bereaved person find hope and comfort in the face of his inner turmoil and confusion? The quasi-depressive state which marks the third stage of grief can be understood in a number of ways. Freud (1917) recognised that some internal work was occurring which was necessary before the person could begin to form new attachments. For him the key feature was *identification* with the lost object; in Klein's (1986) word, the lost person is 'reinstated' in the inner world in the course of healthy grief so that he or she forms part of a composite internal representation of reality.

Melanie Klein (1986) sees the depression and apathy and withdrawal of the bereaved as a regression to infancy, a result of the assault on the security of the inner world which has been so painstakingly built up through childhood. For Klein grief is 'shot through with persecutory anxiety and guilt' (Bowlby 1961a) because the bereaved person is thrown back to the abandonments and failures of early childhood. During the phase of disorganisation the bereaved person is constantly questioning and questing, but 'reality passes its verdict – that the object no longer exists – upon each single one of the memories and hopes' (Klein 1986). Just as the infant, through maternal tolerance and capacity to process conflict and negative affect learns that the lost breast will reappear, that his anger has not destroyed his mother's love, so the bereaved person begins once more to build up his inner world:

> every advance in the process of mourning results in a deepening in the individual's relation to his inner objects, in the

happiness of regaining them after they were felt to be lost. This is similar to the way in which the young child step by step builds up his relation to external objects, for he gains trust not only from pleasant experiences, but also from the ways in which he overcomes frustrations and unpleasant experiences, nevertheless retaining his good objects.

(Klein 1986)

Bowlby is critical of Klein for what he sees as her overemphasis on the persecutory aspect of normal (as opposed to abnormal) grief, and for her neglect of the *reality* of the danger to which the bereaved person is exposed (widowers die of a broken heart more frequently than comparable non-bereaved men). Nevertheless, her account of the impact of death on the internal world is entirely compatible with the Bowlbian view that the work of grief consists of rebuilding a secure inner base, that the building of secure attachment depends on a secure holding environment which in the past has been reliable enough to withstand and process hostility, and that new attachments can only be formed once old ones are relinquished.

A widower – at twenty-six

Jock was a tough shipbuilder from the Clyde. At twenty-six his wife died suddenly of a cerebral haemorrhage, leaving him with six children aged eight to 6 months. He tried for a few weeks to carry on as normal but suddenly took all the children to his sister and brother-in-law and set off for London. There he led the life of a tramp, living on the streets and in doss houses, drinking heavily, fighting a lot and moving on. Eventually he was brought to the emergency clinic of the hospital, where he told his story. He spoke of his feelings of rage and fury towards his wife for abandoning him, about which he felt intensely guilty and about his incomprehension that God (he was a devout Catholic) should have allowed such a thing to happen to him; of the despair and chaos which he felt inside; of his wish to smash anyone and everyone who thwarted or tried to control him; and of his need to drink to blot out the pain of losing the wife whom he loved so much. His drinking and way of life continued, but he went on coming to the clinic to talk. Then, suddenly and without warning he disappeared. A few weeks later he wrote saying that he had returned to Glasgow, had stopped drinking and was now happily looking after the children. A further letter about a year later confirmed that things continued to go well.

Perhaps Jock felt sufficiently 'held' (in the Winnicottian sense) by his weekly contact with the therapist at the hospital to be able to rebuild his inner world so that he could become once more a secure base for his children – leaving his therapist as abruptly as his wife had 'left' him. For Bowlby the opportunity for emotional release is an essential ingredient in healthy mourning, avoiding the defensive manoeuvres which unexpressed emotion requires:

> The behaviour of potential comforters plays a large part in determining whether a bereaved person is sad, perhaps dreadfully sad, or becomes despairing and depressed as well . . . if all goes well, since he will not be afraid of intense and unmet desires for love from the person lost, he will let himself be swept by pangs of grief and tearful expressions of yearning, and distress will come naturally.
>
> (Bowlby 1982a)

MOURNING AND ADULT PSYCHOPATHOLOGY

Bowlby's early studies had convinced him of the far-reaching effects of separation and bereavement in childhood. He was convinced that much of adult psychiatric disability could be traced back to such traumata. This view is supported by recent psychophysiological findings that early separation can have long-lasting effects on the sensitivity of brain receptors, leading to permanently raised anxiety levels (Van de Kolk 1987; Gabbard 1992). Post (1992) has similarly argued that depression in adult life may originate with environmental trauma that is encoded in brain changes in protein and RNA, on the analogy of the 'kindling' phenomenon in epilepsy in which the sensitivity of brain cells becomes progressively greater with each seizure, so that what starts as a response to an environmental stimulus becomes eventually an intrinsic feature of the brain.

Bowlby was also convinced that the response of the adult world to a child's distress had a decisive influence on the outcome of loss. He was implacably opposed to the stiff-upper-lip attitude, and disparagement of 'childishness' which epitomised his generation, class and profession. Love, tenderness, encouragement of emotional expression even if hostile, and acceptance of the life-long imperative for mutual dependency were his watchwords.

Recent epidemiological research (Tennant 1988) suggests that the influence of childhood bereavement *per se* on adult psychiatric disorder is probably less significant than Bowlby imagined. Parental disruption and disturbance is a much more potent cause of difficulty and depression than loss in itself. But, as we shall see in Chapters 6 and 9, the current evidence suggests that Bowlby was right to emphasise the real nature of environmental influence and to make quite sharp distinctions between normal and abnormal developmental patterns, a point which he felt the psychoanalysts consistently fudged. His hunch that loss was a key research issue has been proved right, but in a more subtle way than he might have imagined, and one which is compatible with the Kleinian view from which he was so careful to distance himself. The manner in which a child's carers respond to her or his reactions to loss, whether major or minor – to the anger and pining and demandingness – may crucially influence that child's subsequent development. The establishment of a secure internal base, a sense that conflict can be negotiated and resolved, the avoidance of the necessity for primitive defences – all this depends on parental handling of the interplay between attachment and loss that is the leitmotiv of the Bowlbian message.

COMPANIONSHIP AND ATTACHMENT: A POETIC POSTSCRIPT

Being highly intelligent, very well-organised and slightly obsessional, Bowlby was a master of any topic to which he put his mind: for example, he re-read the whole of Freud during his Stanford fellowship in 1957. The corollary of this was that he tended to avoid those few subjects of which he had only passing or partial knowledge, one of which was English literature (U. Bowlby 1991). Having no such scruples – perhaps to my discredit – I conclude this chapter by considering three classic poems of grief from the English canon, which in their non-scientific way lend some support to Bowlby's thesis on mourning.

Milton's *Lycidas* and Tennyson's *In Memoriam* are both poems by young men about the loss of loved and valued fraternal comrades. It is debatable whether friendship (and sibship) fulfil the criteria of proximity seeking, secure-base effect and separation protest which are the hallmarks of a full-blown attachment relationship. Weiss (1982) distinguishes the companionship provided by friends from the intimacy of adult attachment typically to be found in a sexual partnership. He showed how wives who move because of their husband's job to new towns felt cut off from their friends and bored, but did not experience the specific empty loneliness that widows or separated people feel when loss of a spouse first hits. Similarly, Heard and Lake (1986) write about the need for 'like-minded companions of similar experience and stamina with whom to engage in mutually interesting and enjoyable activities' as part of the 'attachment dynamic'. A cursory glance at any lonely hearts column will attest to the reality of this need. The prime role of friendship seems to facilitate exploratory activity rather than to provide a secure base, although without a secure base no exploration is possible, and many intimate relationships, especially marriage, provide both. It seems likely that friendship or sibship does have a more central role as a source for a secure base in certain circumstances: in adolescence; among comrades in intense and isolated circumstances such as the armed services or mountaineering expeditions; and between siblings when the parental relationship is difficult or defective. The latter was certainly the case for Tennyson, who had an extremely unhappy and tormented childhood which he survived mainly through his writing and intelligence (Hamilton 1986), and, from his teenage years, through his friendship with Arthur Hallam who, although two years younger, became his mentor, sponsor and champion. Hallam's premature death when Tennyson was only twenty-four led to near-breakdown for the poet. *In Memoriam* was started within weeks of the loss, but was only completed and published some thirteen years later.

Milton's *Lycidas* 'bewails' the death of a 'learned friend' (Edward King) drowned in the Irish Sea – like Tennyson's Hallam, a childhood companion and one who shared Milton's radical anti-clericalism. Milton's mother had died a few months earlier; numbed, Milton had apparently been unable to write anything to mark her loss. The scene is pastoral and the two friends are depicted as shepherds. The need at times of grief to return to the good object (breast-hill) is evoked:

For we were nursed upon the self-same hill,
Fed the same flock by fountain, shade, and rill.

The centrepiece of the poem is the attack on the 'corrupted clergy then in their height', drawn as self-serving, ignorant shepherds. Like so many prematurely bereaved people, Milton rails against the injustice of fate: why has *my* loved one died, who did not deserve it, and not those undeserving souls who live on?

'How well could I have spared for thee, young swain,
Enow of such as for their bellies' sake
Creep, and intrude, and climb into the fold! . . .
Blind mouths! that scarce themselves know how to hold
A sheep-hook . . .
The hungry sheep look up, and are not fed,
But swoln with wind, and the rank mist they draw,
Rot inwardly, and foul contagion spread.'

The inner world is contaminated and fouled by the anger and despair of the poet, then projected onto the corrupt priests who are held to blame for the loss.

The action of the poem takes place in a single night in which the poet passes through the stages of sadness, despair, anger, blame and depression until he reaches acceptance, with the help of two images from the natural world. The first are the garlands of flowers with which to 'strew the laureat hearse where Lycid lies', and which serve to link the loss of Lycidas with the natural transience of beauty. In the second he pictures the sun setting over the ocean where Lycidas is drowned, only to rise again the next morning,

and with new spangled ore
Flames in the forehead of the morning sky.

An image of setting and rising, of separation and reunion, has replaced the sense of irretrievable loss. A secure base is re-established, mirroring perhaps the regular appearance and disappearance of the feeding mother. The poet can begin once more to explore, no longer enshrouded, but enveloped by a cloak that moves and lives:

At last he rose, and twitched his mantle blue:
To-morrow to fresh woods and pastures new.

In *In Memoriam* we see many of the same themes. In recalling his love for Hallam, Tennyson is taken back to pre-verbal paradisial times before the loss, reminiscent of the mother's attunement to her baby's needs, which leads, in Winnicottian terms, to the opening out of a transitional space between them. The poet describes the two friends' sense of intuitive, empathic understanding:

Dear as the mother to the son
  More than my brothers are to me . . .
  Thought leapt out to wed with Thought
Ere thought could wed itself with speech.

But then the dreadful boat brings the dead body home. Tennyson contrasts his own empty hands and those reunited with their attachment figures:

Thou bring'st the sailor to his wife
  And travelled men from foreign lands
  And letters unto trembling hands
And, thy dark freight, a vanished life.

Tennyson tackles the tragic implications of monotropism: attachments are not transferable, or only so by a slow and painful process of withdrawal and re-attachment. By contrast, nature becomes an indifferent mother who cares equally and indiscriminately for all her 'children' and has no special affection for any one of them.

Are God and Nature then at strife,
  That Nature lends such evil dreams?
  So careful of the type she seems,
So careless of the single life?

Despair strikes, meaning is destroyed, when the interplay of attachment, with its mutual reinforcement, its linking of inner world and outer reality is disrupted:

'So careful of the type'? But no.
  From scarped cliff and quarried stone
  She cries, 'A thousand types are gone;
I care for nothing, all shall go.'

Loss throws us back to our childhood, to our primary attachments:

> but what am I?
> An infant crying in the night:
> An infant crying for the light:
> And with no language but a cry.

Tennyson begins to think on a new time-scale and to see the possibility of new attachments, as one generation succeeds another:

> Unwatch'd, the garden bough shall sway,
> The tender blossom flutter down . . .

> Till from the garden and the wild
> A fresh association blow,
> And year by year the landscape grow
> Familiar to the stranger's child.

Finally he returns to the image of mother and child, to the hatching of individuality from their symbiotic mixed-upness (Balint 1964). The mother's 'roundness' takes him round the corner of his developmental pathway towards a less despairing separation in which the inner world is strengthened and clarified:

> The baby new to earth and sky
> What time his tender palm is prest
> Against the circle of the breast
> Has never thought that 'this is I'

> So rounds he to a separate mind
> From whence clear memory may begin
> As through the frame that binds him in
> His isolation grows defined.

So it is with grief where, if all goes well, can come a strengthening of the inner world, of memory and definition. As we shall argue in Chapter 8, the importance of telling a story, of 'clear memory' is central to the poet's (and the psychotherapist's) mission.

John Donne's 'A Valediction: forbidding mourning' also concerns a sea voyage, and also uses the image of a 'round' or circle as an antidote to the abyss of loss and separation. This is a poem about anticipatory grief, given by Donne to his wife before setting sail for France in November 1611 (Gardner 1957).

He starts by advocating a slipping away on parting, which he compares with death, rather than an abrupt and emotional separation:

As virtuous men pass mildly away,
   And whisper to their soules to goe
Whilst some of their sad friends doe say
   The breath goes now, and some say no.

He contrasts their love which that of 'dull sublunary lovers', who
lack a secure inner base and who therefore are dependent on
one another's physical presence. They

     cannot admit
Absence, because it doth remove
   Those things which elemented it.

But we . . .
Interassured of the mind,
   Care lesse, eyes, lips, and hands to misse.

He pictures the invisible but precious bonds which link carer and
cared-for, lover and beloved in an attachment relationship as
slender threads of gold:

Our two souls therefore, which are one,
   Though I must goe, endure not yet
A breach, but an expansion,
   Like gold to ayery thinnesse beate.

Then, in another brilliant metaphysical metaphor, he imagines
the internal working model of self and other as the two ends of
a pair of compasses:

Thy soule the fixt foot, makes no show
   To move, but doth, if th'other doe.

And though it in the center sit,
   Yet when the other far doth rome,
It leanes, and hearkens after it,
   And growes erect, as it comes home. . .

Thy firmnes makes my circle just,
   And makes me end, where I begunne.

We have mentioned how Bowlby says little about sexuality and
is at pains to separate 'mating behaviour' from 'attachment
behaviour'. The sexual imagery of this poem – despite appear-
ances to the contrary ladies *do* move, perhaps 'grow erect' even,
the lover 'ending' (that is, in orgasm) where he 'begun' (namely,

was born) – combines in a profound way sexuality and attachment. The rhythm of sexuality, of coming together and separating, is linked both with death and the parting of soul from body at the start of the poem, and with birth at the end. They are held together by the central image of the secure base or 'inter-assurance' of lover and beloved. Seen in this way, attachment is a unifying principle that reaches from the biological depths of our being to its furthest spiritual reaches. The inevitability of loss means that for Bowlby grief sometimes outshines attachment in importance, that his criticisms of psychoanalysis sometimes outweigh his praise, just as for the republican Milton, Satan and the underworld were more vibrant and interesting than the kingdom of God.

Chapter 6

Attachment Theory and personality development: the research evidence

> It is just as necessary for analysts to study the way a child is really treated by his parents as it is to study the internal representations he has of them, indeed the principal form of our studies should be the interaction of the one with the other, of the internal with the external.
>
> (Bowlby 1988a)

One of Bowlby's main reasons for re-casting psychoanalysis in the language of Attachment Theory was the hope that this would make it more accessible for empirical testing. This hope has been fully justified. The past thirty years have seen an explosion of research in infant and child development, a major part of which has arisen directly from the work of Bowlby and Mary Ainsworth in the 1950s and sixties. The aim of this chapter is to show how these findings point to a remarkably consistent story about the emergence of personality, or 'attachment style', out of the matrix of interactions between infant and care-givers in the early months and years of life. The issue of how what starts as interaction becomes internalised as personality is a key question for developmental psychology. Object-Relations Theory rests on the assumption that early relationships are a formative influence on character. I hope to demonstrate in this and the following chapter that Bowlby's movement away from psychoanalysis has come full circle and produced ideas that are highly relevant to, and provide strong support and enrichment for, the psychoanalytic perspective.

As a scientific discipline, Attachment Theory has two great advantages over psychoanalysis. First, it rests on direct observation of parent–child interaction, rather than on retrospective reconstructions of what may or may not have gone in a person's past. Second, it starts from the observation of normal development, which can then be used as a yardstick against which to understand psychopathology, rather than building a theory of normal development from inferences made in the consulting room. It is perhaps no accident that the psychoanalyst with whom Bowlby has most in common, Winnicott, was also keenly aware of normal developmental processes through his earlier work as a pediatrician. Winnicott and Bowlby both believed that their observations of normal development were relevant to psychotherapy, for by getting a picture of what makes a good parent, we are likely to be in a better position to know what makes a good psychotherapist.

MARY AINSWORTH AND THE STRANGE SITUATION

There is an intimate relationship between technology and scientific advance. Galileo's observations depended on the expertise of the sixteenth-century Italian lens grinders; Darwin's discoveries sprang from the navigational and cartographic skills of Victorian maritime imperialism. Ainsworth's 'Strange Situation', 'a miniature drama in eight parts' (Bretherton 1991a) for mother, one-year-old infant and experimenter, has established itself as an indispensable tool in developmental psychology.

Ainsworth devised the Strange Situation in the late 1960s as part of her studies of mother–child interaction in the first year of life. She had worked with Bowlby in the 1950s, then moved to Uganda where she had made naturalistic studies of mothers with their babies, and finally settled in Baltimore, Maryland. Influenced by Attachment Theory, although at first wary of its ethological bias, she was interested in the relationship between attachment and exploratory behaviour in infants, and wanted to devise a standardised assessment procedure for human mothers and their children which would be both naturalistic and could be reliably rated, comparable to the methods used by animal experimenters like Harlow (1958) and Hinde (1982b).

The Strange Situation (Ainsworth *et al.* 1978) consists of a twenty-minute session in which mother and one-year-old child are first introduced into a playroom with an experimenter. The mother is then asked to leave the room for three minutes and to return, leaving the child with the experimenter. After her return and the re-union with the child, both mother and experimenter go out of the room for three minutes, leaving the child on its own. Mother and child are then once more re-united. The whole procedure is videotaped and rated, focusing particularly on the response of the child to separation and re-union. The aim is to elicit individual differences in coping with the stress of separation. Initially three, and later four, major patterns of response have been identified:

1 *Secure attachment* ('B')   These infants are usually (but not invariably) distressed by the separation. On re-union they greet their parent, receive comfort if required, and then return to excited or contented play.
2 *Insecure-avoidant* ('A')   These children show few overt signs of distress on separation, and ignore their mother on re-union, especially on the second occasion when presumably the stress is greater. They remain watchful of her and inhibited in their play.
3 *Insecure-ambivalent (insecure-resistant)* ('C')   They are highly distressed by separation and cannot easily be pacified on re-union. They seek contact, but then resist by kicking, turning away, squirming or batting away offered toys. They continue to alternate between anger and clinging to the mother, and their exploratory play is inhibited.
4 *Insecure-disorganised* ('D')   This small group has recently been demarcated. They show a diverse range of confused behaviours including 'freezing', or stereotyped movements, when re-united with their parent.

In Ainsworth's original middle-class Baltimore sample the proportions were 'B' (secure) 66 per cent, 'A' (avoidant) 20 per cent, and 'C' (ambivalent) 12 per cent. 'D' had not been identified at that stage. Since her original publication, the Strange Situation has been used in well over thirty different studies (Ijzendoorn and Kroonenberg 1988), and is generally accepted as a reliable and valid instrument – comparable perhaps to the widespread use of the Expressed Emotion scales in psychiatry (Leff and Vaughn 1983; see Chapter 9). There are significant cross-cultural variations, so that 'A' (avoidant) classifications tend to be commoner in Western Europe and the United States, while 'C' (ambivalent) is commoner in Israel and Japan. Intra-cultural variation between different socio-economic groups and between disturbed and non-disturbed families is greater than inter-cultural variance.

A whole set of research and theoretical questions follows from the establishment of this robust research tool. What is the meaning of the different patterns of response? Are they stable over time, and if so for how long? Do they predict disturbed behaviour later in childhood? Do they, as psychoanalytic theory might assume, persist into adult life? Can they be related to patterns of maternal–infant interaction in the early months of life? If maternal handling is relevant to classification pattern, what is the relationship between this and the mother's *own* experience of being mothered? If so, what are the psychological mechanisms by which attachment patterns are carried over from one generation to the next? Can patterns be altered by therapeutic intervention? The remainder of this chapter will be devoted to a discussion of these and related questions.

THE ROOTS OF SECURE AND INSECURE ATTACHMENT

Bowlby saw personality development primarily in terms of environmental influence: relationships rather than instinct or genetic endowment are primary. Differing patterns of attachment result from differing patterns of interaction, rather than being a reflection of infant temperament, or instinct. Sroufe (1979) makes an important distinction between 'emergent patterns of personality organisation' as revealed in the Strange Situation, and temperament, the latter representing quasi-physiological styles of behaviour, while the former reflect much more complex habitual relationship patterns. Thus babies may be sluggish, or active, 'cuddly' or non-cuddly, slow or fast, but still be classified as secure. Even more telling is the finding that children have different, but characteristic, attachment patterns with their two parents, and may be classified as secure with one and insecure with the other. This argues strongly that attachment patterns are a feature of the parent–child *relationship*, as yet not 'internalised' at one year, although by 18 months patterns have become more stable, with maternal patterns tending to dominate over paternal.

The Strange Situation research was part of a much larger study in which Ainsworth and her colleagues visited mothers and their infants regularly for periods of observation and rating during the whole of the first year of life. She found that attachment status at one year correlated strongly with the maternal relationship in the preceding twelve months, and this finding has been replicated in several other centres (Main and Weston 1982; Grossman *et al.* 1986; Sroufe 1979). In summary, prospective studies show that mothers of secure one-year-olds are *responsive to their babies*, mothers of insecure-avoidants are *unresponsive*, and mothers of insecure-ambivalents are *inconsistently responsive.*

The key to secure attachment is active, reciprocal interaction (Rutter 1981), and it seems that it is quality of interaction more than quantity that matters – a finding that contradicts Bowlby's earlier view on the causes of maternal deprivation. Passive contact alone does not necessarily promote attachment. Many babies are strongly attached to their fathers even though they spend relatively little time with them, and kibbutzim-reared children are more strongly attached to their mothers than to the nurses who feed them and look after them during the day, but often without much active interaction. In the first three months, mothers of secure infants respond more promptly when they cry; look, smile at and talk to their babies more; and offer them more affectionate and joyful holding. Mothers of avoidant children tend to interact less, and in a more functional way in the first three months, while mothers of ambivalents tend to ignore their babies' signals for attention and generally to be unpredictable in their responsiveness. By the second half of the first year, clear differences can be detected in the babies, and those who will be classified as secure at one year cry less than the insecure group, enjoy body contact more, and appear to demand it less (Bretherton 1991b).

The factor which mothers of insecurely attached children have in common can be understood in terms of Stern's (1985) concept of maternal *attunement.* He shows how sensitive mothers interacting with their children modulate their infant's rhythms so that when activity levels fall and the infant appears bored the mother will stimulate them, and when the child becomes overstimulated the mother will hold back a little so as to restore equilibrium. In *cross-modal attunement* the mother follows the baby's babbling, kicking, bouncing and so on with sounds or movements of her own that match and harmonise with those of the baby, although they may be in a different sensory mode. As he bounces up and down she may go 'Oooooh . . . Aaaaah . . .', matching the tempo and amplitude of her responses to the baby's movements.

This helps, as Stern sees it, in the development of the infant's sense of integrated selfhood. These processes of attunement are impaired in mothers of insecurely attached infants, leading to 'derailment' or mismatching in maternal response (Beebe and Lachmann 1988): thus mothers of ambivalently attached children can be observed to force themselves on their children when they are playing happily, and ignore them when they are in distress.

Brazelton and Cramer (1991) propose a similar model in which they break down the components of secure mother–child inter-active patterns into four main features: synchrony (temporal attunement), symmetry (matching of actions), contingency (mutual cueing), and 'entrainment' (the capturing of each other's responses into a sequence of mutual activity). On the basis of this, play, and later infant autonomy, begins to emerge. Insecure attachments result from intrusiveness or under-responsiveness. They have developed an experimental model of the latter in their 'still face' experiments in which the infant is momentarily presented with an unmoving image of the mother, who is pro-hibited from picking up the baby or responding to it. The baby shows disappointment, gaze aversion and self-soothing strategies, which match those seen in the children of clinically depressed mothers.

As we have seen in the previous chapter, aggression is a major component of the initial response to threatened separation. Both patterns of insecure attachment can perhaps be understood in terms of the interplay between the need for attachment and the aggressive response to the threat of separation. The ambivalently attached child shows overt aggression towards the inconsistent mother who, in the Strange Situation, has just 'abandoned' him for two successive periods (albeit only for 3 minutes – but how was the one-year-old to know that?). It is as if he is saying, 'Don't you dare do that again!', but clinging on at the same time since he knows from experience that she will. The avoidant child shows little overt aggression in the Strange Situation, although these children do show outbursts of unprovoked aggression at home. It may be that the avoidant response is a way of dampening aggression and so appeasing the mother to whom the child needs desperately to feel close, but whom he fears will rebuff him if he reveals his needs too openly, or shows her how angry he feels about being abandoned (Main and Weston 1982).

The clock-watcher

A clinical example of avoidant attachment in adulthood is provided by a patient who, although faithfully reliable in her attendance at therapy, found it difficult to enter affectively into sessions which consisted mostly of a catalogue of the preceding week's events. She was meticulous about timekeeping, kept a close eye on her watch throughout the sessions, because, she said, she was terrified to overrun by a single second. As a solicitor she knew how annoying it was when clients outstayed their allotted time. The effect of this clock-watching was quite irritating to her therapist, who commented that timekeeping was *his* responsibility and tried to persuade her to remove her watch for sessions. It then emerged that her phantasy was that without her watch she would get 'lost' in the session, lose control of her feelings and at just that moment the therapist would announce that it was time to stop; she would then get so angry she would 'disgrace' herself, the therapist would not tolerate this and would break off the treatment. She had been a rather 'good' if distant child who had spent a lot of time on her own, while her older sister had been renowned for her tantrums and angry outbursts. By keeping her distance in a typically avoidantly-anxious pattern, she had maintained some sort of contact with her therapist (and presumably as a child, her parents), while avoiding the danger of threatening her tenuous attachments with her rage. She also kept some sort of coherence in the face of fear of disintegration. The price she paid for this adaptation was affective distancing, low self-esteem ('He would not tolerate me if he knew what I was really like') and the lack of a sense of movement and growth in her life.

THE STRANGE SITUATION AS A PREDICTOR OF SOCIAL ADJUSTMENT

The idea that anxious attachment patterns represent an adaptation or compromise to a sub-optimal environment is borne out by follow-up studies of children classified at one, and tested at pre-school, on school entry and again at ten (Bretherton 1985). At two years, securely attached children have a longer attention span, show more positive affect in free play, show more confidence in using tools, and are more likely to elicit their mother's help in difficult tasks compared with anxiously attached children. Their nursery teachers (blind to attachment status) rate them as more empathic and compliant and higher on positive affect. In peer interaction avoidants are hostile or distant, while ambivalents tend to be 'inept' and to show chronic low-level dependency on the teacher, and to be less able to engage in free play by themselves or with peers.

Evidence that the patterns of behaviour defined by the Strange Situation behaviour carry forward into subsequent development comes from the Grossmans (1991), who have shown that patterns of behaviour on re-union were 87 per cent predictable between one year and six years. They also showed that six-year-olds classified at one year as secure played concentratedly and for longer, were more socially skillful in handling conflict with their peers, and had more positive social perceptions, compared with children who had been rated as insecure as infants. Sroufe (1979) sees secure-rated children as having greater *ego control* and *ego resiliency* than those who were insecure. Secure children were rated by their teachers as neither overcontrolled nor undercontrolled, while avoidants were overcontrolled, ambivalents undercontrolled. Resiliency was inferred from such statements as 'curious and exploring', 'self-reliant, confident'. Stroufe concludes: 'What began as a competent caregiver-infant pair led to a flexible resourceful child. . . . Such predictability is not due to the inherently higher IQ of the securely attached infant, or, apparently, to inborn differences in temperament.'

LANGUAGE, NARRATIVE, COHERENCE

So far we have confined our account to attachment behaviour. As we look now at older children and their mothers, we turn to the trickier but psychotherapeutically more salient topics of the nature of attachment experience, its internal representation and how it manifests itself in language.

Main *et al.* (1985), Bretherton (1991b) and Cassidy (1988) have tried to tap into the child's experience of attachment by the use of play techniques such as a picture completion task, story completion, and puppet interview and story all depicting in different ways episodes of separation and re-union. Children tend to reveal their attachment histories through their play and imaginative activity. Avoidant children at six tend to draw figures with blank faces and no hands, suggesting a lack of responsiveness and holding in their lives. Secure children in response to a picture-story task give coherent, elaborated responses, including references to their own separation experiences, and are able to suggest positive ways in which separated figures could resolve their difficulties. Avoidant children, by contrast, describe separated children as sad, but cannot think of ways to help them. Secure children at six were more able to give a balanced view of themselves as good, but not perfect, while insecure children saw themselves as either faultless or bad. It should be noted that these results were much more consistent for the avoidant than the ambivalent group who gave very varied responses to the play tasks, without a clear pattern emerging. The disorganised group ('D') emerged more clearly in these as opposed to previous studies, showing bizarre or disorganized responses to picture- and story-completion tasks.

Main (1991) presents some remarkable preliminary findings of a follow-up study in which ten- and eleven-year-olds, who had been classified in the Strange Situation at one year, were asked for a spoken autobiography. There was a 75 per cent correspondence between classification at one and at ten. Compared with the insecurely attached, the secure children's stories were consistently more coherent, had greater access to memories, especially of their pre-school years, and showed more self-awareness and ability to focus in on their own thought processes, a phenomenon Main calls 'megacognitive monitoring' – the ability to think about thinking.

The findings so far, which represent more than a decade of 'post-Bowlbian' research into Attachment Theory, can be summarised as follows. Relationship patterns established in the first year of life continue to have a powerful influence on children's subsequent behaviour, social adjustment, self-concept and autobiographical capacity. These effects last for at least ten years. Mother–infant relationships characterised by secure holding (both physically and emotionally), responsiveness and attunement are associated with children who are themselves secure, can tolerate and overcome the pain of separation, and have the capacity for self-reflection.

These results undoubtedly support the view that the early years of life play a crucial part in character formation, and show in a fascinating way the continuity between the pre-verbal infant self and the social self as we commonly conceive it. But two important qualifications need to be noted. First, since the parent–child relationship operates continuously as development proceeds, what we are seeing is not so much the *result* of some irreversible early events as an ongoing relationship with its own 'epigenetic' stability. There is evidence that if a mother's circumstances change – for example, a single parent entering into a stable relationship with a partner – then attachment status for her child may change, in this case from insecure to secure. Similar changes can occur, as we shall see later in the chapter, when mother and infant are both treated with psychotherapy (Murray and Cooper 1992). Second, in presenting these findings the emphasis has been on the contribution of the parent, especially the mother, with the infant's role being relatively passive. Clearly this is a gross oversimplification, and temperamental, or even neurological, factors in the child will play their part in the relationship with the parent, and subsequent social adjustment. Attachment status is quite a crude classification and clearly there will be a spectrum of subtle characterological features within it. Nevertheless, the evidence seems to be that the parent is the determining factor and that a 'good' mother even with a 'difficult' baby will, by one year, be likely to have a securely rather than insecurely attached child. For example, the amount a child cries at one year seems to depend more on the mother than the child: there is a strong correlation between prompt and sensitive maternal *responsiveness* to infant crying in the first three months of life and reduced (as compared with children of less responsive mothers) crying at one year, whereas there is no correlation between the extent of infant crying itself in the first three months and the amount of crying at one year.

This leads us directly to the issue of the inter-generational transmission of attachment. If relationships are in some way internalised by the growing child as 'character', what happens when that child grows up and becomes a parent? We know from Harlow's (1958) experiments that infant monkeys separated from their mothers show, when they become sexually mature, gross abnormalities in mating and parenting behaviour. Can we trace in the infinitely more complex language- and experience-based world of the human primate, connections between a mother's capacity to provide secure attachment for her child, and her experiences with her own mother when she was a child?

THE ADULT ATTACHMENT INTERVIEW

The Adult Attachment Interview (AAI) was devised by Main and her co-workers (1985) as a tool for assessing the working models or inner world of the parent with respect to attachment. It is a semi-structured interview conducted along the lines of a psychotherapy assessment aiming to 'surprise the unconscious' into self-revelation (Main 1991). The subject is asked to choose five adjectives which best describe the relationship with each parent during childhood, and to illustrate these with specific memories; to describe what she did when she was upset in childhood; to which parent she felt closer and why; whether she ever felt rejected or threatened by her parents; why she thinks her parents behaved as they did; how her relationship with her parents has changed over time; and how her early experiences may have affected her present functioning.

The interviews are audiotaped and then rated along eight scales: loving relationship with mother; loving relationship with father; role reversal with parents; quality of recall; anger with parents; idealisation of relationships; derogation of relationships; and coherence of narrative. The 'state of mind with respect to attachment' of the interviewees can then reliably be assigned to one of four categories: *Autonomous-secure*, *Dismissing-detached*, *Preoccupied-entangled* and *Unresolved-disorganised*.

The Autonomous-secure parents give accounts of secure childhoods, described in an open, coherent and internally consistent way. Attachments are valued, and even if their experiences have been negative there is a sense of pain felt and overcome. The Dismissing-detached group give brief, incomplete accounts, professing to having few childhood memories and tending to idealise the past with such remarks as 'I had a perfect childhood'. Preoccupied-entangled parents give inconsistent, rambling accounts in which they appear to be overinvolved with past conflicts and difficulties with which they are still struggling. The Unresolved-disorganised category is rated separately and refers specifically to traumatic events such as child abuse which have not been resolved emotionally.

Several independent studies have shown remarkably consistent correlations between the attachment status of infants in the Strange Situation, and that of their mothers in the AAI. A number of retrospective studies have shown a 70–80 per cent correspondence between infant security and parental attachment status on the AAI. Thus Main and Goldwyn (1984) found that 75 per cent of secure infants had mothers who were rated Secure-autonomous, while mothers of avoidant infants tended to be Dismissing-detached, and ambivalent infants had Preoccupied-entangled parents. The Grossmans found 77 per cent correspondence, and Ainsworth 80 per cent. Even more striking are the findings of Fonagy and his co-workers (Fonagy *et al.* 1991), who administered the AAI to prospective parents during pregnancy and found that the results predicted infant attachment status in the Strange Situation at one year with 70 per cent accuracy. Of insecure infants 73 per cent had insecure mothers, and only 20 per cent of secure infants had insecure mothers, while 80 per cent of secure mothers had secure infants. The influence of fathers appeared to be less: 82 per cent of secure fathers had secure infants, but 50 per cent of insecure fathers still had secure infants. This supports the view that attachment status is a function of the infant–parent relationship, rather than of temperament, and also suggests that maternal, rather than paternal, insecurity is the more potent transmitter of insecure attachment across the generations.

Prospective findings were less clear-cut for the preoccupied parent–ambivalent infant correlation. Many ambivalent children had mothers who were apparently secure when given the AAI in pregnancy. However, Fonagy *et al.* (1992), on reviewing these interviews, found evidence of a certain 'fragility' in the replies of these mothers, suggesting a tendency to idealisation which could easily be mistaken for security. There is some evidence that ambivalent children may have shown physiological immaturity at birth, or are the products of difficult labours, and it is possible that immaturity in the infant may have exposed the mother's 'fragility' in such a way as to produce an ambivalent attachment status at one year.

THEORETICAL INTERLUDE

The findings of this new generation of post-Bowlbian researchers are summarised in Table 6.1 and produce a coherent picture of benign and vicious cycles of security and insecurity. Secure mothers are responsive and attuned to their babies and provide them with a secure base for exploration. They are able to hold

Table 6.1 The continuity of secure and insecure attachment

	Pregnant Mothers	Babies 0–1	Infants 1 year	2-year-olds	6-year-olds	6-year-olds	10-year-olds
Classification	Secure	Responsive mothers – look more, pick up more quickly	Secure	Call for mother when needed, use tools confidently	Concentrated play, socially resilient	Can cope with idea of separation, finds resolution	Coherent memories, stories of conflict resolved
	Insecure-entangled	Inconsistent mothers	Insecure-ambivalent	Inept, low-level dependency	Under-controlled	Varied response	Incoherent stories, no resolution of sadness
	Insecure-dismissive	Unresponsive mothers, 'functional' handling	Insecure-avoidant	Hostile and distant with peers	Over-controlled	Draw pictures with blank faces, no hands, sadness unresolved	Poor recall and poor self-awareness
Test	AAI	Observation of mothers and infants	Strange Situation (SS)	Nursery-school observations	Direct observation, repeat SS	Play tasks picture completion	Spoken autobiography
Reference	Fonagy et al. (1991)	Ainsworth et al. (1978)	Ainsworth et al. (1978)	Bretherton (1985)	Grossman and Grossman (1991)	Main et al. (1985)	Main (1991)

them, delight in them, and cope with their discontent and aggression in a satisfactory way. These mothers have a balanced view of their own childhoods which, even if unhappy, are appraised realistically. Their children, secure as infants, grow up to be well-adjusted socially and to have a realistic self-appraisal and a sense that separation, although often sad and painful, can be responded to positively. Secure mothers and secure children have a well-developed capacity for self-reflection and narrative ability, and convey a sense of coherence in their lives.

Insecure children, by contrast, especially if avoidant, tend to have mothers who found holding and physical contact difficult, who were unresponsive to their infant's needs and not well attuned to their rhythms. These mothers tended to be dismissing about their relationships with their parents and to be unable to tell a vivid or elaborated story of their own childhoods. As they grow up, avoidant children tend to be socially isolated, to show unprovoked outbursts of anger, to lack self-awareness and to be unable to tell a coherent story about themselves.

Are we seeing in these insecure children the roots of adult personality difficulty and neurosis? If so, what can we learn about the mental mechanisms that may underlie these disorders, and do they provide clues as to how psychotherapy might help to reverse them? We shall discuss in the next two chapters the parallels between avoidant strategies in infancy and some of the features of borderline personality disorder, and the possible links between phobic and dependency disorders in adults and patterns of ambivalent attachment in infancy. Our concern here is to try to conceptualise how maternal handling becomes internalised as infant psychology. In Fraiberg's (Fraiberg *et al.* 1975) telling metaphor: 'In every nursery there are ghosts. These are the visitors from the unremembered pasts of the parents; the uninvited guests at the christening.' How do the parental ghosts get incorporated into the internal working models of the infant? Three inter-related ideas can be used to clarify this: avoidance of painful affect (Grossman and Grossman 1991), consistency and coherence of internal working models (Bretherton 1991a), and self-reflection (Fonagy 1991; Fonagy *et al.* 1991, 1992).

As we have seen in the previous chapter, Bowlby views the capacity to 'process' negative affect – to feel and resolve the pain of separation and loss – as a central mark of psychological health. Parents of insecure infants fail to respond appropriately to their infant's distress, either ignoring it (avoidants) or becoming over-involved, panicky and bogged down in it (ambivalents). It seems possible that because these parents have not been able to deal with or 'metabolise' (Bion 1978) their own distress they cannot cope with pain and anger in their infants and so the cycle is perpetuated. The infant is faced with parents who, due to their own internal conflicts or ego weakness, cannot hold (Winnicott 1971) the child's negative feelings of distress or fear of disintegration. The child is therefore forced to resort to primitive defense mechanisms in order to keep affects within manageable limits. Aggressive feelings may be repressed or split off, as in the avoidant child who does not react to his mother's absence but then shows overt aggression towards toys or siblings: or the insecure-ambivalent child who may show overcompliance based on 'identification with the aggressor'. Behavioural manifestations of these parent–child malattunements include such phenomena as gaze aversion, self-injury (such as head banging), freezing or fighting. They may also, as we shall consider further in Chapter 9, be related to such adult maladaptive behaviours as social avoidance, self-injurious behaviour such as wrist cutting, overdosing and substance abuse.

One can imagine continuities between infant physiological experience and psychological structures which evolve through childhood into adult life (see Figure 6.1). From maternal consistency comes a sense of history: the reliability of the mother's response to the infant becomes the nucleus of autobiographical competence. From maternal holding comes the ability to hold one's self in one's own mind: the capacity for self-reflection, to conceive of oneself and others as having minds. The insensitivity and unresponsiveness of the mother of the insecure infant is not necessarily mean or abusive, but rather a failure to see the world from the baby's point of view, to 'take the baby's perspective' (Bretherton 1991a). The mother who cannot act as an 'auxiliary ego' for her child exposes him or her to inchoate and potentially overwhelming feelings when that child is faced, as will be inevitable (and in the case of an insecure mother to an excessive degree), with loss and separation anxiety.

Fonagy (Fonagy et al. 1991) sees coherence as a central feature of parents classified as Secure-autonomous on the AAI:

The coherence of the parent's perception of his past derives

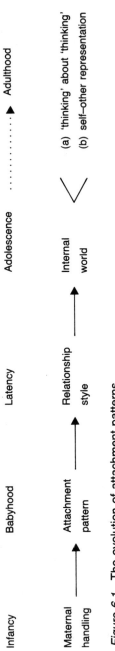

Infancy	Babyhood	Latency	Adolescence	Adulthood
Maternal handling	Attachment pattern	Relationship style	Internal world	(a) 'thinking' about 'thinking' (b) self–other representation

Figure 6.1 The evolution of attachment patterns

from his unhindered capacity to observe his own mental functioning. . . . This coherence is the precondition for the caregiver to be able to provide an 'expectable' or 'good enough' environment for the infant. . . . A child may be said to be *secure* in relation to a caregiver to the extent that his or her mental state will be appropriately reflected on and responded to accurately.

Without some sense of coherence and benignity towards oneself, self-reflection becomes distorted or even impossible, as the following case of borderline personality disorder illustrates.

'I hate myself'

Anna was a single parent in her mid-twenties. She became depressed and suicidal when her child was 6 months old. Her mother had been in hospital a lot when Anna was a small child because of TB, and at one point (when Anna was ten) had left the home for a while to live with another man. Despite this neglect Anna saw her mother as 'perfect', someone whose standards she could never match, and herself as hateful. She had two distinct 'selves': one competent, intelligent, well-organised, cheerful, compliant, pretty; the other dark, despairing, longing to die. In hospital at times she avoided eye-contact, secreted razor blades and frequently cut herself, was morose and monosyllabic, and would occasionally have outbursts of rage. At other times she was a model patient and collaborated enthusiastically with her therapeutic programme. She was discharged from hospital and started weekly analytic therapy, but once more became suicidal and was readmitted. She complained that she found psychotherapy very difficult because it meant that she had to *think about herself*. That entailed getting in touch with her self-hatred:

'Whenever I look into myself I come across the feeling that I want more than anything to die. I am forced to stay alive because of my daughter. Coming to talk to you reminds me of all the things I don't want to think about.'

Her wish to harm herself arose whenever she was faced with painful feelings of separation; for example, when she was on her own in the evenings. The origins of an almost unbridgeable split between her compliant and defiant selves, and the difficulty in reaching her real pain and hope could be seen in terms of insecure-avoidance, and the feeling that she had never felt securely held by her mother as a child, and was reminded of the anxiety and pain of this whenever she was on her own. She needed to be held by the hospital ward – sometimes actually – before she could begin to think about holding herself in mind in therapy, and to feel secure about her capacity to be a mother to her daughter. As suggested by Figure 6.2, her mental state could be represented by a series of parallel concentric circles of holder and held.

Borderline patients like this provide adult examples of the insecure infant with a deficient holding environment, whose mother has been unable to reflect on and so metabolise her infant's feelings of pain on separation, who survives as best she can, using splitting, isolation and self-harm as ways of coping, and who, when she becomes a parent, is in great danger of perpetuating the cycle of insecurity. Ward staff and therapists may then counter-transferentially re-enact a repetition of the unresponsiveness and breaks in care that the patient experienced as a child. Thus Anna became passionately involved with one male nurse – paralleling her long-repressed desire to have an exclusive relationship with her mother – and did very well until he was transferred to another ward, whereupon she took a huge overdose of drugs.

Bowlby depicted healthy internal working models as subject to constant revision and change in the light of experience. Anna exemplified how in pathological mental states there is often a sense of repetitiousness and stuckness in therapy. Bretherton (1987) has speculated about why it might be that internal working models in insecure attachment are particularly resistant to change. She sees mental structures as organised hierarchically from low-level 'event-scripts' (Shank 1982), such as 'When I hurt myself my mother comes to comfort me', through intermediate generalisations like 'My mother is usually there when I need her', to basic assumptions: 'My mother is a loving person. I am lovable and loved.' Insecure individuals not only may have negative core assumptions, but because communication between different levels of the hierarchy is distorted and restricted, may not be able to revise these models in the light of experience. Anna's basic assumption – 'I am hateful' – remained impervious to contrary

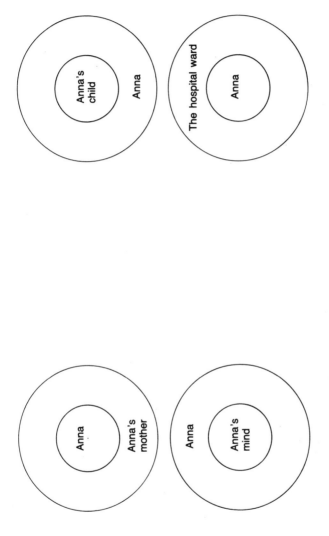

Figure 6.2 Anna and the holding environment

evidence provided by the love of her boyfriend and the care of her therapists:

> What seems to differentiate the Internal Working Models of secure and insecure individuals is in part their content, but also their internal organisation and relative consistency within and across hierarchical levels. . . . Reconstruction of working models cannot be achieved [simply] by 'lifting repression' or removing barriers which allow well-encoded, but hitherto inaccessible information to come into conscious awareness. Something much more akin to complete reorganisation and reinterpretation may be necessary.
>
> (Bretherton 1991a)

THERAPEUTIC IMPLICATIONS

From the perspective of Attachment Theory the process of therapy will require the provision of a secure base, comprising reliability, responsiveness and the capacity to process negative affect, especially in relation to separation and loss. Out of this should emerge an individual with a greater capacity for self-reflection, increased coherence of mental structures and enhanced autobiographical competence. The implications of this for psychotherapy with adults will be considered in the next two chapters. It is beyond the scope of this book to consider the full implications of Attachment Theory for psychotherapy with children, and the reader's attention is drawn to the considerable literature on the subject (Belsky and Nezworski 1988; Greenberg et al. 1988). Three important areas of work will briefly be mentioned.

Lieberman and Paul (1988) have shown that a clinical classification of neurotic disturbance in pre-school children fits well with the categories suggested by Attachment Theory research. They found three basic groups of problematic behaviours: excessive danger seeking, such as wandering off unaccompanied in children whose mothers appeared to discount the attachment needs of their offspring; excessive danger fleeing with punitive mothers who discouraged exploration and illustrated the paradox of clinging to a punitive attachment figure; and children who were 'hypercompetent', equivalent to Bowlby's category of 'compulsive caregiving' (Bowlby 1980) in which there was role-reversal between children and their mothers and inhibition of expression of painful affect.

Informed by attachment theory, several groups have attempted preventive psychotherapy with depressed mothers by working directly with the mother and her infant. Murray and Cooper (1992) describe one such case.

'Uppie . . . uppie'

Following a puerperal depression, Joan had felt unable to get emotionally close to her 18-month-old daughter Sophie, and was frightened that the pattern of distance and lack of trust which characterised her relationship with her own mother was repeating itself. Tested on the Strange Situation, Sophie showed a typical pattern of insecure-avoidance. In the course of brief exploratory-supportive therapy in which Sophie and Joan were seen together, their relationship changed dramatically. In place of distant watch-fulness, Sophie began to approach her mother, asking to be picked up and cuddled, saying 'Uppie, uppie', and was responded to with warmth and affection. At the same time negative feelings became less problematic for both of them. When Sophie cried or was difficult and rejecting, Joan could tolerate this without feeling guilty, and could also allow herself to become irritable with her daughter at times. In parallel with these changes Joan reported an improvement in her relationship with her own mother: here too she could be both affectionate and cross instead of, as before, maintaining a cool distance. At termination, Sophie's re-test on the Strange Situation now showed a pattern of secure attachment. In place of a rigid and restricted pattern of relating, each was able to respond to the other in a more fluid and spontaneous way. This movement from inflexibility towards 'give' and play illustrates Winnicott's (1965) well-known dictum that the essence of psychotherapy is learning to play.

In view of the increasing numbers of adult psychotherapy patients who report sexual and/or physical abuse in childhood, mention must also be made of studies which have approached familial abuse from the perspective of Attachment Theory. 'High risk' (that is, low socio-economic status) parents do not have dispro-portionate numbers of insecure children. The A/B/C ratios remain roughly the same: B, 65 per cent; A, 20 per cent; C, 15 per cent. The proportion of A/C families rises sharply among mothers with major depressive illness, and in families where there is proven sexual or physical abuse. With depressed mothers, 40 per cent of children were insecure-avoidant, and in abusive families 50 per cent are avoidant and 30 per cent disorganised, with only 10 per cent classified as secure (Belsky and Nezworsky 1988). The apparent compliance and conformity sometimes seen in adult patients who have been abused can be understood in the light of Crittenden's (1988) comment that

> Attachment Theory proposed that the maintenance of affectional bonds . . . is essential to the survival of the human species and a compelling individual need. . . . Those people who are most at risk for destroying their love relationships altogether devote the most intense effort towards maintaining the semblance of bonds; inept mothers and their children scrap and feud; mildly abusing mothers and their children are hostile and difficult; but many severely maltreating mothers do not dare challenge the durability of their relationships . . . it is as though they fear that a simple dispute could become an uncontrollable attack on the relationship.

CONCLUSION

Bowlby's grafting of the experimental methods of ethology to the insight of psychoanalysis has born rich fruit. The research we have surveyed in this chapter has begun to lay bare some of the relational elements which provide the foundations of psychological health: a sense of security, of efficacy, of being loved and having the capacity to love, of being a person in the world like others and yet with one's own unique biographical trajectory, of being able to withstand the failures, losses and disappointments that are the inevitable consequence of the 'thousand natural shocks that flesh is heir to'. We have learned about some of the ingredients that make up good parenting: responsiveness, attunement, holding. We turn now to the implications of these findings for psychotherapy, and to further exploration of the relationship – at times avoidant, at times ambivalent – between Attachment Theory and psychoanalysis, in the hope of finding a more secure and coherent synthesis.

Part III

Implications

Chapter 7

Bowlby and the inner world: Attachment Theory and psychoanalysis

[The] early formulations of psychoanalytic theory were strongly influenced by the physiology of the day . . . cast in terms of the individual organism, its energies and drives, with only marginal reference to relationships. Yet, by contrast, the principal feature of the innovative technique for treating patients that Freud introduced is to focus attention on the relationships patients make with their therapist. From the start, therefore, there was a yawning gulf between the phenomena with which the therapist was confronted, and the theory that had been advanced to account for them.

(Bowlby 1990)

Bowlby was primarily a theorist rather than a therapist. Although trained psychoanalytically, and active in the Psycho-Analytical Society from the late 1930s until the late 1950s, where he held high office, he saw himself mainly as a researcher and administrator. Case reports and clinical illustrations are to be found throughout his writings, but, with the exception of his earliest papers, these are almost all based on the work of colleagues or on published articles by other authors. Dreams are nowhere to be found in his work, and he is, for the most part, concerned with observable behaviour rather than the inner world. Nevertheless, Attachment Theory is a child of psychoanalysis and has much to contribute to the theory and practice of psychotherapy. Towards the end of his career Bowlby (1991) wrote, 'my theoretical work has always been directed primarily to my colleagues in the International [Psychoanalytical] Association'. The aim of this chapter is to consider in some detail the relationship between Attachment

Theory, psychoanalysis and contemporary psychoanalytic psychotherapy.

Bowlby's reservations about psychoanalysis come under four
main headings: its neglect of real experience and environmental
influence in favour of overemphasis on autonomous phantasy;
an atmosphere of dogmatism inimical to scientific enquiry; an
outmoded metapsychology; and a lack of experimental observation to underpin its unbridled theorising. All of these objections
may seem to the contemporary observer somewhat overstated,
and we must first place them in an historical context.

HISTORY: BRITISH PSYCHOANALYSIS 1935–60

The atmosphere in the British Psycho-Analytical Society when
Bowlby started training in the mid–1930s was one of ferment and
controversy. The heady excitement of a new science of mind that
went straight to the heart of twentieth century men's and women's
discontents seemed to have generated a hotbed of intrigue, back-
biting, gossip and jockeying for position. The climate resembled
less that of a scientific society than of a family in which a patriarch
was nearing the end of his life with the terms of his inheritance
still undecided.

Ernest Jones had invited Melanie Klein to practise in London
and had entrusted his own two children to her for child analysis
based on her new technique of play therapy. Until the advent of
Klein, the focus of analytical work was predominantly the Oedipus complex. She insisted on the importance and the analysability
of much earlier stages of development, and in particular on the
phantasies and anxieties of the infant in its first two years of life.
As we saw in Chapter 1, Freud tended to regard Klein's views
with some disfavour (Steiner 1985), especially as her ideas about
child analysis differed from those of his daughter Anna, who
saw splitting and other primitive defence mechanisms such as
projective identification proposed by Klein as belonging to a
much later stage of development.

At the time of the arrival of Freud and Anna in London in
the late 1930s the British Society comprised a group of highly
talented and intelligent people, including James Strachey,
Edward Glover, Sylvia Payne, Melanie Klein (Bowlby's supervisor) and Joan Riviere (Bowlby's analyst). A leadership struggle
broke out with an increasing schism between the Kleinian camp,

who were accused of dogmatism and attempts to win students exclusively onto their side, and the more orthodox Freudians, represented by Anna and her followers, together with a third group, who remained non-aligned. Eventually, in 1944, a compromise was reached with the 'gentleman's agreement' (in fact made between three women, Klein, Payne and Anna Freud) between the parties to form separate 'streams' of training and scientific discussion, while remaining united within one society.

Although Bowlby's organisational and intellectual talents were recognised early on – he was appointed Training Secretary of the Society in 1944 (Melanie Klein opposed this on the grounds that he was not a Training Analyst) – he was somewhat at variance with the mainstream of the analytic milieu. His strong commitment to the scientific method, his quintessential Britishness and reserve, his decision to work in child guidance clinics rather than in private practice, set him apart. These very qualities, as well as the fact that he was the son of a famous surgeon, may also have given him the credibility with the medical establishment that was needed for his successful popularisation of psychoanalytic ideas about the importance of infancy, and the mother–child relationship, as a determinant of later mental health.

From early in his psychoanalytic career Bowlby had had misgivings about the way in which analysts downplayed the importance of the environment in the origins of psychological disturbance. Although Freud has been accused of a deliberate and cowardly retreat from his original hypotheses about the adverse effects of childhood seduction (Masson 1985), there is no doubt that he continued to believe that childhood trauma was important, but as the pioneer of a new 'science' he emphasised the primacy of the inner world as the proper domain of psychoanalytic discourse, and this lead was certainly adhered to by his followers. Bowlby writes:

> During . . . 1936–39 I was slowly waking up to the fact that my ideas were developing in a direction very different from those that were accepted truths in the British Psycho-Analytical Society . . . under the influence of Ernest Jones and Melanie Klein it was held that an analyst should concern himself only with the patient's internal world and that to give attention to his real life experiences could only divert attention from what really matters. My experiences in the Child Guidance

Clinic . . . were leading me to an opposite conclusion . . . that one can only understand a person's internal world if one can see how [it] has come to be constructed from the real-life events to which he has been exposed.

(Bowlby 1991; Rayner 1992)

A marked copy of a paper by Bowlby's analyst Joan Riviere contains the following passage:

Psychoanalysis is Freud's discovery of what goes on in the imagination . . . it has no concern with anything else, it is not concerned with the real world . . . it is concerned simply and solely with the imaginings of the childish mind.

(Quoted in Rayner 1992)

In the margin Bowlby has pencilled 'Role of the environment = zero' (Rayner 1992). Bowlby was particularly distressed when the mother of his first training patient in child analysis, a hyperactive little boy of three, was admitted to mental hospital:

When I reported this to Melanie Klein [his supervisor], however, her only concern seemed to be that, since it was no longer possible for me to continue the boy's analysis, another patient must be found for me. The probability that the boy's behaviour was a reaction to the way his mother treated him seemed altogether to escape her.

(Bowlby 1991)

Bowlby consistently stressed the range of environmental traumata to which a developing child can be exposed: actual separations and disruptions in care; threats of separation or suicide by parents; being unwanted, or the 'wrong' sex; suppression of the true facts about parentage (for example, grandfather or uncle the true father, or sister the true mother); role reversal and the 'parentification' of children. His views have been thoroughly vindicated by the recent disclosure of the extent of physical and sexual abuse of children. The evidence that more subtle forms of environmental failure such as parental unresponsiveness and mis-attunement underlie childhood and probably adult psychopathology has been reviewed in the previous chapter. These findings make the polarisation between Bowlby's characterisation of the Kleinians as wholly uninterested in the environment and exclusively concerned with phantasy, and his own insistence on the primacy of environmental failure rather artificial. The Kleinian account is a phenomenological description of mental states found in adult patients, particularly those with borderline pathology, inferring from these what may have gone on in the minds of infants and small children. The Kleinian account contains no clear causal model to account for the phenomena she describes. Bowlby and the post-Bowlbians offer the outlines of an explanation of how such pathological states come about. They suggest that the *capacity* to phantasise and to symbolise, as opposed to resorting to defensive enactments of unmanageable feelings, is itself environmentally sensitive. Parents who can contain and attune to their children have children who can put their feelings into words and who are able to resolve conflict. Those who cannot contain and attune are more likely to have children who are at risk of dealing with their feelings by splitting and projective identification, and so being afflicted by a sense of emptiness and meaninglessness. It is worth noting that Klein, like Freud, assumes that there may be constitutional differences between infants, a point which Bowlby tends to overlook. Westen (1990) has suggested that some babies may have reduced inborn capacities for self-soothing, which would make them more vulnerable to parental deficiencies in containing and calming.

A second area of difficulty about psychoanalysis for Bowlby was its atmosphere of dogmatism and authoritarianism. Peterfreund (1983), who is approvingly cited by Bowlby in several places, decries what he calls the 'stereotyped', dogmatic, 'alogarithmic' approach of traditional psychoanalytic formulation and interpretation. He compares this with the 'heuristic' approach which he and Bowlby advocate, in which patient and therapist find things out for themselves rather than imitating Talmudic scholars burrowing in the obscure texts of the psychoanalytic testament. There is no doubt that at its worst psychoanalysis can degenerate into a mouthing of clichéd formulas by an omniscient analyst who, faced with the pain and complexity of suffering, offers some certainty, however ill-founded, to a confused patient who has no choice but to grasp at straws. The relentless interpretation of the transference may hypnotically open the patient up to layers of regression and dependency which make such interpretations self-fulfilling prophecies. There has been a move towards a much more tentative approach to interpretation in contemporary psychoanalysis (Casement 1985), in which Keats's 'negative capability' – the capacity to allow oneself to be 'in uncertainties, mysteries, doubts, without any irritable reaching after fact and reason' – is valued, and indeed is seen as the hallmark of the 'depressive position' with its emphasis on compromise and reconciliation rather than splitting and false certainties.

Bowlby writes that

> I was dissatisfied with much of the [psychoanalytic] theory . . . being a somewhat arrogant young man . . . I was in no mood to accept dogmatic teaching. My analyst was not altogether happy with my critical attitude and complained on one occasion that I would take nothing on trust and was trying to think everything out from scratch, which I was certainly committed to doing.
>
> (Bowlby 1991)

Bowlby's re-thinking of psychoanalytic metapsychology and terminology has been discussed in the preceding three chapters. Attachment Theory is perhaps best seen as a variant of Object-Relations Theory, using updated terminology and informed by neo-Darwinism. Attachment comprises a distinct motivational system – which includes drive, affect, cognition and behaviour – that parallels and complements sexuality. The main differences between classical Freudian theory, the Object-Relations Theory of Klein, Fairbairn and Winnicott, and Attachment Theory are summarised in Table 7.1. For Bowlby the important issue is not, as the orthodox Freudians thought, sex, but security. Attachment is primary, not a derivative of orality. The organism is not an isolated drive-driven creature in search of an object on whom to discharge his accumulated tension, but a person relating to other persons. Homeostatic and other cybernetic control systems govern his behaviour, just as they do that of other mammals. His relationship to the world is determined not just by unconscious phantasy but also by internal working models which include affective, cognitive and behavioural elements. Aggression is a response to frustration and loss, not an intrinsic property of an individual dominated by the death instinct.

Bowlby's fourth cavil at psychoanalysis was its neglect of direct observation of normal and abnormal children. He felt that reconstructions based on childhood recollections of disturbed patients, while valuable in themselves, did not qualify as a scientific account of what really goes on in real children. He therefore set

Table 7.1 Classical, Object-Relations and Attachment Theories compared

	Classical Freudian theory	Object-Relations Theory	Attachment Theory
Main authors	S. Freud A. Freud	Melanie Klein Donald Winnicott Ronald Fairbairn Wilfred Bion Michael Balint Margaret Mahler	John Bowlby Daniel Stern
1 Models of normal development			
(a) Attachment	Drive-based Aim of drive is 'discharge' Attachment is a 'secondary drive'	Attachment to breast which gratifies But NB Balint's 'clinging instinct'	Intra-personal Primary attachment – continues throughout life
(b) Stages	(i) Pre-Oedipal → Oedipal (phallic) (ii) oral → anal → genital	(i) 1 person → 2 person → 3 person (Balint) (ii) Infantile autism → symbiosis → separation – individuation → rapprochement (Mahler) (iii) Paranoid-schizoid position → depressive position (Klein)	Pattern-recognition → maternal differentiation → set-goal attachment → relationship

Table 7.1 (cont.)

(c) Role of parents in normal development	?inherently traumatic: love of mother versus castration anxiety	inherently traumatic: split between gratifying and frustrating breast, but overcome by (i) holding (Winnicott) (ii) transmuting, 'metabolising' (Bion)	Attunement ⎫ Responsiveness ⎬ overcome Secure base ⎭ frustration of separation
2 *Model of Mind*	conscious/unconscious → id, ego, superego	(i) good object/bad object → whole object (guilt, reparation) (Klein) (ii) libidinal object/anti-libidinal object, libidinal self/anti-libidinal self (Fairbairn)	Internal working models Hierarchical coherence Representation of self and other
3 *Roots of psychopathology*			
(a) Early	Parental ⎫ trauma 'seduction' ⎬ of over- Early loss ⎭ excitement Regression/fixation	Failure of holding transmuting	Lack of responsiveness attunement secure base Failure to cope with loss, separation (based on mother's own experience as a child)

Table 7.1 (cont.)

(b) Later	The Oedipal situation: sibling rivalry, over-involvement with mother, lack of identification with father; Regression/fixation	Failure to progress from paranoid → depressive position; Lack of reparation	Environmental disruption: loss, inconsistency, abuse
(c) Defences	Primitive: Splitting, repression; Intermediate: Isolation, undoing; Mature: Sublimation, humour	Kleinians emphasise splitting and projective identification	'Defensive exclusion' Avoidant, Ambivalent } strategies
(d) Theory of anxiety and aggression	Surplus libido (e.g. Oedipal) → Signal anxiety (loss)	Projection; Aggression; Fear of damage to object	Separation anxiety; Aggression is response to threatened separation
(e) Theory of depression	Identification with lost object. Guilt	Loss; Guilt; Identification with lost object	Loss; Lack of experience of 'metabolising' separation – i.e. depression is abnormal grief
(f) Theory of borderline states	Regression to infantile narcissism	Splitting; Projective identification; Narcissistic defenses	Avoidant anxious attachment; Failure to attune by mother → no self-reflection, lacks coherence

out to study systematically the effects of separating infants and children from their parents, and it was on the basis of those findings that Attachment Theory was born.

BOWLBY AND THE POST-FREUDIANS: THE POST-WAR PERIOD

To continue with our historical account, Bowlby was of course not alone in his dissatisfaction with the state of psychoanalysis in the 1940s and early fifties. During the post-war period several divergent responses can be found within psychoanalysis and psychotherapy in response to the difficulties – dogmatism, obsolete metapsychology and anti-empiricism – with which Bowlby was struggling. The first was the development of Object-Relations Theory, epitomised by the work of Winnicott, Fairbairn and Balint, all of whom were influenced by the Kleinian emphasis on the early infant–mother relationship, but, taking the decisive step of abandoning drive theory altogether, posited *relationships* as primary. Mahler's (1975) direct observations of mothers and infants from a psychoanalytic perspective combined object relations with a degree of empiricism.

A quite different tack was to reject the pseudo-scientific determinism of classical Freudianism altogether, seeing psychoanalysis more as a hermeneutic discipline concerned with meanings rather than mechanisms and emphasising the importance of the creative imagination and spontaneity as the wellspring of the psychoanalytic process (Rycroft 1985). Meanwhile, neo-Kleinian developments concentrated on delving deeper and deeper into the mysteries of the infant–mother relationship in the early stages of life and relating these to the findings of psychoanalysis with psychotic patients (Bion 1978). Finally, there were moves away from the psychoanalytic paradigm altogether, adopting either a family systems approach derived from cybernetics and anthropology (Bateson 1973), or a 'cognitive' approach, based on Piaget and Kelly, in which the logical operations of the mind and the way in which they are organised hierarchically form the basis of psychotherapeutic theory and practice (Beck *et al.* 1979).

Bowlby and Winnicott

Bowlby as a researcher responded to the problems of the psycho-analytic paradigm by moving in the direction of observable behaviour. Attachment, whether secure or insecure, avoidant or ambivalent, can be observed, rated, measured, correlated. By basing his ideas on ethology Bowlby sidestepped the dehumanisation and absurdities of stimulus–response behaviourism, while remaining within the framework of conventional science. Winnicott, an outstanding clinician but an elusive theorist, was wrestling with the same problems but from the perspective of the inner world, developing in his idiosyncratic but highly original way a language of experience directly applicable to the therapeutic situation.

Winnicott and Bowlby had much in common. Both were very 'English' in their background and outlook, in contrast to the European/Jewish/Celtic atmosphere of the Psycho-Analytical Society. Both had had a Cambridge scientific education and were deeply influenced by Darwin. They shared an analyst, Joan Riviere, who, despite her later Kleinian orthodoxy, was firmly interpersonal in her philosophy. With an echo of John Donne, she wrote:

> There is no such thing as a single human being, pure and simple, unmixed with other human beings. Each personality is a world in himself, a company of many. That self . . . is a composite structure . . . formed out of countless never-ending influences and exchanges between ourselves and others. These other persons are in fact therefore part of ourselves . . . we are members of one another.
>
> (Riviere 1927; reprinted 1955)

Winnicott (1965) was therefore paraphrasing Riviere in his famous dictum, 'there is no such thing as an infant . . . wherever one finds an infant one finds maternal care and without maternal care there would be no infant'. Like Bowlby, Winnicott was primarily concerned with the welfare of children, and wrote to an American enquirer about his wartime experiences:

> I became involved with the failure of the evacuation scheme and could therefore no longer avoid the subject of the anti-social tendency. Eventually I became interested in the etiology of delinquency and therefore joined up quite naturally with

John Bowlby who was at that time starting up his work based on the relationship that he observed between delinquency and periods of separation at significant times in the child's early years.

(Rodman 1987)

When Winnicott later was offered the presidency of the Psycho-Analytical Society he accepted, on condition that he have a deputy who would take care of the detailed administrative work. The ever-efficient Bowlby was an obvious choice. They make sparse but polite references to each other's work in their writings. There are many similarities between their theoretical viewpoints, despite the radically different language which each uses. Rycroft's (1985) remark that 'I've always had a phantasy that Bowlby and I were burrowing the same tunnel, but that we started at opposite ends', would be equally true of Bowlby and Winnicott.

Winnicott and Bowlby's responses to the Kleinian domination of the Psycho-Analytical Society can be seen in terms of avoidant and ambivalent attachment. Bowlby, in an avoidant way, distanced himself, expressing neither warmth nor anger, but having little to do with the Society after the 1960s. Winnicott clung ambivalently to his alma mater, and, in his theory of hate, emphasised how identity can be forged through opposition and reaction.

Bowlby and Winnicott's overall view of the infant–mother relationship, and what may go wrong with it, is very similar. Winnicott postulates a 'holding environment' provided by the mother, in which, on the basis of her 'primary maternal preoccupation', she can empathise with the needs and desires of the growing child. The main job of the holding environment is, like attachment, protection, although, in contrast to Bowlby, Winnicott describes this in existential rather than ethological terms: 'The holding environment . . . has as its main function the reduction to a minimum the impingement to which the infant must react with resultant annihilation of personal being' (Winnicott 1965). Winnicott sees 'handling' and 'general management', equivalent to the Bowlbian concept of maternal responsiveness, as the framework within which need can be met. The mother's actual physical holding and handling are primary:

The main thing is the physical holding and this is the basis of all the more complex aspects of holding and of environmental provision in general. . . . The basis for instinctual satisfaction and for object relationships is the handling and general management and care of the infant, which is only too easily taken for granted when all goes well.

(Winnicott 1965)

'Good-enough' holding leads to integration of the infant personality, to a 'continuity of going-on-being', which prefigures Stern's (1985) idea of a 'line of continuity' that is the germ of the sense of coherent self. Where there is such continuity the growing child can cope with temporary separations without resorting to maladaptive defences. Like Bowlby, Winnicott sees the seeds of pathology in failures of the holding environment. Separations may provide the nucleus of later delinquency:

Separation of a one or two year old from the mother produces a state which may appear later as an anti-social tendency. When the child tries to reach back over the gap [i.e., created by the separation] this is called stealing.

(Winnicott 1965)

Although Bowlby and Winnicott are saying something very similar about juvenile theft there is a subtle difference in their language and focus. For Bowlby theft is a sociological phenomenon, which can be well accounted for by the disrupted lives and maternal separations of the thieves' early childhood. Winnicott is reaching towards an understanding of the symbolism of the act of theft itself. He is suggesting that the stolen object stands in for the missing mother which the youth is using to bridge the emotional gap left by her absence. Bowlby is reaching for explanation, Winnicott for meaning. Both, incidentally, tend to ignore other possible aspects of the problem: Bowlby looks exclusively at the childhood experiences of his thieves, and ignores contemporary influences such as housing and unemployment, while Winnicott leaves little room for the many other possible symbolic meanings that an act of theft might represent.

Winnicott goes on to describe how the good mother empathically understands what stage the child's object constancy has reached and so knows how to handle separations: 'She knows she must not leave her child for more minutes, hours, days than the child is able to keep the idea of her alive and friendly' (Winnicott 1965). If this is unavoidable she will have to resort to therapeutic 'spoiling': 'If she knows she must be away too long she will have to change from a mother into a therapist in order to turn the child back into a state in which he takes the mother for granted again' (Winnicott 1965).

Like Winnicott, Bowlby is insistent in his opposition to the notion that children can be 'spoilt' by too much love, and reminds therapists who are working with adults who weep and cling: 'It is perhaps too often forgotten by clinicians that many children when they become distressed and weepy and are looking for comfort are shooed off as intolerable little cry-babies' (Bowlby 1988a).

Winnicott visualises 'two mothers' in the early months of life. The first protects the child from 'impingement' and acts as an 'auxiliary ego' which enables him gradually to build up his own autonomous ego. He calls this the 'environment mother' who offers 'affection and sensuous coexistence'. Within the ambiance created by the environment mother the child then relates to the 'object mother' who can be sucked and bitten, loved and hated. Her response will have far-reaching consequences: overintrusiveness can in a seductive way be as traumatic as neglect, and both can lead to defensive moves such as 'self-holding', disintegration and the development of a false self.

For Bowlby there are also two mothers. The first is equivalent to Winnicott's 'environment mother', the provider of the secure base. The second mother is the companion with whom the child, once a secure base has been established, engages in exploratory play. This 'third mother' is different from Winnicott's second 'object mother' with whom the child engages in orgiastic play. Bowlby seems less interested in orgasmic activities, although the sexual foreplay of trusting adults can be seen as a form of mutual exploration (analogous to the sensuous intimacy of mother and child), which enables a greater build-up of intense pleasure than orgasm not preceded by exploration.

In Winnicott's sophisticated theory of the origins of play he sees the emphatic responsiveness of the mother helping to create a necessary illusion of omnipotence in the infant so that, as a wish begins to form in the child's mind so she begins to answer it – just as the baby begins to feel hungry, the breast appears, as though by magic. In this transitional zone of overlapping phantasy are to be found the origins of playfulness, creativity and, ultimately, culture. Bowlby's 'companion mother' can be seen in similar, if less mystical terms. The post-Bowlbians emphasise the collaborative nature of exploration, the 'zone of proximal development' (Vygotsky 1962), where parent and child interact and in which learning takes place. Stern (1985) sees the task of the mother as maintaining an internal 'line of continuity' for the child, so that she will unobtrusively stimulate the child when his imagination begins to flag, back off when he is playing happily, and dampen his excitement when it threatens to get out of hand. The differing languages of Winnicott and Bowlby reflect the differing foci of their thought. For the Bowlbian, child play and exploration take place 'out there' in the world, while Winnicott's child is concerned with inner exploration, with the world of the imagination 'in here'. The real child is of course engaged in both at the same time. The toddler building and breaking and building again his tower of bricks is simultaneously acquiring Piagetian knowledge of physics – the properties of materials, the mathematics of cubes, the nature of gravity – and in a Freudian sense exploring potency and castration, and the interplay of destruction and reparation of the inner world.

Klein's depressive position becomes in Winnicottian terminology the 'stage of concern'. Here the 'environment mother' and the 'object mother' come together as one person. The environment is necessarily defective: the mother cannot always be perfectly responsive: there will be gaps and breaks and discontinuities of care. The child responds with aggression and rage directed at the 'object mother': she survives the attacks and continues to love her child, and the balance is restored. He now realises that the mother who lets him down is also the one he loves. Clouds of guilt and anxiety appear on his horizon, but also the seeds of gratitude and reparation. For Bowlby, too, the good mother can withstand her child's aggressive onslaughts, and these early experiences lead to a mental set in later life (based on internal working models) that feelings can be expressed and 'processed', conflicts successfully resolved. The anxiously attached child is caught up in a vicious circle (see Figure 7.1) in which he lacks a secure base; feels angry and wants to attack the attachment figure for premature separation; doesn't dare to do so for fear of retaliation or pushing the attachment figure even further away; and so suppresses his feelings of anxiety and rage thereby increasing the sense of insecurity; leading ultimately to an expectation of lack of care, and danger in emotional expression with potentially disastrous implications for self-esteem and intimate

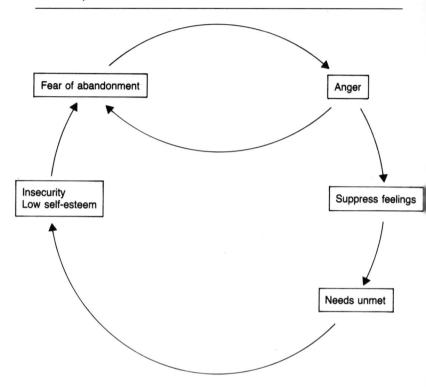

Figure 7.1 The anxiously attached infant

relationships. There is, in this 'Winnicott-type theory' (Bowlby 1988b)

> a massive block against expressing or even feeling a natural desire for a close trusting relationship, for care, comfort and love – which I regard as the subjective manifestations of a major system of instinctive behaviour.

Like Bowlby, Winnicott also repudiates the linear 'monorail' model of development in which the child progresses from oral to anal to genital phases of development:

> Most of the processes that start up in early infancy are never fully established and continue to be strengthened by the growth that continues in later childhood and indeed in adult life, even in old age.

(Winnicott 1965)

Bowlby and Kohut

Bowlby's conviction that attachment needs continue throughout life and are not outgrown has important implications for psychotherapy. It means that the therapist inevitably becomes an important attachment figure for the patient, and that this is not necessarily best seen as a 'regression' to infantile dependence (the developmental 'train' going into reverse), but rather the activation of attachment needs that have been previously suppressed. Heinz Kohut (1977) has based his 'self psychology' on a similar perspective. He describes 'selfobject needs' that continue from infancy throughout life and comprise an individual's need for empathic responsiveness from parents, friends, lovers, spouses (and therapists). This responsiveness brings a sense of aliveness and meaning, security and self-esteem to a person's existence. Its lack leads to narcissistic disturbances of personality characterised by the desperate search for selfobjects – for example, idealisation of the therapist or the development of an erotic transference. When, as they inevitably will, these prove inadequate (as did the original environment), the person responds with 'narcissistic rage' and disappointment, which, in the absence of an adequate 'selfobject' cannot be dealt with in a productive way.

BOWLBY AND CONTEMPORARY PSYCHOTHERAPEUTIC THEORY

There is an inherent dualism in the Freudian project. Freud saw psychoanalysis as a science, and wanted his accounts of psychopathology to have the same status and explanatory power as those of physical medicine. At the same time, as Rycroft (1985) points out, he called his *magnum opus The Interpretation*, not *The Cause of Dreams*, and

> It can indeed be argued that much of Freud's work was really semantic and that he made a revolutionary discovery in semantics, namely that neurotic symptoms are meaningful, disguised communications, but that, owing to his scientific training and allegiance, he formulated his findings in the conceptual framework of the physical sciences.
>
> (Rycroft 1985)

The scientific-explanatory and the semantic-hermeneutic poles of Freud's thought are epitomised in contemporary psychotherapy on the one hand by Kleinian and Lacanian psychoanalysis and on the other by cognitive therapy. In this section I shall first give a brief account of these apparently irreconcilable approaches and then suggest that Attachment Theory provides a possible bridge between them.

Rustin (1991) has described the history of psychoanalysis as moving through the three Kantian categories of truth: scientific, ethical and aesthetic. Freud saw himself as a natural scientist, looking for general truths about normal and abnormal psychology; Melanie Klein's theories were essentially ethical – about destructiveness and splitting and the reconciliation of good and bad in the depressive position; Rustin sees current psychoanalysis as predominantly aesthetic in its orientation. Kant distinguishes aesthetic from scientific or moral judgement in having to do with 'disinterested contemplation of objects of experience, related neither to the goal of interpersonal knowledge of causes, nor to issues of conformity with the moral law' (Rustin 1991). The discovery of meanings is central to this aesthetic sensibility, the prototype of which is to be found within the mother–infant relationship. The mother 'contains' or 'binds' (Bion 1978) infantile sense experiences and mental images; she points, and shapes and names, and so gives meaning to them. Maternal attunement (Stern), secure base provision (Bowlby) and holding environment (Winnicott) are all reaching towards the same idea. The function of the parent, of the therapist and of cultural objects can all be understood in this framework of containment and structuring of inchoate experience.

To illustrate his point Rustin contrasts classical and contemporary psychoanalytic accounts of *Hamlet*. Ernest Jones (1949) saw the play as a quintessentially Oedipal drama in which Hamlet is wracked by his ambivalence towards the father-figures (the Ghost, the King, Polonius), and his simultaneous yearning and rage towards his mother. Williams (Meltzer and Williams 1988) sees the problem of the play centring on Hamlet's search for a vehicle with which to express his grief, anger and ambition. The corrupt world of the court, of institutional power cannot contain this intimacy of the imagination. The play-within-a-play 'catches the conscience of the king', but action – as opposed to thought – spills over into murder and intrigue. Throughout the play

Hamlet, like a patient in therapy, has been struggling to write his story, to find, in Williams' words, an 'aesthetic correlative to image the idea of a new prince' (that is, one not caught up in power and corruption). Dying, he enjoins his faithful Horatio to

> Absent thee from felicity awhile,
> And in this harsh world draw thy breath in pain
> To tell my story.

In this neo-Kleinian perspective, *narrative* becomes a key feature of the psychotherapeutic process. The therapist provides a setting in which thought rather than action can happen, and in which the patient can begin to tell himself his own story, undistorted by repression, splitting and affective distancing. In the Lacanian (Bowie 1991) account too, narrative is central, although a 'story', spoken in words, is seen as the imposition of the *logos*, of phallocentric culture on the primal, pre-verbal unity of mother and child. For the Kleinians there is no such radical rupture with the onset of language: integration is achieved at the advent of the depressive position, rather than thwarted by the insertion of the paternal order.

The aesthetic perspective provides perhaps a much-needed cultural location for psychoanalysis, but what of its claim to be a science, and how do we evaluate one narrative account against another? Are all 'stories' equally valid, or are some more 'true' than others? And what of Bowlby's own comment:

> I believe that our discipline can be put on to a scientific basis. A lot of people think you can't or don't know how to. There are people who think psychoanalysis is really a hermeneutic discipline. I think that's all rubbish quite frankly.
>
> (Bowlby *et al.* 1986)

Bowlby wanted to make psychoanalysis more scientific, claiming to be truer to Freud's intentions and more in touch with his later ideas than were Klein and her followers. He did so at a time when psychoanalysis, partly in spite of itself, was gradually moving away from science and in the direction of hermeneutics and meanings. Attachment theory, like one of Darwin's Galapagos islands, became isolated from the mainland of psychoanalysis, so developing its own ideas and language.

However, to continue the analogy, continental drift has occurred: previously separate areas are now beginning to overlap.

It is here that the recent work of Main (1991), Fonagy (1991) and Bretherton (1991a and b) are so intriguing. As we showed in the previous chapter, the Adult Attachment Interview is a standardised instrument by which an individual's autobiographical narrative *account* of their childhood and attachment history can be linked with their behaviour as parents, and with the security of their children. Clear, coherent stories correlate with securely attached children. Narrative incompetence – inability to tell any sort of story, or embroilment in a muddled and incoherent one – is linked with insecure attachment. The narrative dimension in psychotherapy – helping patients to gain a clearer picture of their life and their early attachments – can be supported on scientific as well as aesthetic grounds. The polarisation between hermeneutics and science implicit in Bowlby's rather intemperate dismissal now looks a lot less clear-cut. Psychoanalysis provides a system of meanings for helping to decode patients' symptoms, but, if we step back from the specific meanings, we find good scientific evidence that narrative capacity, the ability to make meanings out of the inchoate flow of an 'unstoried' life – especially out of loss and disappointment – is associated with healthy psychological functioning.

If hermeneutics is 'rubbish' – a view which, had he lived long enough to consider the implications of Main and Fonagy's work, Bowlby might well have revised – what then of the opposing scientific tendency within psychotherapy? Cognitive therapy, devised by Beck *et al.* (1979), works primarily with cognitions, as opposed to the emotions that are the raw material of psychoanalysis. It is based on the idea that cognitions determine feelings (rather than vice versa), and that if the faulty cognitions which underlie neurotic states can be unearthed and corrected, then psychological health will ensue. There are strong echoes of Bowlbian metapsychology in this model. Mental structures are visualised in a hierarchy of expectations and assumptions, from specific assumptions such as 'When I am distressed I will receive help', to core beliefs such as 'I am lovable and can love'. The internal working models of Attachment Theory are similarly visualised as a set of guiding affective and cognitive models of the world that are more or less subject to revision and updating. Cognitive therapy assumes that in neurosis the normal process of testing and modifying assumptions about the world breaks down, so that, for example, if the core belief in depression is 'I am unworthy of love and deserve rejection', when a fortuitous rebuff occurs this serves to reinforce the faulty belief and to deepen the depression.

In Ryle's (1990) modification of cognitive therapy, cognitive analytic therapy (CAT), he considers that the underlying core beliefs have their origins in disturbed attachment patterns in infancy and early childhood, later perpetuated in adult relationships by a vicious circle of self-fulfilling negative assumptions about the self and the world. Ryles's model of therapy requires a much more active collaborative attitude on the part of the therapist than in traditional analytic therapy. The therapist sets tasks for the patient, such as encouraging them to keep a 'mood diary' and to rate their progress on visual scales, as well as offering the patient a written formulation of the problem and its dynamics and a farewell letter when therapy (which is brief – typically sixteen sessions) comes to an end.

CAT is 'Bowlbian' in three important ways. First in its theoretical eclecticism: Ryle happily marries cognitive science with psychoanalysis in an information-processing model that is very similar to Bowlby's attempt to re-write psychoanalytic defense mechanisms in terms of control theory. Second, Ryle's active therapist is engaging in 'companionable interaction' with the patient just like the secure base mother who actively plays with her child, and meeting the need for affiliation postulated by Heard and Lake (1986). Third, like cognitive therapy, CAT focuses on the need for self-reflection by the patient. This links with Fonagy's account of narrative capacity discussed above. In his model the good mother accurately reflects the moods and wishes of her infant. This mirroring is then internalised as self-reflexive capacity, as the child gradually comes to know about his own internal states. This in turn manifests itself, as development proceeds, in the capacity to verbalise these states, and to 'tell a story' about oneself. The main themes of this autobiographical skill are the history of one's attachments, separations and reunions. Being a brief therapy, CAT highlights and tries to accelerate the emergence of autobiographical competence in a deliberate way rather than assuming that it will be an automatic part of the therapeutic process. Post-Bowlbian research provides a rationale for this in that there is a demonstrable link between the capacity to 'tell one's story' and the development of secure attachment which is an overall goal of psychotherapy.

In summary, Attachment Theory has shown that the emphasis

on narrative and hermeneutics in contemporary psychotherapy can be justified on good developmental grounds. Good mothers help their infants towards personal meanings, which in turn are a basis and mark of secure attachment. Cognitive therapy, although apparently opposed to the narrative approach in its concern with here-and-now cognitions, is also, in its way, a story about the internal world. Its 'basic assumptions' are not far removed from Bowlby's internal working models or the 'representational world' of psychoanalysis.

Freud (1911) always insisted that there were *two* principles of mental functioning, the primary and secondary processes – the visual and the verbal, the imaginative and the rational – and that healthy functioning required a balance between the two. In Humphrey's (1992) re-working of this model there are two channels of information available to the organism, sensation and perception, which tell it about its own internal states and the state of the world respectively. Out of the post-war schisms of psychoanalysis there emerged an unhealthy polarisation between the concern of psychoanalysis with the primary processes and the focus of attachment and cognitive theory on secondary processes. The paradigm of narrative, a blending of sensation and perception, in which the inner world can be described objectively, while the subjective colouring of the outer world is also held up for inspection, is exciting increasing interest in psychotherapy (see Spence 1982; Shafer 1976). The question arises whether a secondary-process type verbal *encouragement* towards self-observation and narrative capacity is likely in itself to be effective, or whether primary-process ingredients, especially the arousal of affect through transference, are also needed. To consider this and other more practical questions we must now turn to a consideration of the specific implications of the Bowlbian perspective for the practice of psychotherapy.

Chapter 8

Attachment Theory and the practice of psychotherapy

The therapeutic alliance appears as a secure base, an internal object as a working, or representational, model of an attachment figure, reconstruction as exploring memories of the past, resistance as deep reluctance to disobey the past orders of parents not to tell or not to remember. . . . Whilst some traditional therapists might be described as adopting the stance 'I know; I'll tell you', the stance I advocate is one of 'You know, you tell me' . . . the human psyche, like human bones, is strongly inclined towards self-healing. The psychotherapist's job, like that of the orthopaedic surgeon's, is to provide the conditions in which self-healing can best take place.

(Bowlby 1988a)

We come now to the core of the book: an attempt to describe Attachment Theory's distinctive contribution to the theory and practice of psychotherapy. Two related concepts have emerged. The first, starting from Object-Relations Theory, but going beyond it, is the idea of the *core state with respect to attachment.* Bowlby sees a person's attachment status as a fundamental determinant of their relationships, and this is reflected in the way they feel about themselves and others. Neurotic patterns can be seen as originating here because, where core attachments are problematic, they will have a powerful influence on the way someone sees the world and their behaviour. Where there is a secure core state, a person feels good about themselves and their capacity to be effective and pursue their projects. Where the core state is insecure, defensive strategies come into play.

Bowlby's concept of defence is different from that of classical psychoanalysis (Hamilton 1985) in that it is not primarily intrapsychic – a way of reducing the internal disruption created by unmanageable feelings – but interpersonal. Secure attachment provides a positive 'primary' defence; 'secondary', pathological defences are methods of retaining proximity to rejecting or unreliable attachment figures. The two main patterns can be formulated along the lines of 'I need to be near to my attachment figures in order to feel safe, but they may reject my advances, so I will suppress my needs both from myself and them, and remain on the emotional periphery of relationships' (avoidant strategy), or 'I need to be near to my attachment figures but they may fail to respond to me or intrude on me in a way I can't control, so I will cling to them and insist on their responding to and caring for me' (ambivalent strategy). Both can be formulated in terms of dilemmas (Ryle 1990) arising out of the need to get close and the imagined dangers of so doing: rejection, abandonment or intrusion. Both lead to inhibition of vital parts of personality functioning. In avoidance, aggression tends to be displaced or split off; in ambivalence, exploration is held back.

The second central concept to have emerged from Attachment Theory is that of *narrative*. A person's core state is a condensate of the history of their primary relationships. If this history is available to them in the form of a personal narrative, then they are likely to feel secure. We have seen in Chapter 6 the evidence that 'autobiographical competence' (Holmes 1992) both results from and contributes to secure attachment. The word 'narrative' derives from *gnathos* or knowing. Psychotherapy is based on the Delphic injunction (Pedder 1982): know thyself. Making the unconscious conscious can be re-formulated as knowing and owning one's story. Attachment Theory has shown that self-knowledge in the form of narrative is associated with a core state characterised by secure attachment. Narrative turns experience into a story which is temporal, is coherent and has meaning. It objectifies experience so that the sufferer becomes detached from it, by turning raw feeling into symbols. It creates out of fragmentary experience an unbroken line or thread linking the present with the past and future. Narrative gives a person a sense of ownership of their past and their life.

Contemporary psychotherapy is characterised by a myriad of different schools and models of the therapeutic process. Attachment Theory should not be seen as yet one more form of psychotherapy, but rather as defining features that are relevant to therapy generally – individual, group, family – akin to Frank's (1986) common factors or 'metamodel' approach to the diversity of therapies. He proposes certain key elements which are shared by all therapies. These include a *relationship* with the therapist, which provides hope or 'remoralisation' – in Bowlbian terms a secure base from which to start to explore the problem; a coherent *explanation* for the patient's difficulties – a shared narrative; and a *method* for overcoming them. Holmes and Lindley (1989) saw the overall goal of psychotherapy as 'emotional autonomy' – the capacity to form relationships in which one feels both close and free, corresponding with Attachment Theory's picture of a secure base facilitating exploration.

This chapter will be devoted to a discussion of five key themes which determine an individual's core state of attachment, and how psychotherapy may help, via the development of a therapeutic narrative, to create secure rather than neurotic (that is, insecure) attachments. These are: the need for a secure therapeutic base; the role of real trauma (as opposed to phantasy) in the origins of neurosis; affective processing, especially of loss and separation; the place of cognitions in therapy; and the part played by 'companionable interaction' between therapist and patient. The main focus will be on individual therapy, but the principles are equally applicable to group therapies, and the chapter ends with a consideration of Attachment Theory in relation to family therapy, of which Bowlby was one of the founding fathers.

1 ATTACHMENT AND THE SECURE BASE IN PSYCHOTHERAPY

Attachment Theory predicts that when someone is faced with illness, distress, or threat they seek out an attachment figure from whom they may obtain relief. Once a secure base is established attachment behaviour is assuaged, and they can begin to explore – in this case, the exploration will be of the situation which has caused the distress and the feelings it has aroused. This would be a simple account of many episodes of brief counselling, and of psychotherapy generally were it not for the question of the nature of the secure base. The establishment of a base depends on the interaction between help-seeker and help-giver. The very fact that someone seeks psychotherapeutic help implies that they will have had difficulty in establishing such a base in the past.

The patient brings with him into therapy all the failures and suspicions and losses he has experienced through his life. The defensive forms of insecure attachment – avoidance, ambivalence, disorganisation – will be brought into play in relation to the therapist. There will be a struggle between these habitual patterns and the skill of the therapist in providing a secure base – the capacity to be responsive and attuned to the patient's feelings, to receive projections and to transmute them in such a way that the patient can face their hitherto unmanageable feelings. To the extent that this happens, the patient will gradually relinquish their attachment to the therapist while, simultaneously, an internal secure base is built up inside. As a result, as therapy draws to a close, the patient is better able to form less anxious attachment relationships in the external world and feels more secure in himself. As concrete attachment to the therapist lessens, so the qualities of self-responsiveness and self-attunement are more firmly established in the inner world.

Freud wrote in 1913: 'The first aim of the treatment consists in attaching . . . [the patient] to the treatment and to the person of the physician.' Psychoanalysts have worried about two aspects of this attachment. First, can healthy, conscious, therapeutic attachment be distinguished from unconscious phantasy-based transferential feelings aroused in the patient by being in treatment? Second, is it the secure base of this relationship and the 'new beginning' (Balint 1968) which provide the main vehicle of cure, or are interpretations and the insight they produce the crucial factors?

The therapeutic alliance and the 'real' relationship

Zetzel (1956) was the first to use the phrase the 'therapeutic alliance' to describe the non-neurotic, reality-based aspect of the therapist–patient relationship (Mackie 1981), a term which is usually used interchangeably with that of the 'working alliance'. Greenson (1967) sees the 'reliable core of the working alliance in the "real", or non-transference relationship'. By 'real' is meant both genuine and truthful as opposed to contrived or phoney, and also realistic and undistorted by phantasy.

In practice these distinctions are not so easy to make. The patient may well have a genuine desire to get better and to collaborate with the therapist in doing so, and at the same time be concealing feelings of despair and disappointment behind an idealising transference. It is certainly the therapist's task to provide a secure base for the patient: to be available regularly and reliably; to be courteous, compassionate and caring; to be able to set limits and have clear boundaries; to protect the therapy from interruptions and distractions; and not to burden the patient with his own difficulties and preoccupations. Since Attachment Theory presupposes that a distressed individual will naturally seek security, the distinction between the 'real' and the transferential relationship becomes less problematic. Dependency on the therapist is not seen as inherently neurotic, but as an appropriate response to emotional distress. The issue is whether the patient has formed a secure or an anxious type of attachment, and if anxious, what pattern. If, for example, there has been major environmental trauma in the patient's life (prolonged separation from parents, or physical or sexual abuse, for example), then the patient is unlikely to find it easy to form a secure base and may in an avoidant way approach therapy and the therapist with suspicion and reserve, and detach himself at the faintest hint of a rebuff, and the 'real' relationship may hang by a thread.

The question of whether attachment to the therapist is merely a necessary first step for the initiation of transference or whether it constitutes a therapeutic element in its own right is usually understood in terms of stages of development. Balint's 'basic fault' patient (that is, one who is severely damaged by early environmental failure) needs a new kind of empathic experience with the therapist which can then be internalised and so provides an inner sense of security which is the precondition of autonomy. In a less damaged 'Oedipal' patient, attachment to the therapeutic environment can be more taken for granted, and the focus will be on the way that the person of the therapist is viewed and treated. Kohut (1977) and Guntrip (1974) have pointed to the difference in technique required for these two types of patient, arguing that more damaged 'borderline' patients require greater acceptance and environmental provision. Kernberg (Bateman 1991) has questioned this, claiming that limit setting and interpretive understanding is even more vital if these patients are to be helped towards adaptation to reality.

Bowlby rejected a simplistic 'stage'-based model of development, but the distinctions which attachment therapy makes between ambivalent, avoidant and disorganised patterns of insecure attachment are relevant here. The disorganised pattern may represent the most disturbed patients who are threatened by too close attachment of any sort, and need a low-key supportive approach (Holmes 1992). The ambivalently attached need a combination of absolute reliability and firm limit setting to help with secure attachment, combined with a push towards exploration. The avoidant group associate close contact with pain and rejection and may experience interpretations as intrusive assaults, and so benefit from a more flexible and friendly therapeutic relationship.

Balint's (1968) distinction between 'ocnophils' (clingers) and 'philobats' (avoiders) corresponds closely with Bowlby's classification of insecure attachment into ambivalent and avoidant patterns. Balint sees many psychoanalysts as 'ocnophilic', clinging to their patients with their interpretations. Like Meares and Hobson (1977) in their discussion of the 'persecutory therapist', he argues that attachment must be sought and accepted as a goal in its own right with more disturbed patients, and that too much interpretation can inhibit a patient's exploration.

Spying or seeking

Annabel was a disturbed young woman living away from home in a bedsitter. She had always felt that her mother favoured her brother over herself. This feeling of exclusion was compounded when, during her teens, her mother became ill and her previously neglectful father had tenderly looked after his sick wife. Annabel confessed to her therapist that one day when alone in the house she had crept into her landlady's part of the house and, searching through her desk, had found some love-letters from her husband and had read them avidly.

A Kleinian interpretation might have focused on the envious 'attack on linking' implicit in this act, trying to help her to get in touch with the angry and destructive impulses which made her feel responsible for her mother's illness. A Bowlbian approach, however, would see the need to maintain a line of attachment as paramount, and would therefore interpret this act as a search for a secure base in her parents' marriage (and by transference in the therapy). Only once this secure base was firmly established would it be appropriate to look at her protest about loss and separation.

As we mentioned in Chapter 3, Attachment Theory is essentially a spatial theory in which the care-seeker is constantly monitoring and adjusting his distance from the care-giver depending on the level of perceived anxiety and the strength of the drive to explore. Balint also emphasises the importance of getting the right distance from the patient, especially if words fail and the patient falls silent. The therapist must be

> felt to be present but must be all the time at the right distance – neither so far that the patient feels lost or abandoned, nor so close that the patient might feel encumbered and unfree – in fact at a distance that corresponds to the patient's actual need.
>
> (Balint 1986)

Therapists and parents

Post-Bowlbian research has begun to provide a picture of the kinds of mother–infant interaction that are likely to give rise to a secure base experience for the growing child. The children of parents who are responsive and attuned and see their infants as separate are likely to be better adjusted socially, more able to reflect on their feelings and to weave their experience into a coherent narrative. The capacity to handle loss and separation with appropriate anger, sadness and reconciliation is associated with secure attachment. These findings can be compared with the Rogerian view that effective therapists show empathy, honesty and non-possessive warmth (Truax and Carkhuff 1967). The good therapist acts, mainly at an unconscious and non-verbal level, like a good parent with his patients. Empathy corresponds with attunement and responsiveness; honesty ensures that negative feelings, especially those connected with loss and separation based on the inevitable failures of the holding environment in therapy (therapist's illness, holidays, memory-lapses and so on), are dealt with openly and without prevarication; non-possessive warmth means that the therapist gets the attachment distance right which means they are containing to the patient without being intrusive.

Based on Attachment Theory research we can identify three component elements which go to make up the secure base phenomenon in therapy: attunement, the fostering of autobiographical competence and affective processing (Holmes 1992). Two case examples will now be given to illustrate the phenomena of attunement and autobiographical competence in therapy. Affective processing will be considered in a later section of the chapter.

Attunement

Stern (1985) sees attunement as the basis for the emerging sense of self in the pre-verbal infant:

> Tracking and attuning . . . permit one human to be with another in the sense of sharing likely inner experience on an almost continuous basis. . . . This is exactly our experience of feeling-connectedness, of being in attunement with another. It feels like an unbroken line. It seeks out the activation contour that is momentarily going on in any and every behaviour and uses that contour to keep the thread of communication unbroken.
>
> (Stern 1985)

For Stern, the emotionally disturbed patient is one whose early experiences lacked this attunement. There is perhaps a faint echo of Hamlet's farewell to Horatio when he compares the need for an attuning parent (or therapist) with

> the continuing physiological need for an environment containing oxygen. It is a relatively silent need of which one becomes aware sharply only when it is not being met, when a harsh world compels one to draw one's breath in pain.
>
> (Stern 1985)

Brazelton and Cramer's (1991) detailed description of secure parent–infant interaction similarly delineates the components of responsive interaction: synchrony, symmetry, contingency and 'entrainment', from which mutual play and infant autonomy begin to emerge (see Chapter 6). These features are equally applicable to therapist–patient interactions. Good therapists find themselves automatically mirroring their patients' levels of speech volume and their posture. Malan's (1976) concept of 'leapfrogging' between patient and therapist is very similar to the idea of contingency and entrainment in which parent and child hook onto each other in sequences of mutual responsiveness. This can be demonstrated immediately in videotapes of therapy, but is less easy to convey in a written account.

Sarah's 'ums' and 'aahs'

Despite marriage, parenthood, a profession and a circle of good friends, Sarah had reached her fiftieth year almost without any sense of who she was or what the meaning and direction of her life should be. In her social self she played the part of a cheerful and active woman constantly fighting off feelings of depression and the wish to end her life. In therapy she returned again and again to the question, 'Who *am* I?'.

She had been brought up in a 'progressive' children's home where her parents were the proprietors. She had always felt that her mother was 'so near and yet so far': she could *see* her, but was expected, from the age of three, to fit in and share a dormitory with the other children, and was not allowed to have any kind of special relationship with her. Her father was harsh, distant, controlling and physically and sexually abusive. She dated the origin of the split between her 'social' and her 'real' self to the age of eight, when she had naïvely tried to disclose her father's abuse but had been disbelieved, and punished by him for what to her was quite inexplicable 'wickedness'. Any attunement between her inner world and the external one was fractured from then on. Peer Gynt-like, she complained that however much she peeled away the onion skin of her existence she could never find her real self.

As therapy progressed she found the 'attuning' sounds of the therapist – the 'ums' and 'aahs', grunts, inhalations and exhalations – immensely comforting. 'They give me a sense that somehow *you know* how I feel, however much you appear distant, rejecting or uninterested (all words she had used about her parents) in your verbal comments.' In fact, it was extremely difficult to tune into this patient, who varied between desperate attempts to draw the therapist into her pain and misery, complaining ('Why aren't you *angry* about the terrible things that happened to me as a child?'), demanding ('I need to know that you *like* me'), and excluding him with a self-absorbed, miserable monologue. Nevertheless, the fact that she *could* complain, demand and moan was, for her, in itself a considerable achievement. She dreamed of the therapist looking at her and knowing, without her having to put it into words, how she felt, and of his gently putting an arm around her in a gesture of protection.

Autobiographical competence

Winnicott (1965) described psychotherapy as 'an extended form of history-taking'. The patient comes with a story, however tentative and disjointed, which is then worked on by therapist and patient until a more coherent and satisfying narrative emerges, which provides an objectification and explanation of the patient's difficulties, and a vehicle or symbolisation which links inner and outer experience (Spence 1982; Shafer 1976). Tulving (Eagle 1988) distinguishes between 'semantic' memory, which is propositional and influences behaviour but which need not necessarily be conscious, and 'episodic' memory, which has a narrative structure and consists of stored chunks of remembered experience. The process of therapy can be seen as one of making 'semantic' memory episodic, of weaving a narrative out of the unconscious attitudes, assumptions and affects which the patient brings to the therapy in the transference, so that they feel they now own them.

The avoidant patient with a dismissing autobiographical style begins to allow some of the pain of separation into consciousness, the ambivalent patient with a preoccupied style can start to feel safe enough to let go of their past anguish. Out of narrative comes meaning – the 'broken line' of insecure attachment is replaced by a sense of continuity, an inner story which enables new experience to be explored, with the confidence that it can be coped with and assimilated. The next example tries to illustrate the immediacy of this process by presenting material from a single session.

Peter: stringing a story together

Peter is a man in his late fifties, now in his second year of weekly therapy. He has a very strong presence: powerful, pugnacious, a self-made man who grew up in the Gorbals, he is now a ship's captain, away from home for long stretches of time. His problems are depression, marital conflict and suicidal feelings which have been present for many years but which came to the surface after the birth of his youngest child.

He starts the session by talking about money. 'I'm like my

father, always worrying about money. I'm feeling good today, I've bought a car cheap, and I've got some work.' But that means another break away from home and from therapy. A lot of therapeutic effort has gone into helping him recognise how he detaches himself from feelings of loss when he goes away. 'I used to pride myself on not bothering to ring home or to miss them when I was away – it's only two weeks, why make a fuss.'

I take up the implication that in one sense therapy has made things more difficult for him now that he is in touch with feelings of loss and separation rather than cutting off from them, and remind him of the misery which he described when as a child he was evacuated to the country during the war, away from the bombs but also from his mother.

'Yes, it was terrible. After a few weeks my mother came to collect me. *Did* she dote on me or what? Everyone says that she did, but I just can't remember.' He then goes on to list a string of incidents which we have already unearthed and discussed from his childhood – playing truant at the age of five without his mother knowing, feeling an outsider among his playmates, learning to establish himself through fighting – 'Who *is* that little boy, I just don't recognise him; *is* that me?' He jokes: 'Oh well, like my father used to say, nostalgia's like neuralgia.'

I suggest that he can't piece himself together, can't identify with the little boy that he was because his mother wasn't there to string the episodes of his life together for him, just as I won't be there when he goes off to work next week.

He protests: 'But I can get what I like from women', and gives several examples to prove his point. I reply by wondering if he feels these women really *know* him, whether he feels that I or his wife know him, if his mother really knew his sadness and fear. Perhaps it was his vitality and strength that she doted on, like the women he can get what he likes from, not his vulnerability.

He then recounts some new history about his mother's childhood, how she was illegitimate, the offspring of his grandmother's second 'husband', how his grandfather had been quite well off, loved opera (as he does) and had taught his mother to play the piano, how she had been only eighteen when she became pregnant by his father and they 'had' to get married.

I suggest that his confusion about whether or not his mother 'doted' on him was perhaps because she was depressed during his infancy, confused in her new 'legitimate' identity, just as he had become depressed after the birth of his youngest child.

There was a pause: it seemed that this had struck a chord. '*Click*: they always used to say what a difficult feeder I was as a baby. My father' (the father who had always told this highly intelligent man what a dunce he was) 'had to buy special milk for me.'

I said: 'So money goes to the heart of your identity. He worked to keep you alive, just as you see me working to keep you alive now.'

He began to weep. I wondered if his sadness was to do with the coming break. 'No,' he said, 'It's gratitude – you seem to *recognise* what I am like.'

Seen from this post-Bowlbian perspective the tension between attachment and interpretation as curative factors in psychotherapy becomes less problematic. The responsiveness of the therapist begins to restore the 'broken line' of the patient's internal world and forms the basis of a secure therapeutic base. This enables the beginnings of exploration which in the setting of therapy takes the form of a narrative in which the therapist's interpretations are an attempt to modify, expand and lend coherence to the patient's story. But the narrative is not just the patient's 'case history'. It is also the history of the therapeutic relationship itself, of the movement from what Balint (1968) calls the 'mixedupness' of patient and therapist to a state of differentiation in which the patient detaches himself from the external support of the therapist and comes to rely on his own internal secure base, with a less fractured line of self.

2 REALITY AND TRAUMA

The notion of the 'broken line' brings us to the question of trauma in the genesis of neurosis. We saw in the last chapter how Bowlby's psychoanalytic education took place in an atmosphere in which the role of external reality was seen as largely irrelevant, compared with the influence of phantasy in mental life. Bowlby found this incomprehensible and reprehensible, and in one sense his life's work could be seen as an attempt to prove Klein wrong on this point.

His model was a rather simple, common-sense one, based on

Freud's early views, in which neurosis is the result of trauma, the facts or emotional implications of which have been repressed. The task of therapy is primarily that of undoing this repression in a non-judgemental and accepting atmosphere. This must be contrasted with Freud's mature views and those of contemporary psychoanalysts. Here the crucial factor is the *interaction* between environmental failure and the child's phantasy life. What makes trauma traumatic is, as Symington (1986) puts it, 'when reality confirms the phantasy'. In the Oedipal situation the child feels that his attachment to the mother is threatened by her relationship with his father. He may harbour feelings of hatred towards him, and have angry outbursts at home or at school. If he is then in reality beaten by his father – say, because of this recalcitrance (or, conversely, there is no father to help him detach himself from his mother) – then his internal world will be deformed and he is likely to be mistrustful of attachment while secretly yearning for it. This will affect his subsequent relationships, which may be characterised by demandingness, violence or detachment. If, on the other hand, his original feelings of fear and rage were accepted by the parents, the outcome will be favourable. A similar story can be imagined about the frustrations of infancy: a mother's actual unreliability and inability to accept the child's protests without retaliation will solidify rather than modify an already split inner world, and lay the foundations for 'borderline' patterns of relationships in which good and evil are kept unstably apart and compromise and balance are inaccessible (see Chapter 9).

Bowlby's own research and the accumulating evidence that parents do indeed abandon, neglect, physically and sexually abuse their children, and often deny that they do so and prohibit protest about the distress they have caused, seems to support his position that trauma and loss are central to the genesis of neurosis. Against this must be set several important qualifications. First, as we saw in Chapter 3, there are not a few resilient children who, despite apparently appalling environmental traumata, appear to come through without major psychological damage (Rutter 1985). Second, seeing people merely as victims of their circumstances, although valid at one level leaves out the idea of *agency*, which is a vital ingredient of psychological health. It also fails to comprehend the way in which pathological patterns, once internalised, are perpetuated by the sufferers themselves: the vicious circles of neurosis in which mistrust breeds disappointment, avoidance invites neglect, clinging provokes rejection, depressive assumptions lead to negative experiences which confirm those assumptions (cf., for example, Beck *et al.* 1979; Strachey 1934; Ryle 1990). Third, merely commiserating with a patient about the ways in which they have been damaged by their parents or by traumatic events does not in itself necessarily produce a good therapeutic outcome. For that to happen there has also to be some re-living (before relieving) of the emotional response to the trauma, and it is a central task of psychotherapy to provide the setting in which this affective processing can take place.

3 AFFECTIVE PROCESSING

Bowlby's early work seemed to imply that separation, at least in the first five years of life, was inherently a bad thing, and that a major task of preventive psychiatry would be to minimise the occurrence and affects of such separations. In his later work, however, there is a shift of perspective so that it is not just the facts of loss and separation, but the nature of a person's emotional response to them that matters. The Adult Attachment Interview findings (Bretherton 1991b) suggest that loss that is either denied (dismissive pattern) or cannot be transcended (pre-occupied pattern) is associated with insecure attachment (see Table 8.1). The way a parent handles a child's response to separation is a key factor here – whether by accepting and encouraging the expression of feelings of anger and sadness, or by sweeping them under the carpet. Bowlby saw the task of the therapist both to encourage appropriate emotional response to past trauma, and to be alert to the ways in which the patient is reacting to the losses and separations in therapy and to encourage discussion and ventilation of feelings about them. His views are well illustrated in his discussion of Charles Darwin's lifelong symptoms of anxiety and psychosomatic illness.

Charles Darwin: loss denied

Bowlby (1990) explained Darwin's lifelong intermittent psychosomatic symptoms of palpitations, paraesthesia, exhaustion and faintness in terms of unmourned loss. His mother died when he was eight. His father, a busy and irascible country doctor, whose

Table 8.1 Clinical aspects of insecure-avoidant and dismissive attachment

	Narrative style	Parenting	Core anxiety	Secondary defense	Transference	Counter-transference	Therapeutic strategy
INSECURELY ATTACHED							
Avoidant	Dismissive	Functional Pushing away	Abandonment	Splitting Denial	Terrified of contact	Bored Angry	Acceptance of rage
Ambivalent	Enmeshed	Inconsistent Intrusive	Impingement	False self Compliance	Terrified of separation	Stifled	Containment

own mother had died when he was a child, handed Charles over to the care of his older sisters, who forbade any mention of their mother's death. So powerful was the effect of this prohibition that, at the age of thirty-three, in a letter of condolence to a friend sympathising about the death of his young wife, he wrote: 'I truly sympathise with you though never in my life having lost one near relation, I daresay I cannot imagine how severe grief such as yours must be.'

Another instance of the repression of painful affect in Darwin's life comes from his granddaughter's account of a family word game in which words are 'stolen' by one player from another if they can add a letter so as to create a new one. On one occasion Darwin saw someone add an 'M' to 'other' to make 'Mother'. Darwin stared at it for some time, objecting: 'There's no such word as MO-THER'! (An unpsychological explanation such as Bowlby's parents might have offered was that Darwin was a notoriously bad speller – Raverat 1952.)

Bowlby sees Darwin's chronic ill health as reflecting two sets of unresolved conflict. The first was his inability to grieve, to bear the pain of the many losses in his life, starting with that of his mother, and including his wife's many pregnancies (sources of great anxiety to Darwin) and the loss of their beloved eldest daughter in 1851. The second was his ambivalent relationship with his overbearing father, whom Charles both revered and feared. Bowlby sees his hesitancy about publication of *The Origin of Species* (it took nearly twenty years between writing the original draft and publication, which was spurred on eventually by competition from Wallace) as reflecting this compliance and defiance in relation to authority. Bowlby's recipe for helping Darwin to overcome his difficulties would have been to 'recognise and gradually counteract the powerful influence . . . of the strongly entrenched Darwin[ian] tradition that the best way of dealing with painful thoughts is to dismiss them from your mind and, if possible, forget them altogether'. Thus does Bowlby recruit Freud to help with the Englishman's Achilles' heel – his fear of feelings.

Bowlby and Winnicott: to commiserate or not?

It is interesting to compare Bowlby's ideas with those of Winnicott on this point. Winnicott opposes any reassurance or commiseration about trauma from the analyst, on the grounds that they may inhibit the affective processing that is needed if therapy is to succeed. He bases this on a rather subtle argument about the infant's necessary illusion of 'omnipotence', based on the mother's sensitive anticipation of his needs so that just as he is, as it were, thinking he might be hungry, the breast miraculously appears, as though by magic. For Winnicott the origins of creativity are to be found in this interplay between mother and child. Like Bion (1978), he also sees the mother helping the infant to deal with bad feelings through her containing and transmuting functions. If the baby feels that his protest and anger are accepted and held, then the environment does not 'impinge' in a traumatic way: 'The ego-support of the maternal care enables the infant to live and develop in spite of his not yet being able to control or feel responsible for what is good and bad in the environment' (Winnicott 1965).

Like Bowlby (but unlike Klein), Winnicott seems to acknowledge that the environment can let the child down, but argues that the child needs to have felt that everything is under his control before he can come gradually to accept his vulnerability:

> The paradox is that what is good and bad in the infant's environment is not in fact a projection, but in spite of this it is necessary . . . if the infant is to develop healthily that everything shall seem to him to be a projection.
>
> (Winnicott 1965)

This viewpoint enables Winnicott to argue the case for an analytic attitude in which the trauma is re-experienced in the transference in such a way that it comes within the area of 'omnipotence':

> In psychoanalysis there is no trauma that is outside the individual's omnipotence. . . . The patient is not helped if the analyst says 'your mother was not good enough . . .'. Changes come in an analysis when the traumatic factors enter the psychoanalytic material in the patient's own way, and within the patient's omnipotence.
>
> (Winnicott 1965)

Winnicott's phrase, 'bringing into omnipotence', is an example of the combination of clinical accuracy with theoretical fuzziness that Bowlby was keen to remedy in psychoanalysis. It also reflects Winnicott's ambivalence about Klein. He is straining both to be true to his clinical experience (that what is good and bad is *not* a projection) and to remain faithful to Kleinian theory (which emphasises the 'omnipotence' of infantile thought). A behavioural way of looking at this is to see it as an example of 'state-dependent learning' – that is, the observation that some things can only be learned, or unlearned, when the emotions associated with them are re-experienced. Humphrey's (1992) recent distinction between perception, an appreciation of the state of the world 'out there', and sensation, the state of things 'in here', is also helpful. While perception is a mirroring of external events that happens willy-nilly if the organism is to survive, and can be conscious or unconscious, Humphrey sees sensation as an active process in which the subject, as it were, presents his feelings to himself and that this is quintessentially a conscious process. One can imagine that sensation is, in the early stages of life, a shared activity between parent and child as the experiences of holding, seeing, feeding and touching are presented to the growing child. As Garland (1991) argues, traumatic events overwhelm the 'stimulus barrier' so that, although perceived, they cannot be sensed. The subject is paralysed by them and cannot actively present them to themselves, while the parent or protector who might help to do so is inevitably absent. The task of therapy then is to 'represent' these traumatic events – via a narrative transformation from 'semantic' to 'episodic' memory – in such a way that they can be sensed, and therefore, by definition, made conscious. This process could possibly be described as 'omnipotent' in so far as any representation or map, including the cerebral 'map' of feelings, is 'omnipotent'. Thus a grain of sand could be said omnipotently to 'contain all heaven'. Here is an example of such emotion recollected in (comparative) tranquillity:

The tonsillectomy

A man in his thirties entered therapy because of his feelings of depression and a failed marriage. His relationships were characterised by avoidant attachment. He was always seemingly throwing away the very things that he wanted. He knew what he did *not* want, but not what he wanted. Whenever his career threatened to take off he would leave his job. A similar pattern affected his relationship with his partner: the closer they became the more likely there was to be a violent argument. He was an only child whose father had been killed in the war, and the origins of this pattern seemed to go back to his mother, on whom he was very dependent, but whom he experienced as intrusive and interfering.

One winter's day as he was waiting for his therapy session he saw the therapist through the closed window breathing steam into the cold air. He found himself worrying that the therapist might have something wrong with his lungs. Suddenly a flood of memories returned a tonsillectomy he had undergone when he was five. Visiting was restricted (these were normal regimes in those pre-Bowlbian days), but he was able to see his mother through a glass window twice a week (it may not have been that bad – this was how he recalled it). He remembered his fury at not being able to go home with her, throwing the toys she had left for him, shouting 'I want my mummy . . .'. As the memories returned so he began to cry profusely. This session was a turning point, enabling him to move from a position of 'I don't want . . .', to 'I want . . .'. The traumatic separation had been re-experienced in the therapy, and no longer needed to be enacted via projective identification (doing to his employers and girlfriend what as a child he had felt had been done to him by his mother) but could be symbolised and so become part of the therapeutic narrative.

Therapists out of touch?

Attachment Theory throws an interesting light on the dilemma posed by the problem of touch in therapy. Bowlby emphasises the importance of real attachment of patient to therapist. Because attachment needs are seen as distinct from sexual or oral drives there is no intrinsic danger of gratification or seduction. Attachment provides a quiet background atmosphere of security within which more dangerous feelings can be safely explored. The patient who asks to touch the therapist, to hold a hand or be hugged, is wanting to get hold of the 'environment mother' who let him down or was absent in childhood, and it may be legitimate in certain circumstances, and with appropriate ethical safeguards (Holmes and Lindley 1989) for the therapist to respond to such a request (Balint 1968). In 'Attachment and new beginning', Pedder (1986) describes how a patient who had been separated from her mother for 6 months in infancy buried her head in the pillow, extending her arms out loosely to either side of the pillow. Her hands moved around restlessly, reaching silently in my direction for some ten minutes. Eventually I said I thought she wanted me to take her hand, though she felt unable to say so, and then I did.

This seemed an important new beginning and she was later able to say how she had been terrified of being too demanding in asking me to hold a hand, fearing I might not trust her and might have mistaken her wish to be held as sexual.

(Pedder 1986)

Secure attachment to the therapist may be part of a 'new beginning' for certain patients, and some physical expression of this can be helpful. But – and here is the dilemma – pain and anguish of separation also need to be re-experienced if the patient is to feel safe enough to form new attachments, secure in the knowledge that, should things go wrong, the loss can be mourned and that he will not be left feeling permanently bereft.

Winnicott's view that trauma needs to be brought 'within the patient's omnipotence' is echoed by Casement (1985) in his discussion of another case in which the patient had asked to hold her therapist's hand. This was a woman who had been badly burned as a child and whose mother had fainted while holding her hand when the burn was being operated on under local anaesthetic. After initially agreeing, Casement later decided not to accede to the patient's request. This withdrawal led to fury and near-psychosis in the patient, but once this had been survived she began rapidly to improve, and it seemed that the uncanny repetition in the transference of the mother's holding and then letting go of the patient, while remaining in a therapeutic context that was basically secure, had contributed to this breakthrough. Casement quotes Winnicott:

the patient used the analyst's failures, often quite small ones, perhaps manoeuvred by the patient. . . . The patient now hates the analyst for the failure that originally came as an environmental factor, outside the area of omnipotent control, but that is now staged in the transference. So in the end we succeed by failing – failing the patient's way. This is a long distance from the simple theory of cure by corrective experience.

(Winnicott 1965)

Bowlby the scientist was always parsimoniously trying to devise a 'simple theory' with which to explain the enormous complexity of intimate human relationships. Attachment Theory, while in general being unworried by physical contact between patient and therapist, does provide a clear rationale for exercising extreme caution in dealing with patients who have been abused in childhood, as the next example illustrates:

Safe breathing: secure base

Sarah, of the 'ums' and 'aahs' discussed above, was increasingly distressed as her elderly mother became ill. This coincided with her therapist having to change the time of her appointments. She started to sob and shake and overbreathe during the sessions. She wrote a poem in which she longed for a pure and childlike intimacy with her therapist. She wanted him inside her, breathing him in through her lungs, rather than taking him in through her mouth or genitals which she saw as sullied and contaminated. She wanted desperately to hold his hand, but he intuitively felt that this would be wrong.

When patient and therapist looked at this together they realised that this was because, as well as being the secure-base mother she so longed for, he also represented the abusive father whom she feared and loathed. Had he held her hand this would have repeated the typical abusive vicious circle in which the child clings ever more tightly to her abuser: the abuse creates a terrible anxiety which leads to attachment behaviour, which provokes more abuse and so on. By holding his hand she would have remained an *object*, albeit one in need of protection, whereas her greatest need was to become the subject of her own life, even though this meant subjecting herself to intense pain and fear. In the end she soothed herself with the idea that if she could feel that she *belonged* for a while in his consulting room, things would be all right. Like Oliver Twist (see Chapter 3), she needed first to find a place to which she could become attached, before she could begin to own her story.

4 COGNITION IN THERAPY

We have argued in the previous chapter that Bowlby's concept of internal working models acts as a bridge between psychoanalysis, which conceives of an internal world populated with objects and their relationships, and cognitive science, which acknowledges internal models of the world in the form of mental representations. Psychoanalysis is concerned with affect-laden sensations which act as a distorting prism as we confront the world; cognitive therapy, with the perceptions and constructions which we put on those sensations and erroneous assumptions which follow from them. Psychoanalysis aims to make the unconscious conscious; cognitive therapy starts from conscious thoughts but then reveals the unexamined assumptions that underlie them. Bowlby provides a bridging language between the two approaches. He sees the neurotic patient as basing his relationship to the world on outdated assumptions; for example, that he will be ignored or let down by people, or that his feelings will be dismissed or ridiculed. While these are, in his view, fairly accurate reflections of the way the person has been treated as a child, they do not necessarily bear any relation to current reality, and can lead to poor adaptation in the form of avoidant or ambivalent relationships.

Two factors are at work in maintaining these outmoded models. The first is defensive exclusion of painful emotions which can be overcome by the kind of affective processing advocated in the previous section. The second, related, phenomenon is the need to preserve meaning and to order incoming information from the environment in *some* kind of schema, however inappropriate.

Liotti (1987; Bowlby 1985) sees these schemata as 'superconscious' (rather than unconscious) organising principles 'which govern the conscious processes without appearing in them', rather as computer programmes determine what appears on the VDU screen without themselves being apparent. An important part of the task of therapy, whether cognitive or psychoanalytic, is to elicit and modify these overarching mental schemata. Given that the patient is likely to become closely attached to the therapist, it is assumed that his assumptions, preconceptions and beliefs will be brought into play in relation to the therapist, and the therapist will re-present them, as they become visible, for mutual consideration. This is Bowlby's version of the phenomenon of transference.

Always too considerate

Rose was in her fifties when she asked for help after splitting up with her second husband. She felt panicky and depressed and did not see how she could cope with being on her own. She had broken the marriage when she suddenly realised how she was compulsively deferential to her husband, and one more unreasonable request from him was the final straw.

As a child her life had changed dramatically when, at the age of seven, her father had walked out. She had been his favourite and every morning had sat on his lap while he fed her titbits. Now he had a new wife and family and she was relegated to occasional weekend visits where she slept in a cold and undecorated room, surrounded, as she saw it, by inaccessible luxury. At the same time her mother became profoundly depressed and developed an hysterical paralysis. When she recovered she had numerous boyfriends, one of whom she eventually married, and who resented Rose and her sisters' presence and insisted they went to bed at five o'clock every evening. Rose soon learned to suppress her own needs and disappointments and discovered in her teens that charm, good looks and compliance were a heady brew and she was able to attract powerful and successful men.

In her early psychotherapy sessions she announced that the last thing she wanted was any long-term commitment, merely a few sessions to 'sort her out'. She was grateful and dutifully took up any tentative suggestion from the therapist – that she might look at her dreams, or anger – with apparent enthusiasm. As the final scheduled session drew near she looked sad and tentative, but insisted that she was 'fine' and that everything was now going well. When challenged, however, she admitted that she did feel nervous about the end of therapy and really wanted to go on, but had 'assumed' that the therapist was far too busy to be bothered with her for more than a few meetings. In this example of ambivalent attachment she had reproduced with the therapist the very pattern of suppression of need, compliance and role reversal (she looking after the therapist) that characterised her relationship with her mother. She carried over into therapy the cognitive assumption 'I will only be loved if I look after others and please them'. This had served her well as an organiser of experience and a way of avoiding painful disappointment and frightening rage, but also acted as a barrier to her achieving what she really wanted and deprived her of feelings of intimacy and ease.

5 COMPANIONABLE INTERACTION

Attachment Theory sees exploratory and attachment behaviour as reciprocal behavioural systems. The securely attached infant feels safe to explore the environment; if danger threatens, exploration is abandoned in favour of proximity-seeking to an attachment figure. In adults, attachment can be differentiated from affiliation (Weiss 1982; Sheldon and West 1989). Affiliative relationships are typically with friends, best 'mates' (an interesting non-sexual use of the term) and comrades and are usually based on mutual exploration of shared interests. Attachment relationships, unlike affiliation, typically provide protection from danger, including the dangers of painful feelings. Thus, as we shall discuss further in the next chapter, Brown and Harris (1978) found that women experiencing loss who had a close confiding relationship with a spouse were protected from depression, while single mothers, even if they had close affiliative-type friendships, were not.

The relevance of this to psychotherapy lies in the likelihood that Heard and Lake's (1986) companionable interaction – synonymous with affiliation – is likely to be a feature of the psychotherapeutic relationship, although it is rarely considered as such by theorists. Freud's early 'training analyses' consisted of a few walks around the Wienerwald (Roazen 1976). A friendship bond undoubtedly does develop in some psychotherapeutic relationships. The tension between the patient's need to see the therapist as a friend, and the professional parameters of the relationship may provide useful transferential material.

Contrasting opening moves

Sarah and Peter, described earlier in the chapter, provide good examples of this point. Sarah would start each session in a bright and breezy way, referring to the weather or to current events as she entered the consulting room. The therapist instinctively did not respond in kind – in a way that would, from the point of view of affiliation, seem almost rude. It was clear from her history that she had always managed to avoid intimacy through group living, and by making sure she was the 'life-and-soul' in any gathering, but always keeping her real self well hidden. Her problem was with one-to-one attachments, not affiliation.

Peter similarly would start his sessions with talk about current politics or sport, but in his case the therapist was prepared to join in, in a limited way, again without this being a thought-out strategy. Eventually, when this was discussed in therapy, what emerged was his desperate need to be liked, and his fear of being an outsider, an emotional orphan whom everyone ignored.

In Sarah's case the therapist was adjusting the therapeutic space so that she could get far enough from him to look at what was going on between them; in Peter's he was encouraging him to affiliate enough for some therapeutic interaction to begin.

In most therapies there is an interplay between attachment and affiliation – which might in different terminology be seen as the interplay between transference and the working alliance. The sensitive therapist, like the good-enough parent, is always alert to the patient's need for security in the face of painful affect on the one hand, and, on the other, their wish to explore in a playful, humorous or companionable way.

The issue of affiliation is even more evident in group and family therapies. Affiliation to group members helps demoralised patients feel that they are of some value and importance, and to overcome isolation. Attachment in group therapy is to the group 'matrix' (derived from the word for mother) that holds its members securely and allows for exploration and affective processing. The family group is an affiliative as well as an attachment system, and much of the effort of systemic therapists is directed towards encouraging family members to do more things together and have more fun (while retaining their individuality and separateness). This chapter concludes, therefore, with a brief consideration of Bowlby's contribution to family therapy.

BOWLBY AND FAMILY THERAPY

In all his vast output Bowlby only published one purely clinical – as opposed to theoretical or research – paper. This was 'The study and reduction of group tensions in the family' (Bowlby 1949a). In it he describes his treatment at the Tavistock Clinic of a disturbed young adolescent boy who was destructive and difficult and failing to reach his potential at school. After two years of individual therapy Bowlby felt he had reached an impasse: there was no improvement, and the boy was becoming increasingly resistant to the therapy. In desperation he took the innovative step of arranging a joint meeting with the boy and his parents, together with a social worker. The meeting lasted two hours. The first hour consisted of a painful reiteration by the parents of their frustrations and disappointments with the boy. Bowlby countered this by suggesting that their nagging had contributed to his behaviour, but suggested that this had to be understood in the context of their own unhappy childhoods:

> After 90 minutes the atmosphere changed very greatly and all three were beginning to have sympathy for the situation of the others . . . they found themselves co-operating in an honest endeavour to find new techniques for living together, each realising that there was a common need to do so and that the ways they had set about it in the past had defeated their object. This proved the turning point in the case.
>
> (Bowlby 1949a)

One senses that here at last Bowlby was allowing himself free rein to do what he really wanted, a process which began in the 1930s when he first began to chafe at the Kleinian bit. Based on Bion's ideas about group therapy he conceptualised the processes involved in family therapy as analogous to individual therapy in which the warring parts of the personality are enabled to communicate more freely with one another and to reach compromise and accommodation. The social optimism of the period (with perhaps also a nod towards Bowlby's surgeon father) is contained within his remark that, once painful and angry feelings are openly expressed,

> the recognition of the basic fact that people really do want to live happily together and that this drive is working for us gives confidence, much as a knowledge of the miraculous healing powers of the body gives confidence to the surgeon.
>
> (Bowlby 1949a)

The paper ends with a section entitled 'Circular reactions in family and other social groups', which is thoroughly systemic in its outlook. Bowlby points out the vicious circles of neurosis in which 'insecure parents create insecure children, who grow up to create an insecure society which in its turn creates more insecure parents', and contrasts this with the virtuous circles of health and the need for 'one great therapeutic endeavour: that of reducing tensions and of fostering understanding co-operation between groups of human beings'.

Although Bowlby did not specifically return to family therapy as a topic after this, he must be credited with having introduced the technique of seeing families together at the Tavistock Clinic, and therefore, alongside Gregory Bateson's Palo Alto group (Bateson 1973), with being the originator of family and systemic therapy which was to become such an important therapeutic mode over the ensuing decades.

Bowlby's ideas have been developed in Britain particularly by John Byng-Hall (1991c), Dorothy Heard (1982) and Robin Skynner (1976). Byng-Hall has addressed the spatial aspect of attachment, which can be illustrated by Schopenhauer's porcupine metaphor as an image for 'too near-too far' dilemmas within families:

> A number of porcupines huddled together for warmth on a cold day in winter; but, as they began to prick one another with their quills, they were obliged to disperse. However the cold drove them together again, when just the same thing happened. At last, after many turns of huddling and dispersing, they discovered that they would be best off by remaining at little distance from one another.
>
> (Quoted in Melges and Swartz 1989)

Byng-Hall (1991a), from a child psychiatry perspective, sees the symptomatic patient in a dysfunctional family behaving like the buffer zone between parental porcupines: when the parents start to drift apart the child will develop symptoms which bring them together, and if they start to get dangerously close he will insinuate himself between them, thereby alleviating the imagined dangers of intimacy. Byng-Hall (1985) sees the presuppositions and assumptions which partners bring from their 'families of origin' into their 'families of procreation' in terms of 'family scripts'; namely, patterns of interaction or 'dance' (Minuchin 1974), which an individual expects of himself and those close to him. The distinction made by Minuchin et al. (1978) between enmeshed and disengaged families (the former tending to occur in anorexia, the latter in behaviour disorders), can be equated in Attachment

Theory terms with ambivalent and avoidant insecure attachment based on the parents' experiences as children and now reproduced with their own offspring.

Perhaps as a counter-balance to Bowlby and Winnicott's emphasis on mothers, Skynner (1976) highlights the role of the father in family attachment patterns. In the early stages of infancy the father's job is to protect the mother–child dyad, to allow attachment to develop and for the mother's 'primary maternal preoccupation' (Winnicott 1965) to flower. Later, he needs to intrude on the intimacy of mother and child, partly in order to make his own relationship with the child and to promote attachment to himself, but also to encourage the process of healthy separation from the mother. The child needs to be able to go off with the father, knowing that he can return to the secure base of the mother when he needs to. Without this Oedipal paternal function the mother will be more likely actively to reject the child, using threats of sending him away or even suicide, which Bowlby sees as a particularly dangerous breeding ground for insecure attachment.

The family therapy perspective shows how attachment patterns perpetuate themselves through the life cycle, event scripts being the psychological equivalent of the genome, or, in Dawkins' (1977) neologism, the 'meme'. The basic aims of psychotherapy – the need to provide a secure base, to help people express and come to terms with anger and disappointment (both of which can be seen in terms of separation protest), to achieve integration and coherence within themselves and their families – represent an attempt to intervene in this cycle, altering not so much an individual personality as a pattern of relating so that good experiences lead, by benign rather than vicious circles, to yet more good experiences, and so on. In this way a healthy social mutation will have occurred and Bowlby's vision of psychotherapy as preventive medicine will, to some degree at least, have been realised.

Chapter 9

Attachment Theory and psychiatric disorder

> Many of the most intense of all human emotions arise during
> the formation, the maintenance, the disruption and the
> renewal of affectional bonds . . . in terms of subjective experi-
> ence, the formation of a bond is described as falling in love,
> maintaining a bond as loving someone and losing a partner as
> grieving over someone. Similarly, threat of loss arouses anxiety
> and actual loss causes sorrow; whilst both situations are likely
> to arouse anger. Finally the unchallenged maintenance of a
> bond is experienced as a source of security, and the renewal
> of a bond as a source of joy.
>
> (Bowlby 1979c)

Social psychiatry is concerned with the ways in which the environment influences the origin, course and outcome of psychiatric
disorders. In his last, and one of his greatest papers, 'Developmental psychiatry comes of age', Bowlby (1988c) bemoans the
'kidnapping' of the label 'biological psychiatry' by those concerned with biochemical and genetic factors in mental illness.
Theories of psychological development, if based on sound ethological and evolutionary principles, are no less 'biological' than
is research in neurotransmitter chemistry. As the quotation above
implies, a key feature of Attachment Theory is its attempt to
combine the psychological and subjective with the biological and
the objective. In Chapter 3 we suggested that psychotherapy
could be seen as a branch of social psychiatry. The integration
of psychodynamic ideas into psychiatry has always been
bedevilled by the difficulty in translating the language of the inner
world into the quantifiable terms of scientific psychiatry. The aim
of this chapter is to explore the meeting points between social

psychiatry research and the recent developments in Attachment Theory discussed in Chapter 6. Out of this encounter there is beginning to emerge the possibility of a more psychologically meaningful psychiatry, and a more scientifically based psychotherapy.

Bowlby compares the role of Attachment Theory in psychiatry with that of immunology in medicine. The comparison is apt, not just because both are concerned with the integrity and security of the individual, but also because immunology, as well as being concerned with specific disorders of the immune system, has a contribution to make to the understanding of a wide variety of medical conditions. Similarly, Attachment Theory has its 'own' disorders to which it is particularly applicable – abnormal grief, neurotic depression, agoraphobia – but can also inform many other aspects of social psychiatry.

Psychoanalytic theorising about the relationship between childhood experience and psychiatric illness – for example, Freud's linking of repressed homosexuality and paranoia – or even more recent speculations about childhood 'theories of mind' (Fonagy 1991) and borderline personality disorder have found disfavour in psychiatric circles for two main reasons. First, psychiatrists tend to use much more tightly defined categories of mental illness than do psychotherapists, for whom, for example, a term such as 'psychotic' is often used in an overinclusive and arcane way. Second, it is very difficult to specify the presence or absence of a category such as 'repressed homosexuality' in a way that lends itself to research. Bowlby's strategy for getting round these difficulties was to concentrate on external, uncontroversial events such as separations. But here too the attempt to relate adult psychological disorder to single events such as childhood separation has been found to be an oversimplification. Apart perhaps from post-traumatic stress disorders there is no one-to-one link between environmental trauma and psychiatric illness. Indeed, given the complexity of psychological development, the variety of experience, and fluidity of meanings by which experience is comprehended, it would be surprising if this were so. A more subtle, if less attractively simple, model of stress, vulnerability and buffering is required.

Attachment Theory is a theory about relationships, based on the idea that human beings evolved in kinship groups and that in the original 'environment of evolutionary adaptedness' (Bowlby

1969b) survival was increased by the maintenance of secure bonds between their members, primarily, but by no means exclusively, between parents and children. The theory, fundamental to social psychiatry, suggests that relationships and their difficulties might influence psychiatric disorder in three distinct but interrelated ways. First, the breaking or disruption of bonds is likely in itself to be a cause of disturbance. Second, the internalisation of disturbed early attachment patterns may influence subsequent relationships in a way that makes a person both more exposed and more vulnerable to stress. Third, a person's current perception of their relationships and the use they make of them may make them more or less vulnerable to breakdown in the face of adversity. We shall briefly consider each of these points, and then proceed to discuss a number of selected psychiatric disorders in the light of them.

Loss

There is strong evidence of the relationship between acute loss and increased vulnerability to psychiatric and physical disorder. Widows and widowers are more likely than non-bereaved people to die themselves from a coronary in the year following the sudden death of their partners from a heart attack. Among depressed patients 60–70 per cent have had an unpleasant loss event (usually involving the loss of or threat to an attachment relationship) in the year preceding their illness, as opposed to only 20 per cent of non-depressed controls. Schizophrenic relapse is often brought on by loss or unexpected change. People who commit suicide or attempt suicide are similarly more likely to have experienced loss than those who do not.

However, as we discussed in Chapter 3, for loss to be pathogenic it has to be in the context of other important variables. Not all those who experience bereavement succumb to depression. Those for whom the loss was sudden and untimely, who had a dependent relationship with the person they have lost, or felt ambivalent towards them, and who lack a supportive relationship and network of friends, are much more vulnerable.

A similar story appears to hold for the long-term effects of childhood loss. Early speculation suggested that childhood bereavement was an important factor in adult depression. While recent research on this point has been contradictory (Tennant

1988: Harris and Bifulco 1991), it does seem clear that the lack of good care that is so often a result of childhood bereavement is a vulnerability factor for depression, and that there are important additive effects, so that loss in adult life, in the presence of vulnerabilities in the personality, makes a person much more likely to become depressed than in their absence.

Attachment styles and vulnerability to psychiatric disorder

We presented in Chapter 6 the evidence that infant attachment patterns persist well into middle childhood, and the Adult Attachment Interview (AAI) data suggest a further continuity of these patterns into adult life. This means, in Western countries at least, that about one-third of adults are likely to have relationships which are characterised by anxious attachment, and this could constitute a major vulnerability factor for psychiatric illness when faced with stressful life events. Using postal questionnaires, Shaver and Hazan (1988; Hazan and Shaver 1987) surveyed a college freshman population and a middle-aged sample about 'romantic attachments' and found remarkable parallels with the Bowlby-Ainsworth classification of infant attachment in the Strange Situation. Of their respondents 56 per cent demonstrated a secure attachment pattern, describing themselves as finding it relatively easy to get close to others, to depend on them, and not worrying about being abandoned or about being intruded upon. Twenty-five per cent showed an avoidant pattern, with difficulty in trusting their partners, and often feeling that their partners wanted more intimacy than they felt able to provide. The remainder (19 per cent) were anxious-ambivalent, often worrying that their partners didn't really love them, and aware that their great neediness and possessiveness often drove potential partners away.

Attachment research on children has shown correlations between attachment styles and social competence. Similar connections can be demonstrated in college students (Kobak and Sceery 1988): those classified as secure on the AAI were rated by their peers as more ego-resilient, less anxious and hostile, and as having greater social support than the anxious-dismissives and anxious-preoccupieds who were less resilient, less supported and more hostile or anxious respectively.

Lake (1985) has pointed to the discrepancy between the frequent invocation of the notion of ego-strength as a mark of mental health, and the lack of a satisfactory definition and operational criteria for its presence. For him ego-strength comprises the ability to form mutually satisfying intimate relationships, the capacity to cope with change, good self-esteem, and a sense of competence. In a similar vein, Holmes and Lindley (1989) define 'emotional autonomy' as the key to mental health and a central goal of psychotherapy:

> Autonomy, in the context of psychotherapy, implies taking control of one's own life . . . emotional autonomy does *not* mean isolation or avoidance of dependency. On the contrary, the lonely schizoid individual who preserves his 'independence' at all costs may well be in a state of emotional heteronomy, unable to bear closeness with another person because of inner dread and confusion. A similar state of emotional heteronomy affects the psychopath who is unaware of the feelings of others. The emotionally autonomous individual does not suppress her feelings, including the need for dependence, but takes cognisance of them, ruling rather than being ruled by them.
>
> (Holmes and Lindley 1989)

Attachment research shows how the psychotherapeutic constructs of ego strength and emotional autonomy have their origins in early familial relationships, and how in turn they affect relationships in adult life. Social psychiatry makes the links between disordered relationships and psychiatric illness, but, as we have seen in Chapter 3, these links are not as straightforward as Bowlby's original analogy between the effects of vitamin deficiency and those of maternal deprivation would imply. Epictetus' doctrine that 'men are troubled not so much by things as by their perception of things' is a reminder that environmental difficulty is *mediated* by a person's state of mind, and that mental set may powerfully influence how a person responds to stress.

Autobiographical competence

Loss and attachment style affect vulnerability to psychiatric disorder by way of the effect on the personality of past difficulty. But a person's current relationships – the support available from family, friends, and neighbours – seem likely also to be important as a source of buffering against the impact of stress. Henderson and his colleagues (Henderson *et al*. 1981) undertook a major study of the relationship between social networks and neurotic disorder in Canberra.

Inspired by Bowlby, Henderson set out to test the 'social bond hypothesis' that deficiency in social relationships, or 'anophelia', is a causal factor in the onset of neurosis. He devised the Interview Schedule for Social Interaction (ISSI) as a way of measuring the adequacy of a person's actual and perceived social support both in the past and in their current situation. Using a General Practice community sample (that is, one with relatively low morbidity), they failed to confirm their original hypothesis, finding *no* association between morbidity and impairment of present or past social relationships. What they did find, to their surprise, was that a person's *perception* of the adequacy of their relationships did, in the face of adversity, have a big impact on whether or not they succumbed to anxiety and depression. In their epidemiological study it was not possible to tease out whether this perception was an accurate reflection of their performance, whether it was a manifestation of a 'complainant attitude' on the part of the affected individual, or whether there was a self-fulfilling pattern in which people who see their relationships as inadequate evoke unsatisfactory responses from their intimates. They conclude that 'the causes of neurosis lie much more within the person than within the social environment', and suggest, rather despairingly, that the attempt to provide good relationships for potential patients is unlikely to be an effective strategy in preventive psychiatry.

Attachment Theory suggests that this pessimistic viewpoint is unwarranted. First, we have seen that secure attachment is associated not so much with the absence of childhood disruption and trauma, as with 'autobiographical competence' – that is, the ability to give a balanced account of difficulty and the capacity for emotional processing of painful events in the past. Second, the evidence is that the 'social environment' *does* influence neurosis, but further back in the causal chain than Henderson was able to look, via the internalisation of childhood attachment patterns. Third, if perception of inadequate relationships is the crucial issue, rather than the relationships themselves, then any psychotherapeutic technique which can alter that perception, whether directly as in cognitive therapy, or indirectly as in analytic and systemic therapies, is likely to be helpful.

Armed with this optimism, let us look now at a number of different psychiatric disorders from the perspective of attachment theory.

ABNORMAL GRIEF

In his early work, Bowlby was keen to establish the reality of childhood mourning in the face of those who disputed whether children were able to experience the same full gamut of emotions as adults (Bowlby 1960d). The fact that adults *do* grieve is in itself evidence for the continuing importance of attachment throughout life. Parkes (1975; 1985; Parkes and Weiss 1983) has shown how the quality of the relationship broken by the death influences the course of mourning. Pathological grief can be divided into four distinct patterns. First is the *unexpected grief syndrome*: major losses which are unexpected or untimely, characterised by shock and disbelief and a persisting sense of the presence of the dead person. In the face of major trauma, securely attached people are as vulnerable as the less secure, and Parkes *et al.* (1991) found that 100 per cent of those referred with abnormal grief to his clinic whose capacity to trust themselves and others was good, had had sudden, unexpected or multiple bereavements. In *delayed grief*, seen typically in people with an avoidant attachment style, the patient characteristically lacks emotional response to the loss, feels numb and unable to cry, and cannot find any satisfaction in relationships or distractions. In the *ambivalent grief syndrome*, the previous relationship was stormy and difficult, often with many quarrels and much misery. Initially, the bereaved person may feel relief, and that they have 'earned their widowhood'. Later, however, intense pining and self-reproach may follow, with the sufferers blaming themselves in an omnipotent way for the death of their partners, based on the earlier unconscious or semi-conscious wishes that they would die. In *chronic grief* the sufferer becomes locked into a state of despair from which there seems no escape. These people have usually shown lifelong dependency on parents and partners. Often such dependency may mask ambivalence, and the unearthing of negative feelings can be the chink through which new life begins to appear.

MRS W: I can't bear to look

Mrs W, a fifty-year-old housewife, had been in a state of chronic grief since the death of her grandmother three years previously. She was unable to carry on looking after the house or caring for her twenty-year-old daughter, herself handicapped with agoraphobia. She was tearful and apathetic, had failed to respond to antidepressants, and her husband and GP were at their wits' end. Referred for psychotherapy, she described how she had to avert her gaze on going past her grandmother's house, tried to avoid going near it although this often meant inconvenient diversions, and could not possibly visit her uncle who still lived there.

When she was a child her father had been away in the war, but on his return when she was four, her mother promptly went off with another man, and she had had no contact with her since. She was brought up by her maternal grandmother to whom she felt close, but who ruled with a rod of iron. When she was eleven, her father remarried and she was summoned to live with him and her stepmother. She was never happy with them, and she spent her teens oscillating between her grandmother and father. At eighteen she left home, made two disastrous marriages, and eventually met her present husband, twenty years her senior, who was very 'good' and 'understanding', but, she felt, was unable to understand her grief and was intolerant of her tears.

Offered brief therapy based on 'guided mourning' (Mawson *et al.* 1981), she brought photographs of her grandmother which, initially, she could only look at with great difficulty. Mixed with her reverence and awe towards her grandmother, a new theme began to emerge – anger at the way her mother had been 'written off' and had become a forbidden subject not to be mentioned in the grandmaternal home. With therapeutic prompting, Mrs W made enquiries about her mother, found that she had died and visited her grave. Then she happened to bump into her maternal uncle at the local supermarket and was able to talk to him for the first time since her grandmother's death. She then went to the house, at first just looking at it from the outside, later going inside. When therapy came to an end after eight sessions her depressive symptoms had lifted and she felt better 'than for years' although she remained overinvolved with her daughter.

DEPRESSION

Attachment Theory has made an important contribution to current thinking about the social causes of depression. Freud's (1917) speculation about the relationship between current loss and melancholia has been repeatedly confirmed by studies showing how adverse life events can precipitate depression. His linking of depression with childhood loss has also been confirmed, although not without controversy. The balance of evidence (Brown and Harris 1978; Tennant 1988) suggests that early loss of their mother, especially if accompanied by disruption and lack of care, makes a person more vulnerable to depression when faced with adversity in adult life. Harris and Bifulco (1991) have tracked the interweaving of social and psychological variables in their Walthamstow study of a group of women who had lost their mothers in childhood. They found, as predicted, that this group of women had significantly raised rates of depression compared with non-bereaved women: one in three versus one in ten. The strand of social causation starts with early loss of mother, whether through death or separation, leading to lack of care in childhood. This is linked, in the teens of the patient-to-be, with high rates of pre-marital pregnancy. This in turn leads to poor choice of partner, so that when these women, often living in disadvantaged circumstances and therefore prone to large amounts of stress, experience loss they are more likely to have unsupportive or non-existent partners, and so to develop depression.

Harris and Bifulco's 'Strand 2', the psychological, centres on a sense of hopelessness and lack of mastery in both the childhood and current circumstances of the depressed patient. As children their depressed patients had not only lost their mothers, but also felt utterly helpless – unable to protest or grieve or retrieve or be comforted, like Bowlby's little patient who, at the age of nine, on the day when his mother died, was told to go and play in his nursery and not to make such a fuss (Bowlby 1979c). When they were adults the feeling of helplessness persisted: when they became pregnant, they coped badly with it. Their perception of their current relationships played a big part in determining whether or not they became depressed; the more helpless they felt, the greater the chance of depression, and when they felt some degree of effectiveness they were protected from it.

Harris and Bifulco (1991) distinguish between a general sense of hopelessness and lack of mastery and what they call 'vulnerable attachment styles' – that is, difficulty in interpersonal relationships. Depression was much more likely in those who showed evidence of poor relating and especially interpersonal hostility. It seems that it is the interpersonal aspect of hopelessness (as opposed to things like managing money and housework) that matters most. We have seen that it is precisely this interpersonal dimension that is formative in insecure attachments: mothers who had difficulty in attuning to their infants and who showed unpredictable hostility were more likely to have anxiously attached children.

Brown and Harris (1978) see *self-esteem* as the key psychological variable in the genesis of depression. As Pedder (1982) points out, to have good self-esteem is to have internalised a two-person relationship in which one bit of the self feels good about another. This is the good internal object of psychoanalytic theory, arising out of the responsiveness of the mother – the mother who not only feeds, but recognises one as a person, is sensitive to one's feelings and moods, whom one can influence, and with whom one can, through play, create and re-create, in the 'present moment' (Hanh 1990), the spontaneity of love.

Brown's group have also suggested a relationship between the age at which the mother is lost, the circumstances of the loss, and subsequent symptom formation. The earlier and more sudden the loss, the more likely the chance of depression, and the greater the chance that the depression will be psychotic rather than neurotic in character. Pedder relates this to the Kleinian notion of the 'depressive position' (see Chapter 5). Children who have not yet developed an internal image of a whole, good mother, safe from destruction by angry attacks, will, when depressed, be more likely to despair and feel overwhelmed with depression. Older children, who do have some sense of a whole mother, or who have had at least an inkling that loss is imminent, will react to her loss with anger and attempts to retrieve her through suicidal gestures or psychosomatic illness. Pedder (1982) relates this to

> several particular clinical situations that must be familiar to many psychotherapists which reflect this protesting state of affairs and make mourning for the lost person very difficult. One is when a parent absents themselves by suicide; another when a marital partner is left unwillingly by the other; or when

a psychotherapist abandons a patient without due warning. In all such cases there is a special problem to internalise any good version of the departing person.

(Pedder 1982)

Bowlby (1980) suggested there were three typical patterns of vulnerable personality arising out of anxious attachment: ambivalent attachment, compulsive care-giving and detachment. The Walthamstow study confirmed the importance of the first two, but found, contrary to expectation, that detachment actually protected against depression. There are two possible explanations for this. One is that their measures were not sensitive enough to distinguish between healthy autonomy (which is a form of mastery) and compulsive detachment (which is not). The second is that detachment may be connected more with borderline personality disorder than depression, a possibility we shall consider below.

Harris and Bifulco (1991) were studying only a small sub-group of depressed patients: although people who have been bereaved in childhood appear to be more vulnerable to low self-esteem and so to depression in later life, the majority of depressives come from intact homes. Parker's Parental Bonding Instrument (Parker 1983) is an attempt, via retrospective accounts, to reconstruct the family atmosphere in patients' childhoods, searching for *qualitative* features of parenting which may predispose to depression. Parker isolates a particular combination of low care and overprotection which he calls 'affectionless control' that is especially corrrelated with neurotic depression: in one study it was present in nearly 70 per cent of patients but in only 30 per cent of controls. Affectionless control conjures up a childhood in which the potential patient lacks a secure parental base, and at the same time is inhibited in exploratory behaviour, thereby reducing the two ingredients of self-esteem: good internal objects and a feeling of competence and mastery.

One of the strengths of Attachment Theory is that it brings together past and present influences, the social and the psychological, providing a comprehensive picture of the varied factors which result in the development of a psychiatric disorder. Bowlby (1988c) gives a vivid picture of this epigenetic process. There is

[a] chain of adverse happenings. For example, when a young woman has no caring home base she may become desperate

to find a boyfriend who will care for her. That, combined with her negative self-image, makes her all too likely to settle precipitately for some totally unsuitable young man. Premature pregnancy and childbirth are then likely to follow, with all the economic and emotional difficulties entailed. Moreover, in times of trouble, the effects of her previous adverse experiences are apt to lead her to make unduly intense demands on her husband and, should he fail to meet them, to treat him badly. No wonder one in three of these marriages break up.

Gloomy though these conclusions are, we must remember that a disastrous outcome is not inevitable. The more secure an attachment a woman has experienced during her early years, we can confidently predict, the greater will be her chance of escaping the slippery slope.

(Bowlby 1988c)

AGORAPHOBIA

In *Separation* (1973a), Bowlby puts forward a theory of agoraphobia based on the notion of anxious attachment. He sees agoraphobia, like school phobia, as an example of separation anxiety. He quotes evidence of the increased incidence of family discord in the childhoods of agoraphobics compared with controls, and suggests three possible patterns of interaction underlying the illness: role reversal between child and parent, so that the potential agoraphobic is recruited to alleviate parental separation anxiety (this may well have happened with Mrs W's daughter in the case described above); fears in the patient that something dreadful may happen to her mother while they are separated (often encouraged by parental threats of suicide or abandonment, Bowlby believed); and fear that something dreadful might happen to herself when away from parental protection.

Central to the theory and treatment of phobic disorders is the idea that painful feelings and frightening experiences are suppressed and avoided rather than faced and mastered. In what Bowlby first described as 'the suppression of family context' (Bowlby 1973a) and later 'on knowing what you are not supposed to know and feeling what you are not supposed to feel' (Bowlby 1988a), he hypothesised that the potentially phobic adult has first been exposed to trauma – such as witnessing parental suicide attempts, or being a victim of sexual abuse – and then subjected to intense pressure to 'forget' what has happened, either by the use of overt threats, as often happens in sexual abuse, or by denial – as, for example, when a grandmother brings up her daughter's illegitimate offspring as one of her own, and the child is led to believe that her true mother is her older sister. The use of denial means that the child does not have the experience of emotional processing of painful affect, and so cannot, as described in Chapter 6, achieve the autobiographical competence that is a hallmark of secure attachment. Liotti (1991) sees in phobic disorders a dissociation between the physiological concomitants of anxiety and the 'meaning structures' that go with them. The events which might make a child anxious cannot be linked up into mental schemata which would enable that child to face and overcome them. When, as adults, such individuals experience shock or conflict, they focus merely on the symptoms of panic, and not on the events which triggered them. He advocates an exploratory form of cognitive psychotherapy which does not merely require exposure to the feared stimulus, but also encourages self-exploration so that emotions and the relationships which evoke them can begin to be linked together in a meaningful way.

Morbid jealousy and agoraphobia

David was a fifty-year-old ex-taxi-driver who developed panic attacks whenever he was separated from his wife, even for half an hour, and could not go out of the house unaccompanied. Her life was made increasingly miserable by his possessiveness, and his ceaseless questioning of her when she returned from brief excursions to visit their daughter. During David's attacks he was convinced that he would die and frequently was rushed to hospital casualty departments with suspected heart attacks. He initially described his childhood as 'all right', that he had few childhood memories, and that 'what's past is past'. Then, in the second session, when asked again about his childhood he began to cry and talked about his terrors on being left alone by his mother who was a night-club 'hostess', about never having known his father, and his misery and confusion about the different men with whom she lived. When it was gently suggested that he must have felt very jealous of these men, and that there might be some connection between this and his present attitude towards his wife, he became extremely distressed and recounted how at the age of twelve he had attacked one of these men with a knife and was taken to a remand home as a result. In subsequent sessions he began to reveal his depression much more openly, and was gradually able to tolerate being on his own for increasing periods of time.

ATTACHMENT STYLES AND EXPRESSED EMOTION IN SCHIZOPHRENIA

It has repeatedly been stressed that Bowlby's early ideas of a simple relationship between, for example, childhood bereavement and depression, maternal deprivation and psychopathy, or anxious attachment and agoraphobia, have had to be modified into much more complex causal models in which early experience, current life situation, adverse events, personality, and mental set all contribute to outcome. It is unlikely that there is a simple relationship between particular attachment patterns in infancy and specific psychiatric diagnoses in adult life.

In considering psychoses, this multifactorial approach has to be further extended to include genetic and biochemical or even infective influences. Nevertheless, social psychiatry has firmly established the importance of the environment in determining the course of schizophrenic illness (Leff and Vaughn 1983). Patients living in families in which there is high 'Expressed Emotion' (EE) – especially high levels of hostility or overinvolvement – are much more likely to relapse than those who live with calmer, less hostile, less overinvolved relations. The effect of EE is not specific to schizophrenia, and also influences, for instance, the course of manic-depression, Alzheimer's disease and diabetes. The prevalence of high EE in the general population is unknown, but in families of schizophrenic patients about one-third are high in EE. It seems at least possible that there is a relationship between EE and anxious attachment, which also affects about one-third of the population. The two main patterns of high EE, hostility and overinvolvement, correspond with those found in anxious attachment; that is, avoidant and ambivalent attachment. The mothers of avoidant infants, it will be recalled, tend to show hostility and to brush their children aside when they approach, while the ambivalent mothers are inconsistent and intrusive. Both patterns can be understood in terms of boundaries. The avoidant mothers feel invaded by their children and tend to maintain a rigid boundary around themselves, and this may lead to hostility when confronted with a mentally ill, and therefore in some ways child-like, grown-up child or spouse. Conversely, ambivalent parents cannot separate themselves from their children, and, if one becomes mentally ill as an adult, the pattern will repeat itself. Such parents cannot draw a firm boundary between themselves and their offspring because of overwhelming feelings of guilt.

Too many telephone calls

Mr P felt intensely guilty when his son Richard developed a severe schizophrenic illness at the age of twenty-two. He blamed himself for being so heavy-handed during Richard's teens, and, as a psychiatric nurse, felt from his reading of Laing and others that he must be a 'schizophrenogenic father'. He tolerated in an almost saint-like way very difficult behaviour from Richard, who would come into his parents' bedroom throughout the night asking for constant reassurance that he was not going to die, on one occasion brandishing a knife. Occasionally Mr P would flip from excessive tolerance into furious outbursts at his son, and then feel even more guilty. When Richard was admitted to hospital and moved later to a hostel, Mr P felt even more guilty, especially as Richard insisted that he hated the hostel and his only wish was to return home to his parents and brothers and sisters (of whom he showed in fact considerable jealousy).

Mr P had himself been an anxious child and had found separations from his mother very difficult, running away from his boarding school where he was sent at the age of nine on several occasions. Therapeutic attempts to create a boundary between Richard and his family were made very difficult because every attempt to do so was immediately interpreted by Mr P as a criticism of his parenting, and as carrying the implication that he was a negative influence on his son. But when it emerged that Richard would phone home from his hostel with unfailing regularity just when the family were sitting down to tea, Mr P was asked to take the phone off the hook for that half hour each evening. With much misgiving and strong feelings that he was rejecting his son, he agreed, without disastrous results, and with a general lightening of the relationship between Richard and his parents. Through this small change the family seemed to have come to accept that a firm boundary can be a mark of loving attachment rather than rejection.

BORDERLINE PERSONALITY DISORDER

Patients with borderline personality disorder (BPD) form an increasing proportion of specialist out-patient psychotherapy practice, and comprise a significant part of the work of in-patient psychiatry, often consuming time and worry disproportionate to their numbers. Despite debate about its validity as a distinct nosological entity (Rutter 1987), BPD is, for the psychodynamically minded, an indispensable concept. It is defined in the *American Diagnostic and Statistical Manual* as comprising a constellation of symptoms and behaviours which include unstable interpersonal relationships, with violent swings between idealisation and devaluation; unstable mood states; self-injurious behaviour, including deliberate self-harm and drug abuse; angry outbursts; identity disturbance with uncertainty about goals, friends, sexual orientation; and chronic feelings of emptiness and boredom. In short, there is an atmosphere of 'stable instability' (Fonagy 1991) about these patients with which most clinicians are familiar.

Empirical studies suggest that these patients have been subjected to high levels of emotional neglect and trauma in childhood, although neither is of course confined to BPD. Bryer *et al.* (1987) found that 86 per cent of in-patients with a diagnosis of BPD reported histories of sexual abuse, compared with 21 per cent of other psychiatric in-patients, and Herman *et al.* (1989) found in out-patient BPDs that 81 per cent had been subjected to sexual abuse or physical abuse or had been witness to domestic violence, as compared with 51 per cent of other out-patients. Of those who had been traumatised in this way under the age of six, the figures were 57 per cent for BPD and 13 per cent for other diagnoses.

Psychoanalysts working with these patients (for reviews, see Fonagy 1991; Bateman 1991) have emphasised the extensive use of projective identification that arises in the transference–countertransference matrix. The therapist is, as it were, used as a receptacle for the patient's feelings and may be filled with anger, confusion, fear and disgust in a way that, for the inexperienced, is unexpected and difficult to tolerate. The patient treats therapy in a very concrete way, and may become highly dependent on the therapist, seeking comfort in fusion with a rescuing object who is, at other times, felt to be sadistic and rejecting. These latter aspects emerge especially at times of breaks, or when the therapist lets the patient down, as inevitably he will through normal human error and the pressure of counter-transference.

With an approach to these patients from the perspective of Attachment Theory two issues stand out. The first concerns the oscillations of attachment (Melges and Swartz 1989) that are so characteristic of BPD, and the related question of why they persist in relationships with their families and partners (and sometimes with their 'helpers') that are so destructive. Here we are reminded of the behaviour seen in rhesus monkeys brought up on wire mothers who, when subjected to physical trauma, cling all the more tightly to the traumatising object (Harlow 1958). According to attachment theory, a frightened child will seek out their attachment figure, and if he or she is also the traumatising one a negative spiral – trauma leading to the search for security followed by more trauma – will be set up.

A second, more subtle conceptualisation of the borderline predicament has been proposed by Fonagy (1991). He suggests that the borderline experience can be understood in terms of the lack in these patients of what he calls a 'mentalising capacity'. By this he means that they lack adequate internal representation of their own or others' states of mind, especially in relation to emotions. A similar idea is contained in Main's (1991) notion of deficits in 'metacognition', the ability to think about thinking. The work of Stern and the post-Bowlbian attachment researchers suggest that maternal responsiveness is internalised by the growing child so that he or she begins to build up an idea of a self that is responded to and understood, and, reciprocally, to be able to understand and take another's point of view. Where there are difficulties in responsiveness, the child is faced with levels of excitation and pain which cannot be soothed and shaped and contained by the parent (perhaps through their own depression or inability to mentalise). Also, to represent to oneself the idea that one's parent might want to hurt or exploit one would in itself be deeply painful. Deprived of the capacity for symbolic representation of their unhappiness, and therefore the opportunity for emotional processing or transcendence, the traumatised child resorts to projective identification in which the intolerable feelings of excitation and pain are 'evacuated' into those to whom he or she is attached. For the child this is the abusing parent who is clung to with 'frozen watchfulness'; for the adult patient it is their intimates, including the therapist. The patient is temporarily relieved of mental pain, at the price of a feeling of emptiness and boredom, to be followed, as the projections are returned or further trauma arises, by yet more episodes of intolerable discomfort leading to more projection.

These speculations are given some substance by a recent Attachment Theory-inspired study by Hobson and his colleagues (Patrick *et al.* 1992), in which they compared a group of twelve borderline psychotherapy patients with a similar number of depressives. They were given Parker's Parental Bonding Instrument (PBI), mentioned above, and Main's Adult Attachment Interview (AAI), described in Chapter 6. Both groups showed Parker's 'affectionless control' constellation of low parental care and overprotection, with the BPD group demonstrating this even more clearly than the depressives, a result also found by Zweig-Frank and Parris (1991). If these retrospective accounts of childhood reflect not just a person's perception of what happened but what actually took place – and there is evidence to suggest that they do (Mackinnon *et al.* 1991) – a picture emerges of parents who were anxious but unable to respond accurately to their children, and, from the child's perspective, of an attachment figure to whom one clings, but who does not assuage one's insecurity (Heard and Lake 1986), with resulting inhibition of exploration.

Even more interesting were the results of the AAI. It will be recalled that this is a psychodynamic snapshot of a person's attachments and reactions to loss in childhood. Based on the coherence and emotional tone of the transcript, the interview is scored not so much for actual trauma as for the way a person describes it – and so is a measure of autobiographical competence (Holmes 1992). There are four possible categories: secure; insecure-dismissive; insecure-preoccupied or -enmeshed; and a fourth category, recognised after the AAI was first developed, unresolved/disorganised/disoriented, which is judged when the subject is talking about past trauma and is rated in parallel to the other categories. Thus someone who can be quite coherent for most of their narrative can still receive an unresolved classification if their story becomes incoherent when they talk about trauma. The results showed that none of the BPD group was secure, and all were classified as enmeshed, while in the depressive group four were enmeshed, six dismissive and two secure. Only two of the depressives were unresolved/disorganised, but nine of the BPDs were so classified.

The combination of enmeshment with disorganisation in relation to trauma suggested that BPD patients were wrestling with an inability to find a way of describing overwhelming mental pain – implying exactly the sort of deficit in mental representation postulated by Fonagy and Main. By contrast, several of the depressives had also been traumatised, but the effect on their linguistic coherence was much less marked.

It is clear from these studies that no one diagnostic entity can be correlated with a particular childhood constellation. 'Affectionless control' occurs in both depressive and BPD; some accounts of BPD stress avoidance, others enmeshment as childhood precursors. But the evidence in general that insecure attachment is an important developmental precursor of psychopathology is increasingly strong. Herman *et al.* (1989) suggest that qualitative differences may relate to different diagnostic outcomes, with the most severe forms of childhood trauma and parental unresponsiveness being linked to multiple personality disorder, less severe forms with BPD, and yet milder types linked to neurotic depression and anxiety. This would be consistent with Pedder's (1982) suggestion along Kleinian lines that the greater the difficulty in integrating a parental good internal object, the greater the likelihood of severe pathology.

The Bowlbian perspective on BPD has several implications for treatment. The patient will lack a sense of a secure base. Extreme forms of avoidance or ambivalence are likely. The patient may resist any emotional involvement in therapy as a defence against the trauma that close relationships have entailed in the past, leaving the therapist with the uncomfortable feeling that he is inflicting therapy on an unwilling subject. Alternatively, the patient may cling to the therapy for dear life, leaving the therapist feeling stifled and guilty about the need to lead their own life. There may be oscillations between these two positions, so that in one session the therapist feels they are really making progress, only to be faced at the next with an indifferent patient, for whom the previous advance appeared to be an illusion. The therapist may feel paralysed, apparently of no value to the patient, and yet meeting with extreme resistance if they attempt to disengage themselves. Throughout, the overwhelming task of the therapist is, as described in the previous chapter, to remain consistent and reliable, responsive and attuned to the patient's emotional states, and to be alert to the unconscious pressure to repeat (often in subtle ways) the punitive and traumatising experiences of intimacy which the patient has come to expect.

Any evidence of mentalisation or symbolisation, however fragile and transient, should be taken as an encouraging sign. This may take varied forms – humour in the session, the bringing of a dream or poem, evidence of self- or other- awareness, an outside interest in a sport or hobby – all suggesting the beginnings of a nascent capacity for exploration that indicate the development of a secure base within the therapy and in the inner world. Although consistency is essential, it is also inevitable that mistakes *will* occur under the intense transferential pressure to which the therapist is subjected. As described in the previous chapter, if handled favourably, these can provide an opportunity for the patient to re-live earlier losses and traumata in a way that they can now be grieved and processed emotionally. This should not lead to complacency on the part of the therapist, however. Winnicott's reminder to omnipotent therapists that 'we help our patients by failing' should be balanced by Bob Dylan's dictum that 'there ain't no success like failure, and failure ain't no success at all'. Finally, therapists should never underestimate the responsibility implicit in allowing attachment to develop in these patients. As Gallwey (1985) puts it:

> Any experience of being taken on, encouraged to become deeply attached, and then terminated suddenly may be catastrophic to patients who have managed to keep themselves going by avoiding precisely that type of hazard, which no amount of interpreting in the short term can possibly alleviate.

ATTACHMENT THEORY AND COMMUNITY PSYCHIATRY

We saw in Chapter 3 how Bowlby's recognition of the traumatic effects of loss and separation led to a revolution in child care, with a move towards home-based treatments and a recognition of the potentially damaging effects of institutions which cannot cater for a child's need to form secure attachments. Although the overall effects of this perspective were undoubtedly beneficial, it was used by many local authorities and government agencies anxious to save money to close down residential homes for children without providing adequate alternatives. Winnicott was sufficiently alarmed by this trend to write to Bowlby in 1955 asking him to tone down his insistence on the dangers of residential care (Rodman 1987).

A comparable revolution has taken place over the past twenty years in the provision of care for the mentally ill. Mental hospitals have been replaced by 'community care', in which patients live with their families or in hostels and group homes, and attend day centers and community clubs. Psychiatric beds are available only for 'acute' episodes of illness or distress, to tide patients through brief periods of crisis. Although many patients have benefited from the enhanced self-respect of living independent lives, there have been losses as well as gains. The emphasis on a version of autonomy that is akin to avoidance has overlooked the continuing need for dependence, which Bowlby saw as lifelong, not confined to the young and the sick. Many patients were intensely dependent on their institutions, and, due partly to their illness, partly to the increasing isolation of modern life, are unable in the 'community' to re-create the network of emotional bonds they found in the mental hospitals.

We have seen repeatedly how there has been a movement from Bowlby's early formulations of a problem in fairly simple and concrete terms, through a series of reservations and doubts, to a much more subtle appreciation of the issues involved. For example, it was not the separation from the mother alone that was damaging when a child went to hospital, but the unfamiliarity of the ward and the punitive discouragement of protest. Similarly, anxious attachment is the result not so much of gross disruptions of care or threats of abandonment (although these are of course harmful), but more a fine-tuned failure of maternal attunement and responsiveness. The problem with institutions is not that they are intrinsically harmful, any more than the 'community' is always beneficial, but the way that care is often delivered in them. We have to look much more carefully at the actual *quality* of experience that a patient has, whether it is in hospital or in 'the community', before deciding whether or not it is bad. Winnicott's list of components of a 'primary home experience' quoted in *Child*

Care and the Growth of Maternal Love (1953b) (see page 43), is as follows. Does the patient have someone to turn to who is specifically orientated towards their needs? Are the patient's basic physiological needs and physical health adequately catered for? Are the patient's needs to hate and to love recognised, and are there clear limits against which the patient can test strengths and weaknesses, and learn to differentiate between reality and phantasy? Is the patient cared for by a team that communicate with one another and in which the 'maternal' and 'paternal' functions are differentiated and harmonious?

Continuity of care is a key issue. In the past the 'stone mother' (Rey 1975) of the institution provided a backdrop of stability for the chronically mentally ill as staff and psychiatric fashions came and went. As patients moved out into the community it was hoped that a network of hostels, day centers, day hospitals, drop-in centers and other facilities could provide a network of care where they would similarly feel at home. These places offer warmth (physical and emotional), security, stimulation and responsiveness: somewhere where one can just 'be'. But these qualities are hard to quantify – and cost money.

The move now is towards discrete 'packages' of care, often on a sessional basis, which are more 'cost-effective' and financially calculable. The Community Care Bill 1993 stipulates that each chronically mentally ill patient shall have a 'care manager' who is responsible for his or her needs and who will arrange such packages of care as are appropriate. On the basis of sound Bowlbian principles, this might be thought to offer the opportunity for a patient to develop a primary attachment bond with a principal care-giver, and to get away from the impersonality and rigidity of institutions. But it may well illustrate the difficulty of translating psychological theories into policy decisions. The reality of the new arrangements is likely to be very far from the Bowlbian ideal. Each care worker will have a large case load of patients living in the community for whom they will be responsible. Staff turnover is likely to be high and the chance of staff burn-out great. Ripped away from the concrete care of a stable if inflexible institution to which they were attached, very damaged patients will be expected to develop an internal secure base which, given the nature of their illness and its antecedents, they are likely to find impossible. The care workers are likely to be working largely alone, unsupported and unsupervised and yet expected to deliver good outcomes. Their position will be not unlike that of the unsupported mothers whom the feminists accused Bowlby of idealising in their critique of maternal deprivation (see Chapter 3). The need for support for carers, and a recognition that psychologically damaged patients who have lost their attachments will need many years of connection to a stable and secure place before that experience can be hoped to be internalised enough for them to 'move on', has not been sufficiently recognised by policy makers in search of quick and easy solutions to the problems of mental illness and personal growth.

A similar conflict between the need for stable attachments and the complexity and commercial pressures of modern life affect acute psychiatric admission wards (Holmes 1993). Two examples illustrate the point. Hospital nurses work on a shift system, which means that a patient newly admitted to hospital may be looked after by an ever-changing group of carers, thereby reinforcing that patient's difficulties in attachment and sense of isolation. Second, the introduction of market forces into health care means that there is a huge pressure for rapid turnover of patients and to increase 'throughput' in psychiatric beds. However, this is inimical precisely to the needs of patients for the gradual formation of an attachment to a ward and to a group of carers, a process which takes much time and professional skill if the many tentative advances and retreats, and the small but significant gains which underlie difficulty and destructiveness, are to be understood. Kernberg (1975) calls these divergent pressures the 'concentric' (that is, familial) and 'non-concentric' (namely, administrative) vectors within a caring environment. It would be Utopian to wish for a system of care in which all non-concentric pressures were subservient to the needs of patients and workers for a secure base within which to work. Nevertheless, for a caring environment to be 'good enough', there has at least to be the opportunity to discuss, protest and mourn the unavoidable limitations of political and social reality, an area where the psychotherapist has, through consultation and conducting sensitivity groups, a vital contribution to make to the practice of general psychiatry. It is to these wider issues and to the social implications of Attachment Theory that, in the final chapter, we shall now turn.

Chapter 10

Attachment Theory and society

Man and woman power devoted to the production of material goods counts a plus in all our economic indices. Man and woman power devoted to the production of happy, healthy, and self-reliant children in their own homes does not count at all. We have created a topsy turvy world. . . . The society we live in is . . . in evolutionary terms . . . a very peculiar one. There is a great danger that we shall adopt mistaken norms. For, just as a society in which there is a chronic insufficiency of food may take a deplorably inadequate level of nutrition as its norm, so may a society in which parents of young children are left on their own with a chronic insufficiency of help take this state of affairs as its norm.

(Bowlby 1988a)

Running throughout Bowlby's life and work there is a strong moral and social vision. His credo might be summarised as follows, couched, as it so often was, in the language of preventive medicine. The emotional deprivation of children is a social ill, distorting and degrading the fabric of social life. It is society's responsibility and duty to remedy this ill by appropriate social medicine. This requires the recognition of the problem through the acceptance of the findings of psychological science; training cadres of child-care workers and psychotherapists who are sensitive to the emotional needs of children and their parents; helping people to find security in their lives through the fostering of close emotional bonds; encouragement of the expression of grief and disappointment when they are disrupted. Devaluation of the need for love and intimacy through the scorning of 'spoiling' and 'dependency' contribute to emotional deprivation. The celebration of mother-love and of our mutual dependency as a species should be encouraged. In these ways the vicious circles of deprivation can be broken, this generation's insecure young people no longer condemned to reproduce their own insecurities in the next.

These attitudes permeate almost every paragraph Bowlby wrote and informed his purposes in whatever sphere they were applied. In two articles written soon after the end of the war (Bowlby 1946b, 1947a) he made his social views even more explicit. In 'The therapeutic approach in sociology' he puts forward his uncompromising environmentalism:

> whether a person grows up with a strong capacity to make good personal relations – to be good – or whether he grows up with a very indifferent capacity for this depends very greatly on something which has never traditionally been regarded as part of ethics – namely on what his relation to his mother was in early life.
>
> (Bowlby 1947a)

He picks up Kurt Lewin's concept of the 'social field' and applies it to delinquency: good environments create good citizens, bad ones, bad. He contrasts three styles of social arrangements: democratic, authoritarian and *laissez-faire*. Only the democratic – one in which leaders and teachers listen and are responsive to the people – is effective:

> Any organisation, industrial, commercial, national, religious or academic, organised on authoritarian lines must therefore be regarded as inimical to the promotion of good personal relations, of goodness. And that goes for our daily lives . . . in so far as we are authoritarian in our attitude towards others we are promoting bad personal relations and evil.
>
> (Bowlby 1947a)

Poised in that statement can be felt the full weight of Bowlby's two contrary sets of experiences. On the one side are his 'town' mother with her overwhelming sense of 'rightness' inherited from 'Grampy', his remote and rather frightening father, the boarding schools, the Navy, the medical hierarchy, the narrow horizons of Psycho-Analytical Society, military authoritarianism; on the other, his intellectual curiosity, inner calm, independence and resilience, his 'country' mother with her love of nature, the 'invisible college' of Army psychiatrists, his personal optimism and that of the times. He continues:

> the drive of the organism towards achieving good personal relations is just as real and persistent as its drive towards physical health. People don't get well because doctors say they ought to get well: they get well because the living organism has a powerful biological drive to throw off noxious influences.
> (Bowlby 1947a)

In his celebration of democracy, Bowlby makes a link between the kind of responsiveness and attunement that good parents provide for their children, and the social arrangements which he saw as most likely to produce flourishing citizens. In 'Psychology and democracy' (1946b), with characteristic boldness and simplicity he tackles the central dilemma of political science: how to reconcile the need for social co-operation with the equally pressing but to some extent incompatible need for individual freedom. He compares the task of the political leader with that of the trusted parent who fosters collaboration among children by showing them that renouncing selfish individual pleasures will result in the ultimately greater enjoyment of shared play. Social co-operation depends on the combination of a population who, through positive childhood experiences, have learned to love and trust, with leaders who, through their democratic attitudes, are prepared to listen to the people, to show they are valued and respected.

All this may sound simplistically anodyne to our late-twentieth-century ears, attuned as we are to the ever-increasing toll of destruction and chaos man has wreaked upon himself and his environment. The Bowlbian ideal of a mother exclusively devoted to the care of her children is, in a contemporary perspective, both unrealistic and undesirable. The pattern of 'absent father – patriarchal society' (Leupnitz 1988) produces mothers who are stretched to their emotional and economic limits, barely able to provide any kind of secure base for their children. New family patterns, unimagined by Bowlby, are emerging, often with fathers who may be biologically unrelated to the children in their care, increasing the likelihood of insecurity or frank physical and sexual abuse. Bowlby's simple formulation of aggression as a response to the threat of loss seems to lack explanatory weight in the face of increasing social chaos. Yet the fundamental principles of

Attachment Theory – that parents need security themselves if they are to provide it for their children, that the threat to security is a potent cause of rage and destruction – remain valid, despite changing conditions. Bowlby may have been mistaken and simplistic in thinking that his experience with disturbed children could be translated simply from the language of psychology to that of sociology, but the challenge thrown down at them by him at the start of this chapter remains.

The Freud (1929) of *Civilization and its Discontents* came late (Pedder 1992) but decisively to the view that destructiveness and aggression were inherent features of the human psyche:

> I can no longer understand how we can have overlooked the ubiquity of non-erotic aggressivity and destructiveness and can have failed to give it its due place in our interpretation of life. . . . In consequence of this primary mutual hostility of human beings, civilized society is perpetually threatened with disintegration.
>
> (Freud 1929)

In his early work (Durbin and Bowlby 1938), Bowlby accounts for aggression in ethological terms as arising from the need for territorial defence and (what amounts to the same thing) defence of breeding and feeding rights. Later, from the perspective of Attachment Theory, he seems to abandon the notion of primary aggressivity altogether, perhaps as part of his overall project to distance himself from the Kleinian approach (Bowlby 1973a). Instead, he sees aggression as springing from insecure attachment. Anxious attachment is a defence, a compromise between the need for security in a dangerous world and the inability of the parent to provide a secure base. Similarly, despair or rage are seen as part of the grief response, frustrated attempts to recover the lost object. In the Bowlbian perspective meaning is imperative: the world must be patterned into some meaningful shape at all costs; what little security there is must be husbanded, shielded from envious eyes; loss cannot be comprehended as total and arbitrary, but construed as recoverable, however much distortion of reality this requires. The avoidant child keeps his distance, warily watching the parent whom he both needs and fears. The ambivalent child clings helplessly to his unpredictable mother. Neither feels free to explore creatively. The disorganised child is defenceless, overwhelmed by stimulus which cannot be organised into any meaningful pattern. Here, where there may have been absolute privation of care in the pre-attachment phase (that is, before six months) may be found the germs of purpose-less destruction and rage.

By analogy, societies can also be seen as dealing with problems of security in many defensive ways. Insularity, suspiciousness, splitting, inability to relate generously, vengeance, chaos, inter-necine struggles, intolerance, exhaustion, corruption – countless examples of these phenomena can be found in social and political life just as much as in individual psychology, and each has its 'meaning', ideologies that evade, justify, excuse. Since, according to Attachment Theory, adults have attachment needs no less press-ing at times of stress than those of children, the same processes which lead to insecure attachment in infants can be seen operating at a societal level. Attachment Theory offers a mechanism that connects the political with the personal. As Marris puts it:

> This is the . . . link between sociological and psychological understanding: the experience of attachment, which so pro-foundly influences the growth of personality, is itself both the product of a culture, and a determinant of how that culture will be reproduced in the next generation – not only the culture of attachment itself, but all our ideas of order, authority, security, and control.
>
> (Marris 1991)

Attachment Theory shows how the minutiae of interpersonal experience become internalised as personality, or attachment style. Much remains to be understood about the precise ways in which handling in the parent–infant relationship influences future character, but there is little doubt that there is a connection between them. Facing outwards as well as in, Attachment Theory also suggests an articulation between intrafamilial experience and social forces. In their personal relationships people face uncer-tainty or security, poverty or riches, loss or plenitude, violence or compassion, unpredictability or responsiveness, neglect or care. This will affect their capacity to care for their children, which in turn affects how secure or insecure those children will be when they become adults. The insecurity or otherwise of its citizens will affect the general cultural and economic conditions of society, and thus the cycle is complete as these factors have their impact on child care in the next generation.

Marris (1991) has used this model of cycles of security or insecurity as a metaphor for the increasing polarisation between the secure and the marginalised in modern societies (and this could be extended to international polarisation between rich and poor nations). On the basis of his work in inner cities, Marris argues that cycles of disadvantage, deriving from social factors which include poverty, poor housing, unemployment, cultural deprivation, educational disadvantage, bad health and diet, are experienced as an emptiness or evacuation of meaning, equivalent to that felt by a bereaved person whose meaning-structures are destroyed by loss. As he puts it:

> the more likely our environment is to engender unintelligible, unexpected, and disruptive events, the less support we have, and the more our confidence in attachment has been undermined or distorted by the experiences of childhood, then the more likely it is that our vital organisations or meaning will be overwhelmed, or crippled in their development. Or to put this the other way about – a society that best protected its members from grief and depression would organise its relationships so that they were as stable, predictable, understandable, and careful of attachments as is humanly possible. And the qualities of behaviour that would need to inform such relationships – sensitivity, responsiveness, mutual understanding, consistency, ability to negotiate – are very much the same as those which create secure attachment. I believe such a familial conception of social order is attractive to most of us: our need to nurture and to be nurtured, to make attachment secure, to see the meaning of our lives confirmed by the meaning of society at large, all respond to it. Yet at the same time we have powerful impulses pulling us in the opposite direction, towards an unequal, unsupportive distribution of uncertainty.
>
> (Marris 1991)

Where security is in short supply it is *contested*, whether in families (Byng-Hall 1991c) or society. For Freud, rivalry and ambivalence are inherent properties of the Oedipal situation and therefore of the human condition. For Bowlby, ambivalence is the result of maternal privation, *not* found with the 'ordinary devoted mother', who is adequately supported by her spouse, family and society. Nevertheless, suboptimal child rearing is widespread, and the ambivalently attached child clings ferociously to a mother whose attention might otherwise be diverted elsewhere – towards her other children, her partner or her own inner concerns. Between parents and children there is an inherent asymmetry. It is a parent's job to provide a secure base for children, but not vice versa. Bowlby repeatedly points to role reversal between parent and child as one of the commoner manifestations of anxious attachment, one that inevitably inhibits the exploratory capacities of the child. Sexual and physical abuse of children are extreme examples of exploitation of this asymmetry. The exploitation of women by men is another example, in which a little boy's helplessness in relation to his mother and the fear that engenders when there is no feeling of a secure base is reversed (and avenged) when he grows up and can use his physical strength to dominate a woman.

So too, Marris argues, in an unequal society, there is competition for security. Security becomes a commodity to which the rich cling, pushing insecurity to the margins of society, which then acts as a buffer zone between themselves and the vagaries of international finance and world trade which determine ultimately their economic fate (Marris 1991). And yet if we take seriously the Bowlbian vision of an essential interdependence of attachments, then this too will be seen as a defensive distortion, a variant of anxious attachment that perverts the notion of a secure base and inhibits the creative development of society. As Rustin (1991) puts it:

> The idea of development and fulfilment of the person through relationship, both internal and external . . . is a distinctively social one. . . . It goes against the widespread idea that society will be better when and if we merely give more opportunity and goods to the individual. It is the quality of relationships that individuals can generally have with others around them . . . which make for contentment and creativity, not merely gratifications of various kinds. The most beautiful house with a swimming pool is obtained at serious psychic price when there has to be an armed man at the gate to keep out intruders. Serious damage must also be done to the quality of experience of 'liberty' when its defence depends on threats to inflict total destruction.
>
> (Rustin 1991)

We are living in an era in which much that we have taken for granted is breaking down. All that is solid melts into air. It is the time of the breaking of nations. Alongside the sense of freedom, the celebration of ethnic and cultural pride and a recognition of the need to mourn past traumata, there is an increase in destructive nationalism and tribal violence. Increasingly polluted by the products of the scramble for security, the Earth itself – Mother Earth – is no longer a safe haven on which we can depend to detoxify our waste and provide a base for new growth (Lovelock 1979).

For Freud, a deep awareness of natural beauty – the oceanic feeling – was an idealisation, a projection of a pure pleasure ego uncontaminated by pain, separation and rage. He was always uncertain about the boundaries between normality and neurosis, and particularly about the distinction between aesthetic experience and pathological states (Rycroft 1985). For Freud, the basic goal of life was the search for happiness based on physical satisfaction – he saw this as inevitably doomed to disappointment. Bowlby's emphasis on security provides a more realisable aim. His vision of the harmonious reciprocity of the responsive mother and her infant offers a metaphor for a balanced relationship between man and his environment that is healthy and not based on splitting and idealisation. A secure child can cope with temporary separation and sub-optimal conditions by healthy protest and non-defensive grief. If a secure base can be achieved, exploration of possible ways out of our political and ecological crisis is possible. In a prescient statement about the dangers of nuclear weapons, Bowlby wrote:

> All our previous experience points inescapably to the conclusion that neither moral exhortation nor fear of punishment will succeed in controlling the use of this weapon. Persons bent on suicide and nations bent on war, even suicidal war, are deterred by neither. The hope for the future lies in a far more profound understanding of the nature of the emotional forces involved and the development of scientific social techniques for modifying them.
>
> (Bowlby 1947a)

A small but significant example of the kind of 'understanding' and 'technique' which Bowlby advocates can be found in Middleton's (1991) description of Sherif's Boys Camp Experiment, in which thirty teenagers were taken for a month's camping in the wilderness by a group of psychologists working as camp attendants. The boys were divided into two groups who ate, slept and played separately. Rather like in Golding's *Lord of the Flies*, two distinct cultures of behaviour, slang and group identity developed. When members of the two groups met, scuffles broke out. The experimenters then arranged for the food lorry to break down some miles from the camp, which meant that the two groups had to collaborate in bringing essential supplies to their base. The results were as follows:

> After some initial prevarication and quarrelling, the two groups coalesced into a larger and sufficiently coherent and cohesive group for this essential task. As this happened the stereotyping, antipathy and intense competition between the groups also dissolved as they worked together in pursuit of their mutual interest.
>
> (Middleton 1991)

The discovery of a superordinate goal enabled the two groups to collaborate. The leadership provided them with a secure base from which they could explore ways collectively to solve their common problem.

The ecological vicious circle the world faces is one in which, confronted with a threat to the environment and therefore to the fundaments of security, nations, and where nations break down tribal groups, fight ever more desperately to extract what resources they can from it. This is rather like the children of abusive parents who, in their fear, cling to the very object that causes their distress. The common objective of global security needs to be made real if this vicious cycle is to be put into reverse, just as the skilled therapist will see that both abusive parent and child are in search of a safety that neither can provide for the other, and, as far as possible will try to remedy this herself, or mobilise others who can do so. If we feel locally secure, with a home base which we know will be respected and protected, there will be less need to project of insecurity onto others. Secure as inhabitants of our locality, we become free to explore our citizenship of the world. As the Sicilian writer Gesualdo Bufalino puts it:

> Now I finally know this simple truth: that it is not only my right but my duty to declare myself a citizen of Everywhere

as well as of a hamlet tucked away in the Far South between the Iblei Mountains and the sea; that it is my right and duty to allow a place in my spirit for both the majestic music of the universe and that of the jet gushing from a fountain in the middle of a little village square, on the far southern bastions of the West.

(Bufalino 1992)

For Freud, our biological heritage was a shackle, creating an inevitable conflict between our selfish and drive-driven nature and the repressions of culture. In his vision of alienation we are prisoners of our paleocortex. Bowlby's more benign picture (the contrast between the two men is partly a reflection of the differing cultural heritage – one a European Jew, the other a member of the English upper middle classes) implies a need to re-establish connections with our evolutionary past. Humans survived and evolved on the basis of bonding and mutual support. Competition and the neglect of these basic ties threaten to destroy us. Nomads and agriculturalists, explorers and stay-at-homes, male and female, men and women of contemplation and of action, pursuers of the inner and outer worlds, psychologists and politicians, yogis and commissars – we all share a need for common security. We are all attached inescapably to an Earth in whose 'environment of evolutionary adaptedness' we originated, and which we now threaten with destruction as we are caught in the vortex of a negative spiral of insecurity.

Chapter 11

Epilogue

Sow a thought and you may reap an act; sow an act and you
reap a habit; sow a habit and you reap a personality; sow a
personality and you reap a destiny.

(Buddhist proverb; Jones 1985)

We ended the previous chapter with a rhetorical flourish which
John Bowlby, however much he approved of its sentiment, would
probably have considered overstated, insufficiently underpinned
by close-grained scientific fact. This is perhaps excusable as we
near the end of this book. As suggested in the Introduction, the
biographer is both patient and therapist to his subject. At the
end of therapy a patient will often yearn for a 'verdict' and ask,
implicitly or explicitly, 'Well, what do you really think of me,
what is your opinion?' But the therapist has already done his
work, said all he can say in the course of the therapy. What
more can he add? In the CAT model of brief therapy (Ryle
1990), this dilemma is met by the introduction of the 'farewell
letter' which the therapist presents to the patient in the penulti-
mate session. This attempts to summarise the patient's strengths
and weaknesses, the progress that has been made in therapy, and
some predictions for the future. This heterodoxy is not, it should
be noted, the exclusive preserve of eclectic therapists like Ryle:
Clifford Scott records that the most moving moment of his analysis with Melanie Klein in the 1930s occurred when she read out
to him a long interpretation she had written over the weekend.
'This was proof that I was in her as well as she was in me'
(Grosskurth 1986).

Here, then, presumptuously perhaps (but is not any therapy –
or biography – an act of presumption?), is an attempt at a farewell

letter for John Bowlby, with which the reader, like the patient in CAT, is also invited to disagree, add to, reject, treasure or do what they will.

Dear John,
We are nearing the end of our time together. I would like to say how much I have enjoyed working with you and how much I have learned from our collaboration. I hope you feel that justice has been done to your work and that the boundaries of privacy which, from an early age, you placed around your feelings have been handled with sensitivity.

Like many outstanding psychologists you come from a background that was not entirely easy, although it offered you many opportunities. Perhaps one of them was the fact that your family was so delightfully unpsychological. As Gwen Raverat, granddaughter of your hero, Darwin, said of her father and his brothers (all of whom were distinguished scientists):

'They had [no] idea of the complications of psychology. They found it difficult to conceive of a mixture of motives; or of a man who says one thing and means another; or of a person who is sometimes honest and sometimes dishonest; because they were so completely single-hearted themselves.
(Raverat 1952)

Perhaps it was because you were so familiar with those to whom psychology is a mystery that you were such a good populariser.

Some of your life's work at least can be understood in terms of the problems which presented themselves to you as a small child. You were the middle boy between a very bright and vigorous older brother and a younger brother who was considered backward. Your compassion for the weak and your undoubted ambition and competitiveness bear the impress of the mould you shared with them. Your father was a distant, awe-inspiring figure, whose voice you are said to have inherited and in whose footsteps you followed into the medical profession. In terms of public recognition your achievements were at least comparable with his, although as it happens, as a resilient and independent-minded person you did not appear to seek or need external approval. Your mother – or, should we say, mothers? – seems in her urban persona to have been rather neglectful and partial in her handling of the children, but was very different on those long holidays which were such an important influence on your life and work. From her you learned the importance of nature, that as creatures we are part civilised, part wild. In middle years you kept the wild side of yourself well hidden, but it was certainly there in your early independence and rebelliousness, and emerged again as you grew older.

I suspect, like many others of your generation, you were very excited when you started your training as a psychoanalyst at the prospect of being able to apply your scientific outlook not just to the external world but also to the inner landscape of feelings. Here, in your own words (Bowlby 1973a), was a continent to conquer. In those days your views were progressive and, while never a Marxist (or indeed an anything-ist), you saw an opportunity to ameliorate psychological as well as material suffering.

Your encounter with psychoanalysis did not really live up to your expectations. Your teachers did not seem particularly interested in trying to change society. They were certainly conservative in their outlook if not in their politics. They ran their society in an authoritarian way and, to succeed, you had to submit to this, even if, as I suspect, your heart was not really in it. Your analyst was Mrs Riviere, your supervisor Melanie Klein. As one of your obituarists put it, 'it is a tribute to [your] independence to point out that neither of these two formidable ladies appear to have had the slightest effect on [your] subsequent development' (Storr 1991). That is not of course quite true because you were, as you yourself later said, determined to prove them wrong. Perhaps you thought you would 'bag' them both, like a brace of pheasants (and you were never happier than after a good day's shooting), with your theory of attachment.

The way you did this was interesting. What you did, in effect, was to appeal over their heads to the higher authority of Freud, much as you might have done as a child when, with your father away at the war in France, you might have wanted some paternal authority with which to out-trump your didactic mother and dominant older brother. First, you emphasised your common scientific outlook with Freud's, in contrast to their lack of scientific understanding. Second, you insisted that they had not really grasped the importance in Freud's late work on attachment (as opposed to instinct), and the role of loss as a cause of neurosis.

You had the social and intellectual self-confidence to challenge psychoanalytic authority – and it certainly needed challenging. But perhaps you missed out on something too. So important was it for you resist what you saw as the negative influence of these wrong-headed ideas – especially the neglect of real trauma in favour of phantasy – that you did not really allow yourself to feel the full emotional impact of psychoanalysis. The imaginative leaps, the heights and depths of emotion, the understanding of how intimate experience is engendered and gendered – you seem to have avoided these. Meanwhile, you built your case, painstakingly and slowly, that psychoanalysis – or the Kleinian version of it, at least – was on a wrong course. The effort of self-control and sustained concentration that this took may have contributed to the impression you gave to some of detachment and even arrogance.

Together with your intelligence and independence you were clearly an excellent organiser and highly efficient. These qualities brought you to the top – or nearly to the top – of your professions of psychoanalysis and child psychiatry. You were Deputy Chairman of the Tavistock and Deputy President of the Psycho-Analytical Society. But something kept you from the summit. Was it your reserve, your lack of overt warmth? Or did you value most strongly the rebellious part of you which wanted to strike out on your own rather than become too identified with an institution? You mistrusted authority, although in your own way you exercised a strong hand in your research group. Running a tight ship always was your style.

Maternal deprivation made your name. What a case you built up for the mother-love which you experienced so intermittently and unpredictably in your childhood. What a devastating criticism and idealisation of motherhood that was! And how the public loved – and hated – you for it. It is a pity that you weren't able to say more about fathers, especially as they are so much more important now in child care than they were when you began your theorising. But the principles of mothering which you put forward remain valid if we speak now instead of parenting, as long as this does not gloss over the fact that the bulk of child care is still done by mothers, who are as vulnerable and unsupported now, although in different ways, as they were when you surveyed the post-war scene in the 1940s.

And loss. What a keen eye for that you had. Your understanding of it may turn out in the end to be your greatest contribution to psychology. And yet how well hidden you kept the losses in your own life that made you so sensitive to others' grief and misery. Was it your father's absence during the war? Or the loss of your younger brother's vigour? Was it your sensitivity to your parents' grief, both of whom had lost parents in their youth – your paternal grandfather's death, your maternal grandmother's preoccupation with the younger children? Or was it Durbin – your Lycidas, a close friend cut down in his prime, trying, tragically, to save another man from drowning?

I wonder what you would have made of our contemporary emphasis on stories and narrative in psychotherapy? You were suspicious of hermeneutics and tried always to stay within the confines of evolutionary science. And yet from your work has come a line of understanding which shows how the capacity for narrative, to link the past with the present and the future in a coherent way, is a continuation of that responsive handling in infancy which you (and Winnicott) saw so clearly were the foundations of security. You made the first entries in the non-verbal grammar of mother–child interaction which is slowly being written. From this has come an understanding that it is the handling of patients by their therapists that matters, not the precision of their interpretations. There is no Bowlbian school of psychotherapy because your emphasis was on the non-verbal language of care-giving. The stories – Kleinian, Freudian or what you will – come later. You were a good story-teller yourself as your books, with their logical progressions and solid factual backing for your theories, attest. You would have agreed that the ability to tell a story is the mark of psychological health. You knew that to be able to talk about pain and loss is the best way to overcome it. You would have been fascinated by the evidence – springing mostly from your work – that securely attached babies become good story-tellers in their teens, and that they in turn have securely attached babies.

I suspect you were one of those people who grow happier as they get older. Towards the end you allowed the twinkle in your eye to show more often. You could finally start to play – your way. Perhaps you hadn't really been able to do this since the thirties. Your battle with psychoanalysis was over and you could be your own man. You returned in your last years to an authority that pre-dated Freud – Darwin, to a Victorian time when progress and order and the power of science were valued, where the battle lines were clear cut, far removed from the chaos and confusion of our post-modernist world.

What of your legacy? Attachment Theory is, as you were, vigorous and independent. If anything, it is likely to come even more into prominence in the 1990s as psychoanalysis struggles with its own need for a secure base, theoretically and economically. The demand for psychological help grows ever stronger as we contemplate the emotional casualties of capitalism; the confusion of psychotherapeutic tongues grows ever louder as the different therapies compete in the marketplace. Your still – but not so small (that 'orotund' charge still rankles) – voice would have been helpful in bringing us back to earth, to the practical questions of who needs help most and with what therapy based on what theory. You would, I think, have taken much satisfaction from the cross-fertilisations stimulated by your work – by analysts like Fonagy and Hobson using the Adult Attachment Interview to study their borderline patients, developmental psychologists like Main and Bretherton beginning to look at object-relations theory.

You were never an intrusive or dependence-creating therapist, despite your insistence on the persistence of dependency needs throughout the life cycle. You have made it so that we can manage without you. You clearly saw the two poles of insecurity – avoidance and ambivalence – and, like the good navigator you once were, tried to steer a true course between them. You could see clearly the 'hardboiledness' (your word) of your affectionless psychopaths of the 1930s reminiscent of the narrow scientism of the behaviourists on the one side, and on the other the clinging adherence to unquestioned shibboleths of the psychoanalytic orthodoxy. You saw behind them to the vulnerability they were defending. You knew that the good therapist has to cultivate a state of 'non-attachment' in which people, ideas, things are neither avoided nor clung to but are seen squarely for what they are. This non-attachment can only grow in a culture of secure attachment to parents and a society that is worthy of trust. You were a good model for such trustworthiness (even if your reliability was a bit *too* much at times for us less organised types!). On the basis of this secure attachment it is possible to face the inevitable losses and failures, the essential transience of things, and to recognise that, if circumstances allow for due grief and mourning, then out of difficulty can come a new beginning.

Yours, with affection and admiration . . .

Glossary of terms relevant to Attachment Theory

ADULT ATTACHMENT INTERVIEW (AAI)   A semi-structured psychodynamic interview in which the subject is encouraged to talk about their early attachments, their feelings about their parents, and to describe any significant losses and childhood traumata. The transcripts are then rated, not so much for content as for style, picking up features like coherence of the narrative and capacity to recall painful events. Subjects are classified into one of four categories: 'Free to evaluate attachment', 'dismissing of attachment', 'enmeshed in attitudes towards attachment', and 'unresolved/disorganised/disorientated'. When given to pregnant mothers the AAI has been shown to predict the attachment status of the infants at one year with 70 per cent accuracy (Fonagy *et al*. 1992).

AMBIVALENT ATTACHMENT   A category of attachment status as classified in the Strange Situation (q.v.). The infant, after being separated and then re-united with its mother, reacts by clinging to her, protesting in a way that can't be pacified (for instance, by arching its back and batting away offered toys), and remains unable to return to exploratory play for the remainder of the test. Associated with mothers who are inconsistent or intrusive in their responses to their babies.

ASSUAGEMENT AND DISASSUAGEMENT   Terms introduced by Heard and Lake (1986) to describe the state of satisfaction or dissatisfaction of attachment needs. The securely attached individual when re-united with an attachment figure clings to them for a few minutes and then, in a state of assuagement, can get on with exploratory activity. If the attachment figure is unable to tolerate attachment behaviour or unavailable, this produces a state of disassuagement of attachment needs associated with defensive manoeuvres such as avoidance or clinging, with consequent inhibition of exploration.

ATTACHMENT   The condition in which an individual is linked emotionally with another person, usually, but not always, someone perceived to be older, stronger and wiser than themselves. Evidence for the existence of attachment comes from proximity seeking, secure base phenomenon (q.v.) and separation protest.

ATTACHMENT BEHAVIOURAL SYSTEM This is conceived to be the basis of attachment and attachment behaviour, and comprises a reciprocal set of behaviours shown by care-seeker and care-giver in which they are aware of and seek each other out whenever the care-seeker is in danger due to physical separation, illness or tiredness.

AVOIDANT ATTACHMENT Together with ambivalent attachment (q.v.), the second main category of insecure attachment delineated in the Strange Situation (q.v.). Here the child, when re-united with its mother after a brief separation, rather than going to her for assuagement (q.v.), avoids too close contact, hovering near her in a watchful way, and is unable fully to resume exploratory play. Associated with mothers who reject or ignore their babies.

BORDERLINE PERSONALITY DISORDER (BPD) A term used rather differently by psychiatrists and psychotherapists to denote a group of difficult and disturbed patients characterised primarily by instability of mood and difficulty in sustaining close relationships. In addition, they often show self-injurious behaviour such as self-harm and drug abuse; have destructive angry outbursts; suffer from identity disturbance with uncertainty about life goals and sexual orientation; and experience chronic feelings of emptiness and boredom. Although a precise definition is difficult, the term captures the sense of an individual who often lives on the borderline of relationships, neither in nor out of them, and, psychologically, on the borderline between neurosis and psychosis.

COGNITIVE THERAPY   A form of psychotherapy associated with the work of Aaron Beck (Beck *et al.* 1979) which focuses on the patient's cognitions (i.e., thoughts) rather than emotions, based on the principle that cognitions determine feelings rather than vice versa. Thus, a depressed person may assume that everything they attempt is bound to fail, and this will lead to feelings of hopelessness and helplessness. In therapy, the patient is encouraged to monitor and challenge these automatic dysfunctional thoughts; for example, questioning whether *everything* they do really is hopeless, or only *some* things, and so begin to build up positive thoughts about themselves.

CONTROVERSIAL DISCUSSIONS (1941–44)   Series of meetings held in the aftermath of Freud's death between two factions, led by Melanie Klein and Anna Freud, in the British Psycho-Analytical Society. The two sides disagreed about theory – especially about the existence or otherwise of the death instinct, and the age at which infantile phantasies could be said to exist. Each side felt that the other had an undue influence over Training Candidates and was trying to denigrate and dismiss each other's theories. Eventually a compromise was reached in which two, and later three, streams of training were created within the society: the Kleinian, the Freudian and a third, non-aligned ('middle') group.

DEPRESSIVE   POSITION/PARANOID-SCHIZOID   POSITION   Melanie Klein's (1986) distinction between a state of mind characterised by splitting (hence the 'schizoid' aspect), in which good and bad are kept separate, and in which bad, persecutory feelings are projected onto the environment (hence the 'paranoid' aspect); and one in which good and bad are seen to be two aspects of the same thing, and which therefore leads to depressive feelings that are healthy and constructive because the sufferer is taking responsibility for their hatred and is appropriately guilty. Klein saw the infant as progressing from the paranoid-schizoid to the depressive position in the course of the early years of life. The move from one position to the other is also a feature of successful therapy. Bowlby differs from Klein in seeing splitting as a response to sub-optimal parenting, a manifestation of insecure attachment, rather than a normal phenomenon. He agrees with Klein about the importance of depression as an appropriate response to loss and separation.

EPIGENETIC   A term coined by Waddington (1977) to describe the development of a differentiated organism from a fertilised ovum. The developing embryo proceeds along a number of possible developmental pathways depending on environmental conditions. Epigenesis may be contrasted with a 'homuncular' (from 'homunculus' or 'little man') model of development in which all the stages of development are already pre-formed. Bowlby applied this distinction to psychological development, and contrasted his own approach in which there are many possible pathways which an individual may take through infancy depending on their interaction with their care-givers, with the classical Freudian approach which sees development in terms of a number of fixed 'stages' through which a person must pass, irrespective of environmental influence. He felt that his approach was more consistent with modern biological thinking, and allowed for a more subtle view of the complexity of interaction between an individual and their environment. Thus 'anxious' attachment, rather than being a 'stage', like the so-called 'oral stage' of development, becomes a possible epigenetic compromise between a child's attachment needs and a parent who is unable fully to meet them. Like Klein's 'positions', but unlike Freud's 'stages', Bowlby's attachment patterns persist throughout life, unless modified by good experiences (which would include successful therapy).

ETHOLOGY   Literally, the study of an individual's 'ethos' or character. Ethology is a biological science which studies animal behaviour in a particular way: the animal is considered as a whole; behaviour is usually studied in natural or wild conditions; there is great attention to the antecedents and consequences of behaviour patterns; the function of any behaviour is considered; and an evolutionary perspective is always taken. An attempt is made to see how the animal views the world from its own perspective and to visualise the internal 'maps' and rules which govern its activities. Ethology is contrasted with behaviourism, which usually concentrates on particular bits of behaviour and does not consider the organism as a whole and is unconcerned with evolutionary considerations. Bowlby saw the methods and theories of ethology as highly relevant to the study of human infants, and this led to a fruitful collaboration between him and the leading ethologist Robert Hinde (see Hinde 1982a and b; 1987).

EXPRESSED EMOTION (EE)   A rating scale initially developed for the relatives of patients suffering from schizophrenia (Leff and Vaughn 1983), but applicable to other disorders including affective illness and Alzheimer's disease, measuring such dimensions as 'hostility', 'warmth' and 'overinvolvement'. Patients whose relatives score high on negative 'expressed emotions' are more likely to relapse from their illness. A link is suggested between anxious attachment and high expressed emotion (see Chapter 9).

INTERNAL WORKING MODELS On the basis of cognitive psychology (see Craik 1943; Beck *et al*. 1979), Bowlby sees higher animals as needing a map or model of the world in the brain, if they are successfully to predict, control and manipulate their environment. In Bowlby's version humans have two such models, an 'environmental' model, telling us about the world, and an 'organismal' model, telling us about ourselves in relation to the world. We carry a map of self, and others, and the relationship between the two. Although primarily 'cognitive' in conception, the idea of internal working models is applicable to affective life. The map is built up from experiences and is influenced by the need to defend against painful feelings. Thus an anxiously attached child may have a model of others in which they are potentially dangerous, and therefore must be approached with caution, while their self-representation may be of someone who is demanding and needy and unworthy to be offered security. The relationship with a person's primary care-givers is generalised in internal working models, which leads to a distorted and incoherent picture of the world, and one that is not subject to updating and revision in the light of later experience. This, in Bowlby's eyes, is the basis for transference, and the task of therapy is help the patient develop more realistic and less rigid internal working models.

MATERNAL DEPRIVATION A catch-phrase summarising Bowlby's early work on the effects of separating infants and young children from their mothers. He believed that maternally deprived children were likely to develop asocial or antisocial tendencies, and that juvenile delinquency was mainly a consequence of such separations. The corollary of this was his advocacy of continuous mother–child contact for at least the first five years of life, which earned him the opprobrium of feminists. Subsequent research has confirmed that lack of maternal care does lead to poor social adjustment and relationship difficulties, but suggests that disruption, conflict and poor maternal handling are more common causes of difficulties in late life than the loss of mother in itself.

METACOGNITIVE MONITORING   Concept introduced by Main (1990) and Fonagy (1991) to denote the ability to 'think about thinking'. Securely attached children and adults are able to reflect freely on their thought processes (e.g., 'I was really upset when my mum and dad split up and felt pretty hostile to all the children at school who seemed to have happy homes'), in contrast to insecure individuals, who tend either to dismiss their thought processes (e.g., 'Oh, the split-up didn't affect me at all, I just concentrated on my football'), or to be bogged down in them ('I can't really talk about it . . . it makes me too upset'). Defects in metacognitive ability are common in pathological states, such as borderline personality disorder, and one of the aims of psychotherapy is to facilitate metacognition.

MONOTROPY   An ethological (q.v.) term introduced by Bowlby to denote the exclusive attachment of a child to its principal care-giver, usually the mother. He was impressed by Lorenz's (1952) studies of geese and their young which suggested that the goslings became imprinted onto a moving object at a sensitive period in the first day or two of life. Bowlby thought that a similar process occurred in humans. In fact, imprinting seems not to be a feature of primate development, where attachments develop gradually and over a wide range from the early months to adolescence. Also, attachment in humans is not so much monotropic as hierarchical, with a list of preferred care-givers, with parents at the top, but closely followed by grandparents, siblings, aunts and so on.

OBJECT-RELATIONS THEORY (ORT)   Attachment Theory is a close relation of, and provides experimental evidence in support of, Object-Relations Theory (Greenberg and Mitchell 1983). This psychoanalytic school is particularly associated with a group of British theorists who include Klein (1986), Fairbairn (1952), Balint (1968) and Winnicott (1965), as well as Bion (1978). In contrast to Freud's early view of the organism as primarily driven by instinct and the need to discharge accumulated psychic energy ('libido'), Object-Relations Theorists see people as primarily seeking a relationship to their 'objects'. There is thus a progression in psychoanalytic thinking, starting with Freud's drive discharge theory, through Object Relations, in which a whole individual is seeking a relationship with an 'object' (i.e., not quite a person), to the reciprocity of care-giver and care-seeker implicit in Attachment Theory and recent developmental psychology.

PARENTAL BONDING INSTRUMENT (PBI)   A questionnaire test, devised by Parker (1983) to try to elicit in a systematic way an individual's perception of their parental relationships in childhood. It gives two main dimensions: 'care' and 'protection'. 'Care' ranges from warmth and empathy at one extreme to coldness and indifference at the other. 'Protection' similarly ranges from over-protection and infantilisation to promotion of autonomy. People with borderline personality disorder and depressive disorders regularly report the constellation of low care and high intrusiveness ('affectionless control'). There is some evidence that such reports of parental behaviour are an accurate reflection of their actual behaviour (Parker *et al.* 1992).

PERCEPTUAL DEFENCE   This, and the related concept of unconscious perception (Dixon and Henley 1991), refer to the apparently paradoxical phenomenon by which an individual can be shown to respond in behaviour to a stimulus without it reaching conscious awareness. Thus, for example, a subject presented with a neutral face and asked to judge whether it is 'happy' or 'sad', will be influenced by the simultaneous presentation of a subliminal word with positive or negative connotations. This provides experimental confirmation of the existence of unconscious thinking. Bowlby (1981c) uses this idea in his discussion of ungrieved loss to suggest that painful feelings are kept out of awareness but may nevertheless influence a person's state of mind and behaviour. By bringing these feelings into awareness – that is, by reducing the extent of perceptual defence – they are then available for processing (cf. 'working through'), leading to a more coherent and better adapted relationship to the world and the self.

SECURE BASE   A term introduced by Ainsworth (1982) to describe the feeling of safety provided by an attachment figure. Children will seek out their secure base at times of threat – danger, illness, exhaustion or following a separation. When the danger has passed, attachment behaviour will cease, but only if it is there to be mobilised if needed will the child feel secure. The secure base phenomenon applies equally to adults. We all feel 'at home' with those whom we know and trust, and within such a home environment are able to relax, and pursue our projects, whether they be play, pleasure-seeking or work.

STRANGE SITUATION   An experimental method devised by Ainsworth (Ainsworth *et al.* 1978) to study the ways in which one-year-old children can cope with brief separations from their care-givers. The child is left first with the experimenter and then alone while the mother goes out of the room for 3 minutes. The child's response to the separation, and more importantly to the re-union, is observed and rated from videotapes. On the basis of this rating children can be classified as secure (usually characterised by brief protest followed by return to relaxed play and interaction) or insecure, the latter being subdivided into avoidant (q.v.) and ambivalent (q.v.) patterns of insecurity. See Chapter 6, page 104, for a more detailed description.

SYSTEMIC   Adjective derived from Systems Theory, a conceptual model used by family therapists (originating with information theory), in which the family as a whole is seen as a quasi-organism, or 'system', with its own rules and ways of behaving. Certain general principles apply to systems whatever their nature, whether they are cells of the body, whole organisms, families or social groups. These include the property of having a boundary, of the need for information flow between different parts of the system, of a hierarchy of decision-making elements, and of 'homeostasis', the tendency towards inertia. Attachment Theory is systemic in that it sees care-seeker and care-giver as a mutually interacting system regulated by positive and negative feedback. Pathological states can result from the operation of such feedback – for example, when a child clings ever more tightly to an abusing parent, because the source of the attack is also the object to which the child is programmed to turn in case of danger.

Chronology

1907 Born, Edward John Mostyn Bowlby, fourth child and second son of Sir Anthony and Lady May Bowlby. Lived at Manchester Square, London.

1914–25 Preparatory school and then Royal Naval College, Dartmouth.

1925–28 Trinity College, Cambridge.

1928–29 Teacher in progressive school for maladjusted children.

1929 Started clinical medical studies at University College Hospital, London, and psychoanalytic training at the Institute of Psycho-Analysis, London. Training analyst, Mrs Joan Riviere.

1933 Medical qualification. Psychiatric training at Maudsley Hospital, London, under Aubrey Lewis.

1937 Qualified as an analyst. Starts training in child analysis, supervisor, Melanie Klein.

1938 Married Ursula Longstaff, by whom two sons and two daughters.

1940 Publication: *Personality and Mental Illness* (with F. Durbin).

1937–40 Psychiatrist, London Child Guidance Clinic.

1940–45 Specialist Psychiatrist, Royal Army Medical Corps, mainly concerned with Officer Selection Boards.

1946 Publication, 'Forty-four juvenile thieves: their characters and home life'.

1946–72   Consultant Child Psychiatrist and Deputy Director, Tavistock Clinic, London, and Director, Department for Children and Parents.

1950–72   Consultant in Mental Health, World Health Organisation.

1951   Publication of *Maternal Care and Mental Health*.

1957–58   Fellow, Centre for Advanced Study in the Behavioural Sciences, Stanford, California.

1956–61   Deputy President, British Psycho-Analytical Society.

1958–63   Consultant, US National Institute of Mental Health.

1969   Publication of *Attachment*, first volume of the *Attachment and Loss* trilogy.

——   Visiting Professor in Psychiatry, Stanford University, California.

1963–72   Member, External Scientific Staff, Medical Research Council.

1972   Commander of the British Empire.

1973   Publication of *Separation*, second volume of the *Attachment and Loss* trilogy.

1973   Travelling Professor, Australian and New Zealand College of Psychiatrists.

1977   Honorary Doctor of Science, University of Cambridge.

1979   Publication of *The Making and Breaking of Affectional Bonds*.

1980   Publication of *Loss*, third volume of the *Attachment and Loss* trilogy.

1981   Freud Memorial Professor of Psychoanalysis, University College, London.

——   Foreign Honorary Member, American Academy of Arts and Sciences.

1987   Celebration of Bowlby's 80th birthday with a conference at the Tavistock Clinic, bringing together researchers and clinicians, entitled 'The Effect of Relationships on Relationships'.

1988 Publication of *A Secure Base*.

1989 Fellow of the British Academy.

1990 Publication of *Charles Darwin, A New Biography*.

—— Dies while in Skye, at his holiday home where much of his writing had been done.

Bibliography

PUBLICATIONS OF JOHN BOWLBY

Personal Aggressiveness and War, (1938) (with E. P. M. Durbin) London: Kegan Paul.

'The abnormally aggressive child', (1938) *The New Era* (Sept.–Oct.).

'Hysteria in children', (1939a) in *A Survey of Child Psychiatry*, pp. 80–94, Humphrey Milford (ed.), London: Oxford University Press.

'Substitute homes', (1939) *Mother and Child* (official organ of the National Council for Maternity and Child Welfare) X (1) (April): 3–7.

'Jealous and spiteful children', (1939) *Home and School* (Home and School Council of Great Britain), IV(5): 83–5.

Bowlby, J., Miller, E. and Winnicott, D. W. (1939) 'Evacuation of small children' (letter), *British Medical Journal* (16 Dec.): 1202–3.

'The influence of early environment in the development of neurosis and neurotic character', (1940) *International Journal of Psycho-Analysis*, 21: 154–78.

'Psychological aspects', (1940) ch. 16, pp. 186–96, in *Evacuation Survey: A Report to the Fabian Society*, Richard Padley and Margaret Cole (eds), London: George Routledge & Sons Ltd.

'The problem of the young child', (1940c) *Children in War-time*, 21 (3): 19–30, London: New Education Fellowships.

'Forty-four juvenile thieves: their characters and home life', (1944) *International Journal of Psychoanalysis*, 25: 1–57 and 207–228; republished as a monograph by Baillière, Tindall & Cox, London, 1946.

'Childhood origins of recidivism', (1945–46) *The Howard Journal*, VII (1): 30–3, The Howard League for Penal Reform.

'The future role of the child guidance clinic in education and other services', (1946a) *Report of the Proceedings of a Conference on Mental Health*, (14–15 Nov.), pp. 80–89, National Association for Mental Health.

'Psychology and democracy', (1946b) *The Political Quarterly*, XVII (1): 61–76.

'The therapeutic approach in sociology', (1947a) *The Sociological Review*, 39: 39–49.

'The study of human relations in the child guidance clinic', (1947b) *Journal of Social Issues*, III (2) (Spring): 35–41.

'The study and reduction of group tensions in the family, (1949a) *Human Relations*, 2 (2) (April): 123–8.

'The relation between the therapeutic approach and the legal approach to juvenile delinquency', (1949b) *The Magistrate*, VIII (Nov.): 260–4.

Why Delinquency? The Case for Operational Research, (1949c) Report of a conference on the scientific study of juvenile delinquency held at the Royal Institution, London 1 Oct., and published by the National Association for Mental Health.

'Research into the origins of delinquent behaviour', (1950) *British Medical Journal* 1 March 11: 570).

Maternal Care and Mental Health, (1951) World Health Organisation, Monograph Series No. 2.

'Responses of young children to separation from their mothers', (with J. Robertson) (1952a) *Courier*, Centre International de l'Enfance, II (2): 66–78, and II (3): 131–42, Paris.

A two-year-old goes to hospital: a scientific film, (with J. Robertson) (1952b) *Proceedings of the Royal Society of Medicine*, 46: 425–7.

'A two-year-old goes to hospital', Bowlby, J., Robertson, J. and Rosenbluth, D. (1952) *The Psychoanalytic Study of the Child*, VII: 82–94.

'A two-year-old goes to hospital: a scientific film', (with J. Robertson) (1952b) *Proceedings of the Royal Society of Medicine*, 46: 425–7.

'The roots of parenthood', (1953) Convocation Lecture of the National Children's Home (July).

Child Care and the Growth of Maternal Love, (1953b) (abridged version of *Maternal Care and Mental Health*, 1951), London: Penguin Books; new and enlarged edition, 1965.

'Critical phases in the development of social responses in man and other animals', (1953c) *New Biology*, London: Penguin Books, pp. 25–32.

'Some pathological processes set in train by early mother–child separation', (1953d) *Journal of Mental Science*, 99: 265–72.

'Research strategy in the study of mother–child separation', (with M. G. Ainsworth) (1954) *Courier*, Centre International de l'Enfance, IV: 105–13.

'Family approach to child guidance: therapeutic techniques', (1955) Transactions of the 11th Interclinic Conference for the Staffs of Child Guidance Clinics, National Association for Mental Health (26 March).

'The growth of independence in the young child', (1956) *Royal Society of Health Journal*, 76: 587–91.

'Psychoanalytic instinct theory', (1956) in *Discussions on Child Development*, vol. 1, J. M. Tanner and B. Inhelder (eds), pp. 182–87, London: Tavistock Publications.

'The effects of mother–child separation: a follow-up study', (with M. Ainsworth, M. Boston and D. Rosenbluth) (1956) *British Journal of Medical Psychology*, XXIX, parts 3 and 4: 211–47.

'An ethological approach to research in child development', (1957) *British Journal of Medical Psychology*, XXX, part 4: 230–40.

Can I Leave my Baby?, (1958a) The National Association for Mental Health.

'A note on mother–child separation as a mental health hazard', (1958b) *British Journal of Medical Psychology*, XXXI, parts 3 and 4: 247–8.

Foreword to *Widows and their Families* by Peter Marris, (1958c) London: Routledge & Kegan Paul.

'The nature of the child's tie to his mother', (1958d) *International Journal of Psycho-Analysis*, 39, part V: 350–73.

'Psychoanalysis and child care', (1958e) in *Psychoanalysis and Contemporary Thought*, J. Sutherland (ed.), London: Hogarth Press.

'Ethology and the development of object relations', (1960a) *International Journal of Psycho-Analysis*, 41, parts IV–V: 313–17.

'Separation anxiety', (1960b) *International Journal of Psycho-Analysis*, 41, parts II–III: 89–113.

Comment on Piaget's paper: 'The general problems of the psychobiological development on the child', (1960c) in *Discussions on Child Development*, vol. 4, J. M. Tanner and B. Inhelder (eds), London: Tavistock Publications.

'Grief and mourning in infancy and early childhood', (1960d) *The Psychoanalytic Study of the Child*, XV: 9–52.

'Separation anxiety: a critical review of the literature', (1961a) *Journal of Child Psychology and Psychiatry*, 1 (16): 251–69.

Note on Dr Max Schur's comments on grief and mourning in infancy and early childhood, (1961b) *The Psychoanalytic Study of the Child*, XVI: 206–8.

'Childhood mourning and its implications for psychiatry', The Adolf Meyer Lecture, (1961c) *American Journal of Psychiatry*, 118 (6): 481–97.

'Processes of mourning', (1961d) *International Journal of Psycho-Analysis*, 42, parts IV–V: 317–40.

'Defences that follow loss: causation and function', (1962a) unpublished.

'Loss, detachment and defence', (1962b) unpublished.

'Pathological mourning and childhood mourning', (1963) *Journal of the American Psychoanalytic Association*, XI (3) (July): 500–41.

Note on Dr Lois Murphy's paper 'Some aspects of the first relationship', (1964a) *International Journal of Psycho-Analysis*, 45, part 1: 44–6.

Security and Anxiety: Old Ideas in a New Light, (1964b) Proceedings of the 15th Annual Conference of the Association of Children's Officers.

Darwin's health (letter) (1965) *British Medical Journal* (10 April), p. 999.

Foreword to *Brief Separations* (1966) by C. M. Heinicke and I. J. Westheimer, New York: International Universities Press; London: Longmans Green.

'Effects on behaviour of disruption of an affectional bond', (1968a) in *Genetic and Environmental Influences on Behaviour*, J. M. Thoday and A-S Parkes, pp. 94–108, Edinburgh: Oliver & Boyd.

'Security and anxiety', (1968b) chapter in *The Formative Years*, London: BBC Publications.

'Affectional bonds: their nature and origin', (1969a) in *Progress in Mental Health*, H. Freeman (ed.), London: J. & A. Churchill.

Attachment and Loss, (1969b) vol. 1, *Attachment*, London: Hogarth Press; New York: Basic Books; Harmondsworth: Penguin Books, 1971; 2nd edn, 1982.

'Types of hopelessness in psychopathological process', (1969c) (with F. T. Melges) *Archives of General Psychiatry*, 20: 690–9.

'Psychopathology of anxiety: the role of affectional bonds', (1969d) in *Studies of Anxiety*, M. H. Lader (ed.), *British Journal of Psychiatry*, Special Publication no. 3.

'Reasonable fear and natural fear', (1970) *International Journal of Psychiatry*, 9: 79–88.

'Separation and loss within the family', (1970) (with C. M. Parkes), in *The Child in his Family*, E. J. Anthony (ed.), New York: J. Wiley; Paris: Masson et Cie; and in *The International Yearbook for Child Psychiatry and Allied Disciplines*, vol. 1, pp. 197–216.

Attachment and Loss, vol. 2, (1973a) *Separation: Anxiety and Anger*, London: Hogarth Press; New York: Basic Books; Harmondsworth: Penguin Books, 1975.

'Self-reliance and some conditions that promote it', (1973b) in *Support, Innovation and Autonomy*, R. Gosling, (ed.), pp. 23–48, London: Tavistock Publications.

'The family for good or ill', (1973c) Report on a seminar given in the Department of Psychological Medicine, University of Otago Medical School, New Zealand Department of Psychological Medicine.

'Problems of marrying research with clinical and social needs', (1974) in *The Growth of Competence*, K. J. Connolly and J. S. Bruner (eds), pp. 303–7, London and New York: Academic Press.

'Attachment theory, separation anxiety and mourning', (1975) in *American Handbook of Psychiatry* (2nd edn), vol. VI, *New Psychiatric Frontiers*, David A. Hamburg and Keith H. Brodie (eds), ch. 14, pp. 292–309.

Bindung, translation of *Attachment*, (1975) Munich: Kindler Verlag.

'Responses to separation from parents: a clinical test for young children', (with M. Klagsbrun) (1976a) *British Journal of Projective Psychology and Personality Study*, 21 (2): 7–27.

'Human personality development in an ethological light', (1976b) in *Animal Models in Human Psychobiology*, G. Serban and A. Kling (eds), pp. 27–36, New York: Plenum Publishing Corp.

'The making and breaking of affectional bonds, (1977) I Aetiology and psychopathology in the light of attachment theory, II Some principles of psychotherapy', *British Journal of Psychiatry*, 130: 201–10 and 421–31.

'Attachment theory and its therapeutic implications', (1978) in *Adolescent Psychiatry: Developmental and Clinical Studies*, vol. 6, S. C. Feinstein and P. L. Giovacchini (eds), pp. 5–33, New York: Jason Aronson.

'On knowing what you are not supposed to know and feeling what you are not supposed to feel', (1979a) *Canadian Journal of Psychiatry*, 24 (5): 403–8.

'Psychoanalysis as art and science', (1979b) *International Review of Psycho-Analysis*, 6, part 3: 3–14.

The Making and Breaking of Affectional Bonds, (1979c) London: Tavistock Publications.

Continuing commentary on article by D. W. Rajecki, M. E. Lamb and P. Obmascher, 'Toward a general theory of infantile attachment: a comparative review of aspects of the social bond', (1979d) *The Behavioural and Brain Sciences*, 2: 637–8.

'By ethology out of psychoanalysis: an experiment in interbreeding', (1979e) (The Niko Tinbergen Lecture, *Animal Behaviour*, 28, part 3: 649–56.

Attachment and Loss, vol. 3, *Loss: Sadness and Depression*, (1980) London: Hogarth Press; New York: Basic Books; Harmondsworth: Penguin Books, 1981.

'Perspective: a contribution by John Bowlby', (1981a) *Bulletin of the Royal College of Psychiatrists*, 5 (1) (Jan.).

Contribution to symposium, 'Emanuel Peterfreund on information and systems theory', (1981b) *The Psychoanalytic Review*, 68: 187–90.

'Psychoanalysis as a natural science', (1981c) *International Review of Psycho-Analysis*, 8, part 3: 243–56.

'Attachment and loss: retrospect and prospect', (1982a) *American Journal of Orthopsychiatry*, 52 (4): 664–78.

Epilogue, (1982b) *The Place of Attachment in Human Behaviour*, Colin Murray Parkes and Joan Stevenson-Hinde (eds), pp. 310–13, New York: Basic Books; London: Tavistock Publications.

'Caring for the young: influences on development', (1984a) in *Parenthood: A Psychodynamic Perspective*, Rebecca S. Cohen, Bertram J. Cohler and Sidney H. Weissman (eds), ch. 18, pp. 269–84, The Guilford Psychiatry Series, New York: Guilford Press.

Discussion of paper, 'Aspects of transference in group analysis' (1984b) by Mario Marrone, *Group Analysis*, 17: 191–4.

'Violence in the family as a disorder of the attachment and caregiving systems', (1984c) *American Journal of Psychoanalysis*, 44: 9–27.

'Psychoanalysis as a natural science', (1984d) *Psychoanalytic Psychology*, 1 (1): 7–21.

'The role of childhood experience in cognitive disturbance' (1985) in *Cognition and Psychotherapy*, Michael J. Mahoney and Arthur Freeman (eds), ch. 6, pp. 181–200, New York and London: Plenum Publishing Corp.

'Processi difensivi alla luce della teoria dell'attaccamento', (1986a) *Psicoterapia e Scienze Umane*, 20: 3–19.

Figlio, K. and Young, R. (1986b) 'An Interview with John Bowlby', *Free Associations*, 6: 36–64.

'Defensive processes in the light of attachment theory', (1987a) in *Attachment and the Therapeutic Process*, D. P. Schwartz, J. L. Sacksteder and Y. Akabane (eds), New York: International Universities Press.

'Attachment', 'Phobias', (1987b) in *The Oxford Companion to the Mind*, R. Gregory (ed.), Oxford and New York: Oxford University Press.

A Secure Base: Clinical Applications of Attachment Theory, (1988a) London: Routledge.
'Changing theories of childhood since Freud', (1988b) in *Freud in Exile*, E. Timms and N. Segal (eds), pp. 230–40, New Haven and London: Yale University Press.
'Developmental psychiatry comes of age', (1988c) *American Journal of Psychiatry*, 145: pp. 1–10.
'The role of attachment in personality development and psychopathology', (1989) in *The Course of Life*, vol. 1, 2nd edn, S. Greenspan and G. Pollock (eds), ch. 6, pp. 229–70, Madison, WI: International Universities Press.
Charles Darwin: A New Biography, (1990) London: Hutchinson.
'The role of the psychotherapist's personal resources in the therapeutic situation', (1991) *Tavistock Gazette* (Autumn).

GENERAL WORKS

Ainsworth, M. (1969) 'Object relations, dependency and attachment: a theoretical review of the infant–mother relationship', *Child Development*, 40: 969–1025.
—— (1982) 'Attachment: retrospect and prospect', in C. M. Parkes and J. Stevenson-Hinde (eds), *The Place of Attachment in Human Behaviour*, London: Tavistock.
—— (1989) 'Attachments beyond infancy', *American Psychologist*, 44: 709–16.
Ainsworth, M., Blehar, M., Waters, E. and Wall, S. (1978) *Patterns of Attachment: Assessed in the Strange Situation and at Home*, Hillsdale, NJ: Erlbaum.
Anderson, J. (1972) 'Attachment out of doors', in N. Blurton-Jones (ed.), *Ethological Studies of Child Behaviour*, Cambridge: Cambridge University Press.
Andry, R. (1962) 'Paternal and maternal roles in delinquency', in *Deprivation of Maternal Care: A Reassessment of its Effects*, Geneva: World Health Organisation Publications.
Balint, M. (1964) *Primary Love and Psychoanalytic Technique*, London: Tavistock.
—— (1968) *The Basic Fault*, London: Tavistock.
—— (1986) 'The unobtrusive analyst', in G. Kohon (ed.), *The British School of Psychoanalysis*, London: Free Associations.
Bateman, A. (1991) 'Borderline Personality Disorder', in J. Holmes (ed.), *Textbook of Psychotherapy in Psychiatric Practice*, Edinburgh: Churchill Livingstone.
Bateson, G. (1973) *Steps Towards an Ecology of Mind*, London: Paladin.
Beck, A., Rush, A., Shaw, B. and Emery, G. (1979) *Cognitive Therapy of Depression*, New York: Guilford.
Beebe, B. and Lachmann, F. (1988) 'The contribution of mother–infant mutual influence to the origins of self–object representation', *Psychoanalytic Psychology*, 5: 305–37.

Belsky, J. and Nezworski, T. (1988) *Clinical Implications of Attachment*, Hillsdale, NJ: Erlbaum.

Bettelheim, B. (1960) *The Informed Heart*, New York: Free Press.

Bion, W. (1978) *Second Thoughts*, London: Heinemann.

Birtchnell, J. (1984) 'Dependence and its relation to depression', *British Journal of Medical Psychology*, 57: 215–25.

—— (1988) 'Defining dependence', *British Journal of Medical Psychology*, 61: 111–23.

Bowie, (1991) *Lacan*, London: Fontana.

Bowlby, U. (1991) Personal communication.

Brazelton, T. and Cramer, B. (1991) *The Earliest Relationship*, London: Karnak.

Bretherton, I. (1985) 'Attachment Theory: retrospect and prospect', in I. Bretherton and E. Waters (eds), 'Growing points of attachment theory and research', *Monographs of the Society for Research in Child Development*, 50: 3–35.

—— (1987) 'New perspectives on attachment relations: security, communication and internal working models', in J. Osofsky (ed.), *Handbook of Infant Development*, New York: Wiley.

—— (1991a) 'Pouring new wine into old bottles: the social self as Internal Working Model', in M. Gunnar and L. Sroufe (eds), *Self Processes and Development*, Hillsdale, NJ: Erlbaum.

—— (1991b) 'Roots and growing points of attachment theory', in *Attachment Across the Life Cycle*, C. M. Parkes, J. Stevenson-Hinde and P. Marris (eds), London: Routledge.

Brown, G. and Harris, T. (1978) *The Social Origins of Depression*, London: Tavistock.

Bryer, J., Nelson, B., Miller, J. and Krol, P. (1987) 'Childhood sexual and physical abuse as factors in adult psychiatric illness', *American Journal of Psychiatry*, 144: 1426–30.

Bufalino, G. (1992) 'An island between heaven and hell', *Guardian*, 21 May.

Byng-Hall, J. (1980) 'Symptom bearer as marital distance regulator', *Family Process*, 19: 335–65.

—— (1985) 'The family script: a useful bridge between theory and practice', *Journal of Family Therapy*, 7: 301–5.

—— (1991a) 'The application of attachment theory to understanding and treatment in family therapy', in *Attachment Across the Life Cycle*, C. M. Parkes, J. Stevenson-Hinde and P. Marris (eds), London: Routledge.

—— (1991b) 'Memorial service for John Bowlby: address', *Tavistock Gazette* (Autumn).

—— (1991c) 'An appreciation of John Bowlby: his significance for family therapy', *Journal of Family Therapy*, 13: 5–16.

Byng-Hall, J. and Stevenson-Hinde, J. (1991) 'Attachment relationships within a family system', *Infant Mental Health Journal*, 12: 187–200.

Casement, P. (1985) *On Learning from the Patient*, London: Tavistock.

Caspi, A. and Elder, G. (1988) 'Emergent family patterns', in *Relation-*

ships within Families: Marital Influences, R. Hinde and J. Stevenson-Hinde (eds), Oxford: Oxford University Press.

Cassidy, J. (1988) 'The self as related to child–mother attachment at 6', *Child Development*, 59: 121–34.

Chodorow, N. (1978) *The Reproduction of Motherhood*, Berkeley, CA: University of California Press.

Craik, K. (1943) *The Nature of Explanation*, Cambridge: Cambridge University Press.

Crittenden, P. (1988) 'Maternal antecedents of attachment quality', in *Clinical Implications of Attachment*, J. Belsky and T. Nezworski (eds), Hillsdale, NJ: Erlbaum.

Darwin, C. (1872) *The Expression of the Emotions in Man and Animals*, London: John Murray.

Dawkins, R. (1977) *The Selfish Gene*, Oxford: Oxford University Press.

Dixon, N. (1971) *Subliminal Perception: The Nature of a Controversy*, London: McGraw-Hill.

Dixon, N. and Henley, S. (1991) 'Unconscious perception: possible implications of data from academic research for clinical practice', *Journal of Nervous and Mental Disease*, 79: 243–51.

Eagle, M. (1988) 'Psychoanalysis and the personal', in *Mind, Psychoanalysis, and Science*, P. Clark and C. Wright (eds), Oxford: Oxford University Press.

Fairbairn, R. (1952) *Psychoanalytic Studies of the Personality*, London: Tavistock.

Ferenczi, S. (1955) *Final Contributions to the Problems and Methods of Psychoanalysis*, London: Hogarth.

Fonagy, P. (1991) 'Thinking about thinking: some clinical and theoretical considerations in the treatment of a borderline patient', *International Journal of Psycho-Analysis*, 72: 639–56.

Fonagy, P., Steele, M. and Steele, H. (1992) 'Maternal representations of attachment during pregnancy predict the organisation of infant–mother attachment at one year of age', *Child Development* (in press).

Fonagy, P., Steele, M., Steele, H., Moran, G. and Higgins, A. (1991) 'The capacity for understanding mental states: the reflective self in parent and child and its significance for security of attachment', *Infant Mental Health Journal*, 12: 201–18.

Fraiberg, P., Adelson, E. and Shapiro, V. (1975) 'Ghosts in the nursery: a psychoanalytic approach to the problem of impaired infant–mother relationships', *Journal of the American Academy of Child Psychiatry*, 14: 387–422.

Frank, J. (1986) 'Psychotherapy: the transformation of meanings', *Journal of the Royal Society of Medicine*, 79: 341–6.

Freud, S. (1910) 'Leonardo da Vinci and a memory of his childhood', *Standard Edition of the Complete Psychological Works of Sigmund Freud*, SE 9, London: Hogarth.

—— (1911) 'Formulations on the two principles of mental functioning', SE 12, London: Hogarth.

—— (1913) 'On beginning the treatment', SE 12, London: Hogarth.

—— (1917) 'Mourning and melancholia', SE 14, London: Hogarth.

—— (1926) *Inhibitions, Symptoms, and Anxiety*, SE 20, London: Hogarth.

—— (1929) *Civilisation and its Discontents*, SE 21, London: Hogarth.

Frost, R. (1954) *Collected Poems*, London: Penguin.

Gabbard, G. (1992) 'Psychodynamic psychiatry in the "decade of the brain"', *American Journal of Psychiatry*, 149: 991–8.

Gallwey, P. (1985) 'The psychodynamics of borderline personality', in *Aggression and Dangerousness*, D. Farrington and J. Gunn (eds), London: Wiley.

Gardner, H. (1957) *The Metaphysical Poets*, London: Penguin.

Garland, C. (1991) 'External disasters and the internal world', in *Textbook of Psychotherapy in Psychiatric Practice*, J. Holmes (ed.), Edinburgh: Churchill Livingstone.

Gathorne-Hardy, J. (1992) *Gerald Brennan*, London: Sinclair.

Grant, S. (1991) 'Psychotherapy with people who have been sexually abused', in *A Textbook of Psychotherapy in Psychiatric Practice*, J. Holmes (ed.), Edinburgh: Churchill Livingstone.

Greenberg, J. and Mitchell, S. (1983) *Object Relations in Psychoanalytic Theory*, London: Harvard University Press.

Greenberg, M., Cummings, M. and Cicchetti, B. (1988) *Attachment in the Preschool Years: Theory, Research and Intervention*, Hillsdale, NJ: Erlbaum.

Greenson, R. (1967) *The Technique and Practice of Psychoanalysis*, New York: International Universities Press.

Grosskurth, P. (1986) *Melanie Klein: Her World and her Work*, Cambridge, MA: Harvard University Press.

Grossman, K. and Grossman, K. (1991) 'Attachment quality as an organiser of emotional and behavioural responses in a longitudinal perspective', in *Attachment across the Life Cycle*, C. M. Parkes, J. Stevenson-Hinde and P. Marris (eds), London: Routledge.

Grossman, K., Grossman, K. and Schwann, A. (1986) 'Capturing the wider view of attachment: a re-analysis of Ainsworth's Strange Situation', in C. Elzard and P. Read (eds), *Measuring Emotions in Infants and Children*, Cambridge: Cambridge University Press.

Guntrip, H. (1974) *Schizoid Phenomena, Object Relations and the Self*, London: Hogarth.

Hamilton, V. (1985) 'John Bowlby: an ethological basis for psychoanalysis', in *Beyond Freud: A Study of Modern Psychoanalytic Theorists*, J. Reppen (ed.), New York: Analytic Press.

—— (1986) 'Grief and mourning in Tennyson's In Memoriam', *Free Associations*, 7: 87–110.

—— (1991) 'Personal reminiscences of John Bowlby', *Tavistock Gazette* (Autumn).

Hanh, T. N. (1990) *Present Moment, Wonderful Moment*, Berkeley, CA: Parallax Press.

Harlow, H. (1958) 'The nature of love', *American Psychologist*, 13: 673–85.

Harris, T. and Bifulco, A. (1991) 'Loss of parent in childhood, attachment style and deprivation in adulthood', in *Attachment Across the*

Life Cycle, C. M. Parkes, J. Stevenson-Hinde and P. Marris (eds), London: Routledge.

Harris, T., Brown, G. and Bifulco, A. (1987) 'Loss of parent in childhood and adult psychiatric disorder: the role of social class position and premarital pregnancy', *Psychological Medicine*, 17: 163–83.

Hazan, C. and Shaver, P. (1987) 'Romantic love conceptualised as an attachment process', *Journal of Personal and Social Psychology*, 52: 511–24.

Heard, D. (1978) 'From object relations to attachment theory: a basis for family therapy', *British Journal of Medical Psychology*, 51, 67–76.

—— (1982) 'Family systems and the attachment dynamic', *Journal of Family Therapy*, 4: 99–116.

—— (1986) 'Introduction' to new edition of *The Origins of Love and Hate* by Ian Suttie, London: Free Association Books.

Heard, D. and Lake, B. (1986) 'The attachment dynamic in adult life', *British Journal of Psychiatry*, 149: 430–8.

Henderson, S., Byrne, D. and Duncan-Jones, P. (1981) *Neurosis and the Social Environment*, Sydney: Academic Press.

Herman, J., Perry, C. and Kolk, B. (1989) 'Childhood trauma in Borderline Personality Disorder', *American Journal of Psychiatry*, 146: 490–5.

Hinde, R. (1982a) 'Attachment: some conceptual and biological issues', in *The Place of Attachment in Human Behaviour*, C. M. Parkes and J. Stevenson-Hinde (eds), London: Tavistock.

—— (1982b) *Ethology*, London: Fontana.

—— (1987) *Individuals, Relationships and Culture: Links between Ethology and the Social Sciences*, Cambridge: Cambridge University Press.

Hinde, R. and McGinnis, L. (1977) 'Some factors influencing the effects of temporary infant–mother separation', *Psychological Medicine*, 7: 197–212.

Holmes, J. (1991) *A Textbook of Psychotherapy in Psychiatric Practice*, Edinburgh: Churchill Livingstone.

—— (1992) *Between Art and Science*, London: Routledge.

—— (1993) 'Psychotherapeutic aspects of the acute psychiatric admission ward', unpublished.

Holmes, J. and Lindley, R. (1989) *The Values of Psychotherapy*, Oxford: Oxford University Press.

Hopkins, J. (1990) 'The observed infant of attachment theory', *British Journal of Psychotherapy*, 6: 460–70.

Horney, K. (1924) 'On the genesis of the castration complex in women', *International Journal of Psycho-Analysis*, 5: 50–65.

—— (1932) 'The dread of women', *International Journal of Psycho-Analysis*, 13: 348–60.

Horowitz, M. (1988) *An Introduction to Psychodynamics*, London: Routledge.

Humphrey, N. (1992) *A History of the Mind*, London: Chatto & Windus.

Hunter, V. (1991) 'John Bowlby: an interview', *Psychoanalytic Review*, 78: 159–65.

Ijzendoorn, M. and Kroonenberg, P. (1988) 'Cross cultural patterns of attachment: a meta-analysis of the Strange Situation', *Child Development*, 59: 147–56.

Jones, E. (1949) *Hamlet and Oedipus*, London: Gollancz.

Jones, K. (1985) *Buddhism and the Bombs*, Preston: Buddhist Peace Fellowship (UK).

Kernberg, O. (1975) 'A systems approach to priority setting of interventions in groups', *International Journal of Group Psychotherapy*, 25: 251–75.

King, P. and Steiner, R. (1990) *The Freud–Klein Controversy 1941–5*, London: Routledge.

Klein, M. (1986) *The Selected Melanie Klein*, J. Mitchell (ed.), London: Penguin.

Kobak, R. and Sceery, A. (1988) 'Attachment in late adolescence: working models, affect regulation, and representations of self and others', *Child Development*, 59: 135–46.

Kohut, H. (1977) *The Restoration of the Self*, New York: International Universities Press.

Kraemer, S. (1991) 'Personal reminiscences of John Bowlby', *Tavistock Gazette* (Autumn).

Kuhn, T. (1962) *The Structure of Scientific Revolutions*, Chicago: University of Chicago Press.

Lake, B. (1985) 'The concept of ego-strength in psychotherapy', *British Journal of Psychiatry*, 147: 411–28.

Leff, J. and Vaughn, C. (1983) *Expressed Emotion in Families*, New York: Guilford Press.

Leupnitz, D. (1988) *The Family Interpreted*, New York: Basic Books.

Lieberman, A. and Pawl, J. (1988) 'Disorders of attachment in the second year: a clinical developmental perspective', in *Attachment in the Preschool Years: Theory, Research and Intervention*, M. Greenberg, B. Cicchetti and M. Cumming (eds), Hillsdale, NJ: Erlbaum.

Lieberman, A., Weston, D. and Paul, J. (1991) 'Preventive intervention and outcome with anxiously attached dyads', *Child Development*, 62: 199–209.

Liotti, G. (1987) 'The resistance to change of cognitive structures: a counterproposal to psychoanalytic metapsychology', *Journal of Cognitive Psychotherapy*, 1: 87–104.

—— (1991) 'Insecure attachment and agoraphobia', in *Attachment across the Life Cycle*, C. M. Parkes, J. Stevenson-Hinde and P. Marris (eds), London: Routledge.

Lorenz, K. (1952) *King Solomon's Ring*, London: Methuen.

Lovelock, J. (1979) *Gaia*, Oxford: Oxford University Press.

Mackenzie, M. (1991) 'Reminiscences of John Bowlby', *Tavistock Gazette* (Autumn).

Mackie, A. (1981) 'Attachment theory: its relevance to the therapeutic alliance', *British Journal of Medical Psychology*, 54: 203–12.

Mackinnon, A., Henderson, S. and Andrews, G. (1991) 'The Parental Bonding Instrument: a measure of perceived or actual parental behaviour', *Acta Psychiatrica Scandinavica*, 83: 153–9.

Mahler, M., Pine, F. and Bergman, A. (1975) *The Psychological Birth of the Human Infant*, London: Hutchinson.

Main, M. (1990) *A Typology of Human Attachment Organisation Assessed with Discourse, Drawings and Interviews*, New York: Cambridge University Press.

—— (1991) 'Metacognitive knowledge, metacognitive monitoring, and singular (coherent) vs multiple (incoherent) models of attachment: findings and directions for future research', in *Attachment across the Life Cycle*, C. M. Parkes, J. Stevenson-Hinde and P. Marris (eds), London: Routledge.

Main, M. and Goldwyn, R. (1984) 'Predicting rejection of her infant from mother's representation of her own experience: implications for the abused-abuser intergenerational cycle', *International Journal of Child Abuse and Neglect*, 8: 203–17.

Main, M., Kaplan, K. and Cassidy, J. (1985) 'Security in infancy, childhood and adulthood. A move to the level of representation', in 'Growing points of attachment theory and research', I. Bretherton and E. Waters (eds), *Monographs of the Society for Research in Child Development*, 50: 66–104.

Main, M. and Weston, D. (1982) 'Avoidance of the attachment figure in infancy', in *The Place of Attachment in Human Behaviour*, C. M. Parkes and J. Stevenson-Hinde (eds), London: Tavistock.

Malan, D. (1976) *Towards the Validation of Dynamic Psychotherapy*, Chichester: Plenum.

—— (1991) 'John Bowlby remembered', *Tavistock Gazette* (Autumn).

Marris, P. (1991) 'The social construction of uncertainty' in *Attachment across the Life Cycle*, C. M. Parkes, J. Stevenson-Hinde and P. Marris (eds), London: Routledge.

Masson, J. (1985) *The Assault on Truth*, London: Penguin.

Mawson, D., Marks, I., Ramm, L. and Stern, R. (1981) 'Guided mourning for morbid grief: a controlled study', *British Journal of Psychiatry*, 138: 185–93.

Mead, M. (1962) 'A cultural anthropologist's approach to maternal deprivation', in *Deprivation of Maternal Care: A Reassessment of its Effects*, Geneva: World Health Organisation Publications.

Meares, R. and Hobson, R. (1977) 'The persecutory therapist', *British Journal of Medical Psychology*, 50: 349–59.

Melges, F. and Swartz, M. (1989) 'Oscillations of attachment in Borderline Personality Disorder', *American Journal of Psychiatry*, 146: 1115–20.

Meltzer, D. and Williams, M. (1988) *The Apprehension of Beauty*, Perthshire: Clunie Press.

Menzies-Lyth, I. (1988) *Containing Anxieties in Institutions*, London: Free Association Books.

—— (1989) *The Dynamic of the Social*, London: Free Association Books.

Middleton, P. (1991) 'Some psychological bases of the institution of war' in *The Institution of War*, R. Hinde (ed.), London: Macmillan.

Minuchin, S. (1974) *Families and Family Therapy*, London: Tavistock.

Minuchin, S., Rosman, B. and Baker, L. (1978) *Psychosomatic Families*, Cambridge, MA: Harvard University Press.

Mitscherlich, A. (1962) *Societies Without the Father*, New York: Schocken.

Murray, L. and Cooper, P. (1992) 'Clinical application of attachment theory and research: change in infant attachment with brief psychotherapy', *Journal of Child Psychology and Psychiatry* (in press).

New, C. and David, M. (1985) *For the Children's Sake*, London: Penguin.

Newcombe, N. and Lerner, J. (1982) 'Britain between the wars: the historical context of Bowlby's theory of attachment', *Psychiatry*, 45: 1–12.

Oakley, A. (1981) *Subject Women*, Oxford: Martin Robertson.

Parker, G. (1983) 'Parental "Affectionless Control" as an antecedent to adult depression', *Archives of General Psychiatry*, 40: 956–60.

Parker, G., Barret, R. and Hickie, I. (1992) 'From nurture to network: examining links between perception of parenting received in childhood and social bonds in adulthood', *American Journal of Psychiatry*, 149: 877–85.

Parker, G. and Hadzi-Pavlovic, D. (1984) 'Modification of levels of depression in mother-bereaved women by parental and marriage relationships', *Psychological Medicine*, 14: 125–35.

Parkes, C. M. (1964) 'The effects of bereavement on physical and mental health', *British Medical Journal*, 2: 274–9.

—— (1971) 'Psychosocial transitions: a field for study', *Social Science and Medicine*, 5: 101–15.

—— (1975) *Bereavement: Studies of Grief in Adult Life*, London: Penguin.

—— (1985) 'Bereavement', *British Journal of Psychiatry*, 146: 11–17.

Parkes, C. M. and Stevenson-Hinde, J. (1982) *The Place of Attachment in Human Behaviour*, London: Tavistock.

Parkes, C. M., Stevenson-Hinde, J. and Marris, P. (eds) (1991) *Attachment across the Life Cycle*, London: Routledge.

Parkes, C. M. and Weiss, R. (1983) *Recovery from Bereavement*, New York: Basic Books.

Parsons, T. (1964) *Social Structure and Personality*, New York: Free Press.

Patrick, M., Hobson, P., Castle, P. *et al.* (1992) 'Personality Disorder and the mental representation of early social experience', Paper presented to the MRC Child Psychiatry Unit at the Institute of Psychiatry, London.

Pedder, J. (1982) 'Failure to mourn and melancholia', *British Journal of Psychiatry*, 141: 329–37.

—— (1986) 'Attachment and new beginning', in *The British School of Psychoanalysis*, G. Kohon (ed.), London: Free Association Books.

—— (1987) 'Some biographical contributions to psychoanalytic theories', *Free Associations*, 10: 102–16.

—— (1992) 'Psychoanalytic views of aggression: some theoretical problems', *British Journal of Medical Psychology*, 65: 95–106.

Peterfreund, E. (1983) *The Process of Psychoanalytic Therapy*, Hillsdale, NJ: Analytic Press.

Phelps-Brown, H. (1992) Personal communication.

Pines, M. (1991) 'A history of psychodynamic psychiatry in Britain', in *A Textbook of Psychotherapy in Psychiatric Practice*, J. Holmes (ed.), Edinburgh: Churchill Livingstone.

Post, R. (1992) 'Transduction of psychosocial stress into the neurobiology of recurrent affective disorder', *American Journal of Psychiatry*, 149: 999–1010.

Raverat, G. (1952) *Period Piece*, London: Faber.

Rayner, E. (1992) 'John Bowlby's contribution, a brief survey', *Bulletin of the British Psycho-Analytical Society*, 20–3.

Rey, H. (1975) Personal communication.

Riviere, J. (1955) 'The unconscious phantasy of an inner world reflected in examples from literature', in *New Directions in Psychoanalysis*, M. Klein, P. Heimann and R. Money-Kyrle (eds), London: Hogarth.

Roazen, P. (1976) *Freud and his Followers*, London: Penguin.

Roberts, G. (1992) 'The origins of delusion', *British Journal of Psychiatry*, 161: 298–308.

Robertson, J. (1952) *Film: A Two-Year-Old Goes to Hospital*, London: Tavistock.

Rodman, D. (1987) *The Spontaneous Gesture*, Cambridge, MA: Harvard University Press.

Rustin, M. (1991) *The Good Society and the Inner World*, London: Verso.

Rutter, M. (1972) 'Maternal deprivation reconsidered', *Journal of Psychosomatic Research*, 16: 241–50.

—— (1979) 'Maternal deprivation 1972–1978, new findings, new concepts, new approaches', *Child Development*, 50: 283–305.

—— (1980) 'Attachment and the development of social relations', in *The Scientific Foundations of Developmental Psychiatry*, M. Rutter (ed.), London: Heinemann.

—— (1981) *Maternal Deprivation Reassessed*, 2nd edn, London: Penguin.

—— (1985) 'Resilience in the face of adversity: protective factors and resistance to psychiatric disorder', *British Journal of Psychiatry*, 147: 598–611.

—— (1986) 'Meyerian psychobiology, personality development and the role of life experiences', *American Journal of Psychiatry*, 143: 1077–87.

—— (1987) 'Temperament, personality, and personality disorder', *British Journal of Psychiatry*, 150: 443–58.

—— (1990) *Essays in Honour of Robert Hinde*, P. Bateson (ed.), Cambridge: Cambridge University Press.

Rutter, M. and Quinton, D. (1984) 'Long-term follow-up of women institutionalised in childhood', *British Journal of Developmental Psychology*, 18: 225–34.

Rycroft, C. (1985) *Psychoanalysis and Beyond*, London: Chatto.

—— (1992) Personal communication.

Ryle, A. (1990) *Cognitive Analytic Therapy: Active Participation in Change*, Chichester: Wiley.

Schank, B. (1982) *Dynamic Memory: A Theory of Reminding and Learning in Computers and People*, Cambridge, MA: Cambridge University Press.

Shafer, R. (1976) *A New Language for Psychoanalysis*, London: Yale University Press.

Shaver, P. and Hazan, C. (1988) 'A biased overview of the study of love', *Journal of Social and Personal Relationships*, 5: 473–501.

Sheldon, A. and West, M. (1989) 'The functional discrimination of attachment and affiliation', *British Journal of Psychiatry*, 155: 18–23.

Skynner, R. (1976) *One Flesh, Separate Persons*, London: Constable.

Spence, D. (1982) *Narrative Truth and Historical Truth: Meaning and Interpretation in Psychoanalysis*, New York: Norton.

Spitz, R. (1950) 'Anxiety in infancy', *International Journal of Psycho-Analysis*, 31: 138–43.

Sroufe, A. (1979) 'The coherence of individual development', *American Psychologist*, 34: 834–41.

Steiner, R. (1985) 'Some thoughts about tradition and change arising from an examination of the British Psycho-Analytical Society's Controversial Discussions 1943–1944', *International Review of Psycho-Analysis*, 12: 27–71.

Stern, D. (1985) *The Interpersonal World of the Infant*, New York: Basic Books.

Storr, A. (1991) 'John Bowlby', *Munks Roll*, London: Royal College of Physicians.

Strachey, J. (1934) 'On the nature of the therapeutic action of psychoanalysis', *International Journal of Psycho-Analysis*, 15: 127–59.

Sutherland, J. (1991) 'Reminiscences of John Bowlby', *Tavistock Gazette* (Autumn).

Suttie, I. (1935) *The Origins of Love and Hate*, London: Kegan Paul.

Symington, N. (1986) *The Analytic Experience*, London: Free Association Books.

Tennant, C. (1988) 'Parental loss in childhood', *Archives of General Psychiatry*, 45: 1045–55.

Tinbergen, N. (1951) *The Study of Instinct*, Oxford: Clarendon Press.

Tizard, B. (1977) *Adoption: A Second Chance*, London: Open Books.

Trowell, J. (1991) 'Personal reminiscences of John Bowlby', *Tavistock Gazette* (Autumn).

Truax, C. and Carkhuff, R. (1967) *Towards Effective Counselling and Psychotherapy: Training and Practice*, Chicago: Aldine.

Van de Kolk, B. (1987) *Psychological Trauma*, Washington, DC: American Psychiatric Press.

Vaughn, B. and Egeland, B. (1979) 'Individual differences in infant–mother attachment at twelve and eighteen months', *Child Development*, 50: 971–5.

Vygotsky, L. (1962) *Thought and Language*, Cambridge, MA: MIT Press.

Waddington, C. (1977) *Tools for Thought*, London: Cape.

Webster, C. (1991) 'Psychiatry and the early National Health Service: the role of the Mental Health Standing Advisory Committee', in *150*

Years of British Psychiatry, G. Berrios and H. Freeman (eds), London: Gaskell.

Weiss, R. (1982) 'Attachment in adult life', in *The Place of Attachment in Human Behaviour*, C. M. Parkes and J. Stevenson-Hinde (eds), London: Routledge.

Westen, D. (1990) 'Towards a revised theory of borderline object relations: contributions of empirical research', *International Journal of Psycho-Analysis*, 71: 661–93.

Winnicott, D. (1965) *The Maturational Process and the Facilitating Environment*, London: Hogarth.

—— (1971) *Playing and Reality*, London: Penguin.

Wolkind, S., Hall, F. and Pawlby, S. (1977) 'Individual differences in mothering behaviour', in *Epidemiological Approaches in Child Psychiatry*, P. Graham (ed.), London: Academic Press.

Wright, K. (1991) *Vision and Separation*, London: Free Association Books.

Zetzel, E. (1956) 'Current concepts of transference', *International Journal of Psychoanalysis*, 37: 369–76.

Zweig-Frank, H. and Parris, J. (1991) 'Parents' emotional neglect and overprotection according to recollections of patients with BPD', *American Journal of Psychiatry*, 148: 648–51.

Index